SLEEP TALK

SLEEP TALK

A BREAKTHROUGH TECHNIQUE

FOR HELPING YOUR CHILD COPE WITH

STRESS AND THRIVE THROUGH

DIFFICULT TRANSITIONS

LOIS V. HADDAD, R.N.

with Patricia Wilson and Judith Searle

CB
CONTEMPORARY BOOKS

Library of Congress Cataloging-in-Publication Data

Haddad, Lois Y.
    Sleep talk : a breakthrough technique for helping your child cope
with stress and thrive through difficult transitions / Lois Y.
Haddad, with Patricia Wilson and Judith Searle.
      p.   cm.
    ISBN 0-8092-2800-9
    1. Mental suggestion.   2. Child rearing.   3. Parent and child.
I. Wilson, Patricia, 1936– . II. Searle, Judith.   III. Title.
BF1156.S8H33   1999
649'.64—dc21

                                            99-13967
                                                    CIP

Interior design by Susan H. Hartman

Published by Contemporary Books
A division of NTC/Contemporary Publishing Group, Inc.
4255 West Touhy Avenue, Lincolnwood (Chicago), Illinois 60646-1975 U.S.A.
Printed in the United States of America
International Standard Book Number: 0-8092-2800-9

99 00 01 02 03 04 LB 18 17 16 15 14 13 12 11 10 9 8 7 6 5 4 3 2 1

If you treat an individual as he is, he will remain as he is. But if you treat him as if he were what he ought to be and could be, he will become what he ought to be and could be.

Johann Wolfgang von Goethe

The main fact of life for me is love or its absence. This is a generalization for which I can think of no exception. Whether life is worth living depends for me on whether there is love in life. Without a sense of it, or even the memory of an hallucination of it, I think I would lose heart completely.

R. D. Laing
The Facts of Life

When you plant lettuce, if it does not grow well, you don't blame the lettuce. You look for reasons it is not doing well. It may need fertilizer, or more water, or less sun. You never blame the lettuce.

Yet if we have problems with our friends or our family, we blame the other person. But if we know how to take care of them, they will grow well, like the lettuce. Blaming has no positive effect at all, nor does trying to persuade using reason and arguments.

This is my experience.

No blame, no reasoning, no argument, just understanding.

If you understand, and you show that you understand, you can love, and the situation will change.

Thich Nhat Hahn
Peace Is Every Step

CONTENTS

Foreword   IX

Acknowledgments   XIII

Introduction   I

1 New Tools for Difficult Times   13

2 How Sleep Talk Works   31

3 Seven Steps to Success with Sleep Talk   39

4 Scripts for Different Ages and Stages   49

5 Sleep Talk Before Birth   61

6 Sleep Talk and Your Infant or Toddler   79

7 Sleep Talk and Your Preschool Child   97

8 Sleep Talk and Your Child in Day Care   119

9 Sleep Talk and Your School-Age Child   139

10 Sleep Talk and Your Adolescent   171

11 Sleep Talk and Responsibility   195

12 Sleep Talk and Recreation   219

13 Sleep Talk and Special Needs   237

A Final Note   263

Appendix A: Additional Sample Scripts on Recreation   265

Appendix B: Master Index to Scripts   271

Index   281

FOREWORD

I have spent most of my professional career working with families in crisis, with families struggling to live with the broken dreams of parents and their children, facing the realism of squandered opportunities and/or unrealized hopes and expectations. It is heartbreaking and often very uncomfortable to examine the path and the trail of these dreams. One after another, the dreams become chipped, scratched, cracked, and then shattered as the failures of the child mount. They cascade, to bury the love and the tenderness which these parents felt for the sweet baby and the toddler before the changes and the misadventures began. Those loving feelings have slowly changed into fear and trepidation—fear that any thought or word uttered between them may launch a diatribe of epithets and accusations, further distancing the parents from the child.

I earn my living in psychology, and I feel the challenge of healing the chasms of separation. I would much prefer to be invited to bolster and to encourage a healthy and supportive relationship. I would like to show families how to take the strength of a close relationship and make it closer, to make it more exciting and more productive. Psychologists have the ability to do *that*, too! However, we are overwhelmed by the need to treat the diseased relationships and have little time or opportunity to nourish the healthy relationships in this world.

When Lois Haddad asked me to read her manuscript for this book, I was busy, and there seemed little time to devote to the additional commitment of reading another book on "self-help" or "do-it-yourself" counseling. As I was in the process of writing a manuscript of my own, however, I agreed to give it a go. And, to my surprise, this book is not an easy fix but a down-to-earth approach to a very serious dilemma.

I believe that this book will help families nourish the parent-child relationship, building on the tenderness and the loving, hopeful expectations of parents for their children. With these rather simple but powerful exercises, the partnership of parent and child can begin, or be nourished . . . or both. Utilizing the suggestions in this book will help parents, at nearly any stage of a relationship, to strengthen the relationship and to enrich it.

Contributions of positive expectations can be put into the relationship in a form acceptable to the child. As the child accepts the inputs and feels energized to fulfill the suggestions, the child can act consciously to make the expectations be unanimous in the relationship. That is, the child can be on the team and feel a part of the team. The child can and will be determined to develop and exhibit the behavioral and personality traits so dear to the hearts of the parents.

While this may all sound very clinical and stilted, it is not. Here is a simple, straightforward, easy-to-understand, and easy-to-use tool to build teamwork between parent and child. The beauty of this approach is that it works! In my opinion it should be considered by parents everywhere to be a valuable aid to reach out to those persons most precious and dear to them, their children. As the bond and the relationship builds and bears the fruit of results, they become self-reinforcing and self-energizing.

My wife and I use Sleep Talk with our daughter. We have used it since reading the book, and we are very pleased with the results.

I look forward to the time when I can begin to help families build on the strong, positive relationships that can be initiated and nourished by techniques such as Sleep Talk. Try it. Once the team is humming, professionals in family counseling can work on a higher level to help strengthen the family.

George H. Tucker, Ph.D.

ACKNOWLEDGMENTS

I would like to give thanks to my family, cowriters, agent, publisher, and friends:

To my mother, who gave me my highest compliment: "Lois, finish your book. No one takes care of the children like you do."

To my children: my greatest appreciation is for their willingness to be who they are regardless of judgment from others. I consider this one of their highest attributes.

Without George, I would never have had these children.

Without my children, I would never have had this information.

Without Jack Gutman, this book would never have been written.

Without Patricia, this book would never have been started.

Without Judith, this book would never have been finished.

Without Al Melrose, I would never have survived.

I owe much to the care and attention of my agent, Betsy Amster, and my editor, Kara Leverte.

From Jo-Helen Steckbauer, Charli Williams, and Jack Stanley, I received the support to keep me on track.

Thank heavens for Terri LaMantain, Carol Blakeslee, and especially Julie Wheelock for their superb secretarial skills.

I owe much to my clients and their wonderful children: Sue, Terry, Bonnie, Lori, Tori, Paul, Sharlene.

Isaac Newton wrote: "If I have seen further than others, it is by standing upon the shoulders of giants."

Some of my giants are David Cheek, M.D., Jim Newman, Angeles Arrien, Andrew Galambos, Ayn Rand, David Bresler, M.D., Sam Stanley, and Maria Montessori.

INTRODUCTION

A few summers ago when my son T.J. and I were visiting friends in Florida, I observed the difficulties that Lisa, the daughter of a close friend of mine, was having with her two sons. Her three-year-old, Mike, was so terrified of the water that his screaming and fussing prevented any conversation among the mothers watching our kids playing and enjoying the water. Mike's mom was on call every moment he was anywhere near the lake, and his behavior soon became an ordeal for everyone within earshot.

Lisa's other son, Kevin, who was ten, had a different problem, but his behavior was equally troubling. He seemed driven to excel in everything he tried, and when he didn't get his way, he lashed out at others and made life miserable for everyone in the vicinity. An attitude adjustment was definitely needed, and Lisa was obviously at her wit's end.

I told her I might be able to suggest something that would help Kevin, and she said she'd try anything. And while we were at it, did I have any ideas for helping Mike get over his fear of the water?

I told her about the Sleep Talk technique I had developed, in which a parent reads a prepared script to a sleeping child who is having difficulties in a particular area.

The brain is a powerful organ even at rest. It accepts suggestions in the sleep state. With Sleep Talk, it receives and accepts honest, positive information because the "why it won't work" objection is not present. When a mother tells her son positive things while he's awake, he can choose to negate everything she says. But in the sleep state, when she tells him how special he is and how much he means to her, the information is accepted, and changes in behavior begin to happen.

I wrote out the following Sleep Talk script for Lisa to read to Mike, to help him get over his phobia about the water:

《 *Mike, this is your mommy.*
I want to let you know how much I love you.
I want to let you know how proud I am that you are my son.
I want to let you know how proud I am of your courage
     when you are around water.
You are careful and keep yourself safe.
You take a deep breath and relax.
Thank you for your effort in learning to swim.
You are very brave.
You have a fun time.
Thank you for being my son.
I love you.
Sweet dreams. 》

When you script one child, it's important not to leave out other siblings. So, even if Kevin had not had an immediate problem with his attitude, I would have offered Lisa a general "bonding with a parent" script to read to him. The following script was designed to offer Kevin an alternative to the negative attitude that was causing difficulties for him:

《 *Kevin, this is your mother.*
I want to let you know how much I love you.
I want to let you know how proud I am that you are my son.

*I am proud of you when you wake up in the morning with
  your smiling, shiny face.
Seeing you happy makes my heart sing.
People comment on what a gentleman you are.
You are fun to be around.
I enjoy being with you.
When you are calm and confident, you feel good about who
  you are, and that makes me happy.
Thank you for being in my life.
I love you.
Sweet dreams.* »

I gave Lisa directions on how to deliver these scripts, and a few days later, T.J. and I left the lake.

I didn't hear from Lisa again until a few months later, when I got a letter from her. She had "felt like a fool," she wrote, "reading in the dark to two boys who were sound asleep," but she followed my directions to read to them five nights in a row. Even though she didn't have much confidence that this would have any effect, she kept on reading the scripts even beyond the fifth night.

Before she started the Sleep Talk, she'd noticed that certain things caused Kevin to have a fit:

"For example, Kevin loves to bike race on Friday nights. In the past, when he asked if he could go racing and we weren't able to do it, he would pitch a fit, rant and rave, and cry for a while. I would end up yelling at him and sending him to his room. A couple of weeks ago, after I'd been reading his script for about ten days, he asked if we could go racing on Friday night. I told him I didn't think it was a good idea, since the next day he had his first football game and I wanted him to get a good night's rest.

"He said to me, 'OK, Mom, I'll race another night.' I almost fell over. I wanted to go over and feel his head to make sure he was all right.

"Another thing: Kevin would always have to be called four or five times in the morning before he would get out of bed and get ready for school. I would end up fighting with him all morning, and when I finally left the house for work, I felt as though I had already worked half the day. Now Kevin wakes up the first time I call him. He gets dressed, comes in, and tells me what he would like for breakfast. He finishes getting ready and sits and waits until it is time to go or watches TV. My mornings are so nice. I still have ten or fifteen minutes just to relax before we even leave the house. There is no stress at all. What a joy!

"During football practice, I noticed when he was not playing that he did not run around the way he used to, but sat and paid attention to what was going on. He was always ready to go right back on the field when the coach called him.

"These things might not seem like much to other people, but it sure has made a difference in our home."

And what about Mike, Kevin's three-year-old brother? Had the Sleep Talk been effective in dispelling his fear of the water? I read on in Lisa's letter:

"Mike has always had a fear of water since he was little. He did not like to get his hair wet, and he would not go anywhere near the pool. If someone took him into the water, he would start shaking and want to get out. Since I began using Sleep Talk with him, he started wearing his life jacket and would swim around the shallow end of the pool. At the lake, he would swim around as long as he could touch the bottom.

"Two weeks ago, we were at the lake, and he said, 'Mom, watch this!' He went down the steps and started swimming toward the deep end. At home, he now goes all over the pool with his jacket on. At the lake, he wants you to put him out of the boat so he can swim to the dock.

"You won't believe it, but over the weekend, Mike took off his life jacket and dog-paddled across the pool. I thought I was going to faint.

"This has been the nicest month ever for our family.

"Lois, I don't know how to thank you enough for what you've done for my kids. I wish I'd had this years ago. I'm still talking to them, but with much more feeling, and once in a while I add a few extra words to what you gave me in the beginning. I think Kevin is going to turn out to be a special little boy because of what you did.

I really enjoy being around him now that we don't fight the way we used to. He is making straight As at school and doing fantastic in football."

Over the years, I have seen variations on this story repeated many times. And every report of success is music to my ears. As a nurse, a mother, and a counselor, I have explored many ways to help the people whose lives have touched my own, and Sleep Talk offers parents the most powerful tool I know for enriching both their children's lives and their own.

Developing this technique has been a labor of love over many years, and I've encountered many frustrations and blind alleys along the way.

The UCLA Pediatrics Ward

When I started my nursing career in the UCLA pediatrics ward, I was fresh out of nursing school, and I had never seen a child die. I had never even seen a child with cancer. The year was 1958, and many medical techniques that are standard today were just being developed. The first two months that I worked on pediatrics, I personally got eight kids ready for open-heart surgery, and only three of them came back.

I had a hard time with that. Why would God have children die? Beautiful, wonderful children. I was struggling to find a way to keep on doing my job—not to just burn out with the terrible percentages of kids who didn't make it.

When I started working in the pediatrics ward, I had no family in Southern California, no ties at all. So, I often worked double shifts. I'd finish my regular shift, which was from 3:00 to 11:00, then work an additional shift of private-duty nursing a couple of times a week. With this kind of schedule, I got a crash course in pediatrics, and two weeks before my twenty-first birthday, I was made head nurse.

Aware that I still had a lot to learn, I was paying close attention to what was happening with the kids I was taking care of, and I noticed that when they had pain, they complained about it; when they didn't have pain, they didn't complain. This was in contrast to hospitalized adults, who complained all the time.

At that point in my life, I wasn't aware of all the ways illnesses serve adults, how what psychologists call "secondary gain" works (the incidental advantages an illness can offer in our lives). But I was aware that these kids not only had a better ability to express their needs, but they also healed faster than adults. The remarkable thing was that they did not need to be told how to do this.

Fascinated by what the mind was able to do, I began reading everything I could find on visualization and imagery. My work with visualization became an important part of my therapeutic process, and it provided much of the basis for the Sleep Talk techniques I developed later.

I noticed that keeping the kids busy and involved seemed to speed up the healing process. I began telling them stories, and I discovered that their pain lessened when their minds were stimulated and they became involved with the story. They were also more cooperative when I conjured up tales or games that enlisted their imagination.

In addition to telling them stories, I would rock them endlessly and sing to them. Even when kids had tubes in them or were encased in casts, I'd rock them. If that rocking chair had had a meter on it, I probably would have set some kind of record. The physical closeness in this process was good for me, too, especially since I was living so far away from my family in the South.

During this time, we had a nine-year-old patient who had burns over 60 percent of his body. He'd had a lot of grafting and a lot of surgery, and he was in isolation, in a room where we could watch him through a pane of glass. Whenever the staff needed to go into his room, we'd have to put on scrubs and a mask and a hat. So, all he ever got to see were these white figures moving around him.

This was 1958 or 1959, and most of his burns were on his extremities. The standard treatment then was to wrap up his arms and his legs, and we would go in every now and then with normal saline and wet him down, so he was constantly lying in a wet bed.

The worst part was changing his dressings. None of the nonstick materials that are now standard were available back then. So, we would have to undo his old bandages, and that process would take off any scab that had formed over the burn. What we'd be faced with was an open wound that was seeping and smelly.

With burn patients, progress depends a great deal on the kind of nursing they get, and seeing this boy's reaction to our efforts to help him was discouraging. Of course, every time we would go in, he knew what was coming, and he was terrified. We would give him a shot of Demerol and then do what we had to do. Things got to a point where I wondered whether we were going to heal him or make a drug addict out of him. He would be screaming all the time, fighting us all the way, and his grafts weren't taking.

Everyone who has burned a finger on a hot stove knows that burns are the most painful of injuries, and this boy was in agony much of the time. I asked myself, What can I do so that nursing care is even possible with this boy? I realized I needed some way to address his psyche.

At that time, I was dating a medical student, and he and I would have discussions about whether there was anything you could say to a boy like this that might help him. I felt it was essential not to tell him anything that wasn't true. In those days, there wasn't a lot of emphasis in medicine on the role of the immune system, but we were aware of the part the body's immune system played in healing. It seemed to me that it might be possible to put this in terms a nine-year-old could understand: that his body wanted to get well and was working to heal him.

So, I began, as I was putting him to bed, to tell him stories along those lines and say things like, "Thank you for cooperating with your treatment," and "I'm proud of your willingness to do what it takes to get better." When he went in to have further skin grafts, I would talk to him about how his body was going to accept them and how the grafts would heal rapidly to a healthy pink (the way they look when the blood supply is getting to the surface of the wound).

I was really flying blind at this time, trying to do something for this boy that wouldn't usurp either his doctors' or his parents' role. What I was doing was outside normal medical practice for those days, but I figured that what I was telling him couldn't hurt him.

Who can say whether what I did made a crucial difference? But the boy shifted toward assisting in his own healing, his grafts began to take, and eventually he was discharged from the hospital.

The fact that I happened to be head nurse on the 3:00 to 11:00 shift may also have contributed to the Sleep Talk techniques I developed later. The hours I worked made me especially aware of children's psychological receptivity at the end of their waking cycle. My responsibilities included finishing up treatments and getting kids settled in their rooms when they came back from the surgeries. After they were fed and their parents had left for the evening, there would be a period of crying and upset and distancing. During this time, I'd walk them and rock them and sing to them and tell them how wonderful they were and how they were going to get well. By the time the 11:00 shift came on, they would all be asleep.

My experiences with the children who were my patients set me thinking about the ways people can assist in their own healing, and the work I did with them became the basis for the Sleep Talk techniques I developed after I had children of my own.

Refining Sleep Talk in the Home "Laboratory"

Feeling as I did about children, I knew my own parenting would have a strong element of responsibility to love and teach and learn from my children. George, my husband, has been as committed as I am to Trey, Tara, and Briana, the three children of our marriage, and T.J., our adopted son. As each of our children arrived, we honed our skills in parenting, and I began using visualization techniques with them early.

By this time, I had great confidence in the power of the mind to heal, and when Briana, our youngest daughter, was about three, an incident occurred that put my skills to a critical test. The family car was loaded up with picnic gear, and we were about to set out for a day at the beach. As we left the house, each of us laden with last-minute totes, Briana, who was wearing beach thongs, could not stop the heavy door from swinging back against the wall—except with her foot. The metal strip on the base of the door scraped off the top layer of flesh from her toes to the top of her arch.

Immediately I sat down on the steps and told her to make the pain go away. Briana sat down, cradled her foot in her arms, and began rocking back and forth saying, "Go away pain, pain go away. Go away pain, pain go away."

The hurting stopped.

I looked at her foot and said, "Briana, you forgot to stop the bleeding."

Briana addressed her foot: "Stop bleeding, stop bleeding, stop bleeding."

And it did.

We washed the foot, put a large Band-Aid on it, and proceeded to the beach.

When I talked recently with the adult Briana (now a lawyer) about this experience, she told me, "I remember what it felt like to stop the bleeding. I'm still good at doing things like that. Pain, for instance—I can withstand it better than anybody I know because I go 'within' and let the pain drip out."

By the time Briana had the incident with her foot, I had already started using Sleep Talk with the children. The first time I used it was with our middle child, Tara, after two young girls who had been living with our family were suddenly taken away by their father. Tara, who was then four, was especially upset about their leaving.

The parents of the two visiting children had been friends of ours. The husband—I'll call him Bill—had been having an affair. His wife, whom I'll call Marge, found out about it, got a gun, and shot Bill. But then her gun jammed and, seeing that she'd only wounded him, she went and got another gun, preparing to shoot him again. But before she could open fire, Bill got a gun, shot her, and killed her. People outside their house saw the whole sequence through the open windows.

While Bill was recovering from his wounds, his two daughters, ages one and three, came to live with us. During that time, we became a family with five children. Bill's older daughter, Susie, suffered from night terrors, and she would be screaming, "Please don't hurt me. I'll be good. Don't hurt me like you hurt Mom." So, I would get up with her, or George would, or both of us would, and we'd rock her and talk to her endlessly, and that seemed to help.

After Bill's kids had lived with us for almost a year, he came and took them away abruptly one day. This was a shock to Tara, who began having night terrors of her own because the kids she'd come to see as her sisters were suddenly gone. So, I began getting up and talking with Tara. And I just fell into using techniques from affirmations, talking to her as she was falling back to sleep. And then after she was asleep, I'd sit by the bed and continue talking to her, saying, "I love seeing your happy, smiling face." She was hurt and sad, basically in a state of depression. But nobody talked about treating depression in a child, not in those days. And I could see that what I was doing made a difference to her. That's really where Sleep Talk began.

Seeing how well this technique was working with Tara, I began doing similar work with our younger daughter, Briana, in relation to whatever would come up in her life. By then she was two, and at that age she was always running, falling, and hitting her head. She always seemed to have a bump or a bruise, so I began using Sleep Talk for her healing. This prepared her to stop the bleeding when the door injured her foot.

The important point here is that you need to build the bridge that will allow that sort of communication, that sort of acceptance. Many years later, when Briana had finished law school and was getting ready to take the bar exam, she called me and said, "Mom, talk to me over the phone. Just talk to me and program me for success."

Because we'd had this history, she could ask for the help she needed whenever and however she needed it. And I admit it's thrilling for me to have my adult daughter call and ask me for help that I can offer her. She's living on her own now, but she still calls to tell me she loves me, she calls me to ask for help—and she doesn't ask for money.

Sharing Sleep Talk Techniques Beyond the Family

When Briana was in elementary school, one of her friends fell in the playground and broke her right arm. The other children ran back to the office for help, and Briana stayed with her friend. When the teacher arrived, she found the two girls sitting against the fence. Briana was holding her friend's left hand and moving it over the injured arm saying, "Let the pain drip out your elbow. Let the pain drip out your elbow."

The girl's mother called me afterward and said, "I cannot thank you enough for what Briana did. When my daughter gets hurt, she is an absolutely hysterical child. Today she was calm all the way to the hospital. When they were taking the x-rays and setting her arm, she stayed in control the whole time. You've got to tell me how Briana does this."

I explained something about the work I was doing, and the woman asked me to teach her, which I did. Soon I began offering private seminars in visualization and imagery in Orange County and San Diego County, and it seemed natural to incorporate the Sleep Talk work into that as well as into my counseling in the stress management area. During the summers, I was asked to teach the same material at conferences associated with the Policy Analysis for California Educators (PACE) seminars designed to enhance motivation and achievement among teenagers. In order to serve my clients through a wider variety of approaches, I also undertook professional training in biofeedback.

Interrupting and Transforming the Vicious Cycle

We're all familiar with vicious cycles, and any parent can offer a list of painful examples. Mike, Lisa's three-year-old son, got into a vicious cycle because of his phobia about the water. Sleep Talk opens the possibility of not only halting a vicious cycle in your child's behavior but also establishing in its place what I call a "benevolent cycle"—a cycle that builds through the power of love. This benevolent cycle is fueled by both your love for your child and your child's love for you, and the deepening love and trust on both sides is the basis for the significant behavioral changes Sleep Talk brings about.

The techniques I describe in this book act as a kind of nuclear-powered submarine—working below the surface of consciousness to move both you and your child toward positive destinations. Fueled by love—which expands exponentially as each of you becomes more aware of the other's trust and respect—your child's behavior is likely to undergo a transformation. (You may notice some positive changes in your own, as well.)

Throughout this book, I offer examples of the way Sleep Talk can reverse negative patterns in your child's behavior toward family members, friends, teachers, and the world at large. There seems to be no area in which productive applications are not possible. The chapters that follow offer suggestions for ways Sleep Talk can help you improve your child's health, self-confidence, personal relationships, school performance, and achievements in extracurricular activities. I also present sample scripts applicable to a wide variety of situations.

The most important single fact about Sleep Talk is that it works. Like Lisa, you will see the evidence in your own family very quickly. I wish I could be there to witness your excitement when you understand from direct personal experience how much these techniques can add to the quality of your child's life—and your own.

1

NEW TOOLS

FOR

DIFFICULT TIMES

"Lois, I need your help."

My friend's voice on the phone sounded tense.

"Of course, Melanie, what can I do?"

"I've just come from a conference at Kelly's school—you know she's in second grade now—and her teacher says my daughter is painfully shy, just can't bring herself to participate in class. And when Kelly does talk, she holds her head down and won't look at anyone. I'm wondering if that Sleep Talk work of yours could help her."

Even though Melanie had previously asked me a lot of questions about the Sleep Talk work I'd done with my own children, I'd always had the impression that she was somewhat skeptical of the whole idea. I realized she must be extremely concerned about Kelly to be willing to give it a try now.

I wrote a program on shyness, encouraging Kelly to be more assertive and to raise her hand in class when she knew the answers. (See Chapter 9 for this script.)

"What you need to do," I told Melanie, "is to copy this program down on a three-by-five card. Take a flashlight into her room with the card an hour or two after she's gone to sleep, and read it to her once every night for five nights in a row."

Three days later, Melanie called me.

"Lois, I think it may be working. Last night after I finished reading the card and was leaving Kelly's room, she sat up in bed—still asleep—and I heard her mumble, 'You're proud of me, Mom.' Would you say that's a good sign?"

"Absolutely," I said. "It means she's hearing you."

"Is there anything else I should be doing?"

"No, keep reading that card to her for two more nights, then take a couple of nights off before you read it to her again."

I had another call from Melanie about a week later.

"You're not going to believe this, Lois—I'm not sure I believe it myself! I just had a call from Kelly's teacher. I can tell you her exact words—they're burned into my memory forever: 'Whatever work you're doing with Kelly about her shyness is really paying off. She's raising her hand in class. She looks me in the eye when she talks to me. She's full of beans—eager to participate in everything.'" Melanie took a deep breath. "Can you believe that?"

"I believe it," I said. "I've seen it happen with a lot of kids, my own included. I'm so pleased it's working for you and Kelly."

Three months later, Melanie called me again. As soon I heard her voice, I knew something was troubling her. Finally she came out with it.

"We need a new program for Kelly. I'm getting these behavior slips from the school that indicate she's now talking too much, bossing everyone around. She knows her material—smart as a whip—but now she's letting everyone know it. I think we need some balance here."

By now, Melanie was familiar with the way Sleep Talk scripts need to be written, and together we created a new script for Kelly to provide balance.

This is what we wrote:

《 *Kelly, this is your mom.*
I want you to know how much I love you.

> *I want you to know how proud I am that you are my*
> *daughter.*
> *I appreciate your being so well behaved.*
> *I am proud that you know the answers at school.*
> *I know that you can be assertive, or say what you need to*
> *say, and there are times when you listen.*
> *I am proud when you listen.*
> *Thank you for being my daughter.*
> *I love you.*
> *Sweet dreams.* »

This new script did just what we hoped it would do. Kelly was still able to express herself in class, but she began making different choices about when and how loudly to speak.

Now, three years later, I'm still getting periodic reports from Melanie about Kelly's progress. At ten years old, she's still rather quiet but has a lot of friends. She's attending a new school this year, and all reports from her teachers are extremely positive.

Even though Melanie's suggestions in the Sleep Talk scripts encouraged Kelly to try out different behaviors in her school situation, the responsibility—and the choice—remained Kelly's. The love Melanie expressed for her daughter was combined with a strong sense of respect for Kelly's ability to adjust her own behavior in appropriate ways.

You may have all the love in the world for your child, but there are still times when, like Melanie, you need help. When your child behaves in ways that bring ineffective results for her, you as a parent can step in with skills that help her change this behavior to something that will better serve her. In any stressful situation, a parent can offer important information, and the skills this book describes have the power to stimulate in any child the kind of mental openness that will allow her to take in and process this information.

Parents and children experience many stresses in their lives and in their relationships at the best of times, and modern life has turned up the heat on all of us even further. Two-career families, single-parent families, and reliance on day care, sitters, and nannies make the need for strong parenting skills more urgent than ever. Our children depend on us for guidance, and they are eager to follow suggestions that we offer in a spirit of love and respect.

The Power of Sleep Talk

The power of Sleep Talk to rebond parent and child after the inevitable stresses of the day is the basis for all the positive changes I have seen this amazing technique bring about.

Essentially, here is how it works:

Your child is finally asleep, after a day that has taken its toll on him as well as on you. If it has been one of *those* days, your child may have driven you crazy, and he has probably felt equally frustrated with you. But seeing him in his bed, looking cherubic, it's impossible to feel anything but love for him, quite apart from his behavior.

You are ready now to dump the garbage of the day and help your child do the same. Through reaffirming your love for him and your pride in him, you allow him to truly *hear* you on the deepest level, and you clean the slate for the next day's activities.

Because the first words of your Sleep Talk script have made clear to him that in your deepest heart you love and respect him *just as he is*, he is able to trust your practical advice about ways he might better deal with the tricky process of growing up.

When we sense that we are truly loved for ourselves, in our essence, we are able to risk trying something new. This is a truth many of us know intellectually, but Sleep Talk offers parents a way to get beyond the child's usual objections to any given suggestion for changing attitudes or behaviors. When alternative modes of behavior are offered to a sleeping child in a context of love and approval *as though they were already a fact*, the usual defenses are disarmed, and the child is able to "own" the new way of being in a context of self-respect.

For you as a parent, too, the experience of reading the script provides a powerful renewal of your joy in loving and guiding your child. It strengthens the commitment between parent and child in much the same way a renewal of marriage vows strengthens the bond between husband and wife.

The payoff to all this is in the feedback you get from your child, her confidence that you love her and are proud of her, her "living out" in her waking life the behaviors you have already credited to her in your Sleep Talk script.

I spoke in the Introduction about interrupting vicious cycles and replacing them with benevolent cycles. These are only words unless we actually involve ourselves in the process. It is the *experience* of the way the Sleep Talk process plays out in practice with your own child that offers you an incredible return on the small investment of time and energy required to put this powerful tool into action.

Strengthening the Bond Between Grandfather and Grandson

Patricia Wilson, one of this book's coauthors, has been using Sleep Talk with her own children for many years. Now a grandmother, she is one of the most skillful practitioners of the technique I know, and she is a living embodiment of the "each one teach one" philosophy I prize so highly.

Here is her story about the way Sleep Talk skills she shared with her husband helped him change a problematic relationship with his grandson:

"We were sitting in a tiny restaurant in Baja, Mexico, with our two grandsons, four-year-old Jimmy and nineteen-month-old Joey.

"I heard Jimmy say, 'Granddaddy, you're my friend, aren't you? My best friend!' I watched as Jimmy put his arms around my husband, Chuck.

"Chuck was beaming. When he was able to get my attention without the boys' hearing, he whispered, 'Did you hear what Jimmy just said to me? It's the exact same thing I read to him last night in his Sleep Talk.'

"As I shifted my attention back to our hyperactive grandson, he was singing Chuck a song he'd just made up about how his granddaddy was his 'New Best Friend.'

"When Jimmy was in preschool, his mom, our daughter Wendy, was continually getting notes and calls from his teachers complaining about his aggressive behavior and lack of attention. He could not sit still, would not follow directions. When he came to visit us, he was always into things, and Chuck had trouble accepting this whirling dervish into our household. His solution was to use stern looks, continual corrections, and removal of privileges in an attempt to control Jimmy.

"But this approach to grandparenting did not prove very effective, and Chuck was unhappy about the quality of his relationship with the boy. Since Chuck knew I was involved in writing the Sleep Talk book, he decided to try using one of Lois's scripts on Jimmy during the five days the boys were visiting us.

"The scene in the restaurant that I described took place on the third day of their visit, after Chuck had read Jimmy's script on the two previous nights while I read one to Joey dealing with health.

"Chuck chose a program that addressed bonding and added a few statements to Lois's script. This is what Chuck read to Jimmy each night after he fell asleep:

« *Jimmy, this is your granddaddy.*
I want you to know how much I love you.
I want you to know how proud I am of you.
You are a wonderful grandson and friend.
You are a good friend to me.
I appreciate all the help you give me.
You help me around the house.
You help with Joey.
You help at the pool.
You help in the car.
Thank you for your help.
Your calm, relaxed manner and energy makes me smile.
Thank you for being my grandson, and friend.
I am proud of you, and I know you are proud of yourself.
I love you.
Sweet dreams. »

"Now watching the two of them holding each other and enjoying each other, I felt elated.

"Chuck continued to read that same program to Jimmy for the last three nights he was with us, and the changes in Jimmy's behavior were striking. He actually looked at us when we talked to him.

He no longer ignored such requests as 'Please pick up your toy' or 'Would you please come to the table for dinner.'

"Most important of all, the mutual affection between Chuck and Jimmy was thrilling to see.

"After Jimmy had been home with his parents for a few weeks, his mom phoned, and we chatted about the boys. I asked how Jimmy was doing, and Wendy said she could see distinct changes. She told me, 'I talked to his preschool teacher yesterday, and she said he's like a different kid.' "

One of the things I love about Patty's story is the way it illustrates the transformation in both child and adult. Not only did Jimmy discover the pleasure of having a "new best friend," but also Chuck discovered the joy of *being* a best friend to his grandson.

One of the most delightful aspects of Sleep Talk for a parent or grandparent is the pleasure of using these new skills to participate in and support the child's natural maturing process. Those of us who enjoy gardening know about the care we take with a plant, making sure it gets the right amount of water and sunlight and enrichment in its soil, and how satisfying it is to see it finally come into flower. Watching the effects of Sleep Talk on a child is akin to this, only a thousand times more exciting.

Avoiding the Mistakes Our Own Parents Made

Most of us become parents without any special training for the role. We love our kids, and we have every intention of doing our best. If we have some reservations about how our own parents brought us up, we are resolved to do better by our own kids and not repeat the mistakes our parents made.

But what happens when we get frazzled and overwhelmed? You guessed it: we fall right back into the patterns our parents used on us, appropriate or not. We're doing the best we can (just as our parents did, we now realize), though we may sometimes have a sinking feeling that our best isn't really good enough.

There is a way out of this vicious cycle, and that is to learn skills that can set us on a different road. After all, if no one ever taught us to swim and we watched our own parents floundering whenever

they tried, it's not really our fault that we can't swim. But instead
of spending our energies complaining that we don't know how,
doesn't it make sense just to sign up for some lessons?

To my mind, parenting skills are a lot easier to learn than swimming. And this book teaches the basics of these skills in the sim-
plest and most practical way I know. Through practicing Sleep Talk,
you learn these skills almost the way a child learns a foreign language—by osmosis. What's more, you don't have to continually
ask, "How am I doing?"

Your child's response will give you fast and unmistakable
feedback.

You've already seen examples of some of these parenting skills
in the Sleep Talk stories I've told you. Let me sum up a few of them:

- learning to dump the emotional garbage of the day (through
  acknowledging and expressing your love for your child)

- refocusing your energies in a positive way (so that any criti-
  cism gets focused on what a child *does* rather than who the
  child *is*)

- recognizing the truth of the old saying, "you will catch more
  flies with honey than with vinegar" (as Chuck certainly learned
  through the pride he expressed in Jimmy)

Sleep Talk and Troubled Families

Whenever I give workshops on Sleep Talk, someone invariably asks,
"But what about dysfunctional families—families in which alco-
holism or drug abuse or domestic violence is part of the scene? Can
Sleep Talk really help in situations like that?"

My answer is, *It can't hurt.*

I'm not going to pretend that these techniques are a cure-all, but
even in troubled families, I believe that parents at some level want
to do better by their kids. And these techniques can help them see
that they aren't stuck with doing what was done to them. Sleep Talk
can serve as an opening wedge—a way to interrupt a destructive

cycle and put something positive in its place. I believe we all want to see our kids happy and flourishing, and when you start something that steers them in that direction, the process feeds on itself.

Parents Need Healing, Too

Sometimes even conscientious parents have unreasonable feelings of inadequacy about their child-raising abilities.

My neighbor, Jennifer, for example, tearfully confided in me some years ago about her long-term guilt over her six-year-old son, Devlin. It began with Devlin's premature birth and Jennifer's despair at believing her three-pound-seven-ounce son wouldn't know who his mother was, since he was in another hospital, being kept alive by machines. She couldn't stop thinking about what she might have done to cause his premature birth and her anguish at not being there to bond with him during those first precious days of his life.

"When Devlin was two months old," she told me, "he would roll away from me after nursing, as if to say, 'You left me when I was born.' Even though I was feeling utter joy that he had survived, and survived with flying colors, I still couldn't help feeling guilty. You'd think by now I'd have gotten over this feeling—he's six years old. But I'm aware that, of all our four kids, he's by far the most withdrawn and introverted. That bothers me, too. I still feel it's somehow my fault."

I suggested Jennifer try a Sleep Talk program on self-confidence and taught her how to deliver it. I explained that it was important to identify herself as his mom and tell him how much she loved him and how proud she was that he was her son. Then she should tell him how wonderful he was and what a joy he was to have in the family, and that he was potentially great because he had the ability to do all he desired. Always, I said, she should end with the Sleep Talk signature: "I love you. Sweet dreams."

Within four weeks of working with the Sleep Talk program, Devlin became an A student, and with his new level of self-confidence, he continued to maintain this level of academic work. He also

became a valuable player in several sports and a soloist in the All
American Boys' Chorus.

Now, eight years later, Jennifer tells me her fourteen-year-old
son is witty, outgoing, exceptionally bright, accepting of everyone—
and very loving toward his mother.

I am aware that her gain is at least equal to his—her obsessive
guilt is a thing of the past.

When to Begin Sleep Talk

Another question I'm frequently asked in my seminars is, "How
early can a parent begin Sleep Talk work with a child?"

My answer may surprise you: *After conception.*

During pregnancy it is helpful for both mother and father to talk
to the unborn child and express love and confidence in the child's
coming to an easy, full-term birth in good health. In Chapter 5, I
offer scripts for both parents to read to the child during the mother's
pregnancy.

Barbara began using Sleep Talk techniques while she was pregnant with the second of her three daughters. Mindful of the difficulties she had experienced during her first pregnancy, she took one
of my classes, hoping to learn some techniques that would make
this second pregnancy less problematic. In her work with me, she
learned to control her thoughts, adjust her attitude, even talk to
her growing fetus. The experience was such a revelation that she
continued to use the techniques with her children throughout their
growing up.

Can prenatal Sleep Talk really help?

Again I reply, *It can't hurt* (and I suspect it might help at least
as much as that mobile you're taking so much trouble choosing, to
hang over the baby's crib).

Remember, these scripts are designed as much to help the parent as to help the child. I believe that had Jennifer been able to
read an appropriate script to Devlin when she could first spend
time with him after his premature birth, she might have eliminated
both her own extended guilt and his early tendency toward with-

drawal. In Chapter 6, I offer scripts for newborns (as well as for their older siblings).

Even in babyhood, whether the child understands the actual language or not, she is able to pick up on a parent's feelings of love and pride, and the scripts in Chapter 6 can start you in the right direction early. If your child is adopted, as our son T.J. is, using appropriate scripts early on can be especially helpful for making him feel loved and valued in his new family.

Don't underestimate the importance of this preverbal level of communication. It establishes the foundation for a solid relationship with your child.

The Child Teaches the Parent

Sometimes your baby's responses can surprise you. From the time she was born, Barbara's first child, Georgia, suffered from many allergies, and nothing Barbara could do had any visible effect on them. Georgia was continually plagued with ear infections, and she seemed to have a "clogged" head or runny nose all the time. Barbara didn't want to subject her to surgery or tubes in her ears to relieve the earaches, so Georgia was constantly on medication.

In a Sleep Talk script, Barbara spoke to her daughter: "Georgia, give me some information so I'll know what to do to help you get well."

Georgia began refusing her bottle of milk. She would even toss it out of her crib. But if Barbara put juice in the bottle, Georgia would accept it.

As soon as Barbara got the message and removed dairy products from the baby's diet, her allergic reactions cleared up, and the medications for her ear infections were no longer needed. Georgia became a happy, healthy child.

Barbara still has the three-by-five card with the script written in red ink that she and I planned more than eighteen years ago.

Remember my saying earlier that the child teaches the parent as much as the parent teaches the child? The process can start a lot earlier than you expect.

Dealing with Serious Health Issues

By the time her third daughter was born, Barbara was an old hand at Sleep Talk techniques. She always took a lot of care to get the scripts exactly right and would go from room to room at night with her three-by-five cards so she would be sure to say the words correctly.

Her skills were put to a major test when eight-year-old Maureen, her youngest, began having grand mal seizures. The first doctor to whom Barbara took the girl predicted that Maureen would always have the seizures, and he wanted to put her on daily medication.

Barbara's response was to change doctors. There are differences of opinion among doctors about the best treatment for Maureen's condition, and the new doctor advised an intensive regime of vitamin therapy. Barbara added to this a Sleep Talk script that encouraged Maureen to make her body and mind well. For three months, Barbara read the following words to her daughter every night, giving her permission to heal herself:

《 *Maureen, this is your mom.*
I want to let you know how much I love you.
I want to let you know how proud I am that you are my
   daughter.
I want to let you know how much I appreciate it when you
   keep your body in balance.
I appreciate the responsibility you take in keeping your body
   strong and healthy.
Thank you for making the decision to be well.
I love you so very much.
I am so very proud of you.
Sweet dreams. 》

With Barbara's two-step program—involving Maureen's brain and Barbara's love—things began to happen. The seizures stopped. Maureen's personality changed from irritable to happy and healthy.

Watching this transformation, I was powerfully aware of the distance the Sleep Talk techniques had come from my first tentative efforts in the UCLA pediatrics ward.

When Maureen was sixteen, eight years after her original diagnosis, I interviewed her about her personal experience of the Sleep Talk scripts her mother had used to help her heal.

Maureen told me the techniques had now become so familiar that she wasn't always conscious of using them. But when her friends asked about how she dealt with pain, anxieties, sports, dancing, or schoolwork, she realized she actually made daily use of the tools her mom had taught her.

One skill she often uses is to "go within" to handle any problem that comes up.

"All my friends know not to bother me or talk to me right after I have been hurt or need to handle an important situation," she said. "They just know! I do self-talk. I visualize myself before cheerleading, basketball, or dancing. I tell myself I know the plays or routines. I practice in my head, doing it the way I want it done. I also use 'going within' for comfort—for example, when I go to the dentist. And I've taught a lot of my friends to self-talk and be more confident."

And how is her relationship with her mother?

"I can tell my mom anything," she says. "We have a great relationship."

Like her two sisters, Maureen is remarkable for her independence, her ability to make good decisions, and her gift for sustaining friendships. All three girls have a powerful bond of love with their mother.

It was especially gratifying for me to hear Maureen talk about passing on to her friends some of what she learned from her mom. If she decides one day to become a mother herself, I can imagine her bringing up a second generation of healthy, positive Sleep Talk kids. Talk about benevolent cycles!

Everyday Uses for Sleep Talk

Not every family has the health challenges that Barbara had to meet. But most parents need effective tools to deal with such everyday problems as a child's discouragement.

In search of ways to better serve my counseling clients, I was sitting in the office of Dr. Jack Gutman, a physician specializing in sports medicine. As we discussed what happens when an athlete "hits the wall," my mind was going a mile a minute, looking for correspondences with the emotional stresses that my clients reported. When our consultation was finished, I asked about Jack's family.

He had two daughters, he told me, one six and the other twelve. Twelve-year-old Molly was an accomplished pianist. "In fact," he said, "she was in the National Piano Competition this past October. She came in third but hasn't touched the piano since. No amount of begging, pleading, or bribing on my part has made any difference. She hasn't played in five months."

"Molly 'hit the wall,' " I said. "You need to learn Sleep Talk."

"What's Sleep Talk?"

I described the technique, then said, "You love Molly a lot, don't you?"

"More than anything in the world," he said. "Both my daughters."

"Do you think a child can be loved too much?"

"Too much? No, of course not." He laughed. "None of us can be loved too much."

I suggested, "Even though you know how much you love Molly, you need to keep reminding her." To do this, I explained, he would need to separate who Molly is from what her performance was. And he could accomplish this by reminding her that he loves her and is proud that she is his daughter.

I wrote out the following script and explained how Jack should deliver it:

≪ *Molly, this is your father.*
I want to let you know how much I love you.
*I want to let you know how proud I am that you are my
    daughter.*
*I want to let you know what fun it is for me to hear you play
    the piano.*
You play the piano beautifully.
I love hearing you play the piano.
When you play the piano, magical things happen for me.

> *When you play the piano, magical things happen for other*
> *people. We all enjoy hearing you play the piano.*
> *Thank you for being such an accomplished pianist.*
> *Thank you for being in my life.*
> *Thank you for playing the piano for me.*
> *I love you.*
> *Sweet dreams.* »

"I'll do this," Jack said, "but I have to tell you, I can't believe it will work. My wife and I have tried every single thing we know to get through this."

"Yes," I said, "but you haven't tried *this* yet. If you'd known about it, you would have done it first."

He called me the next morning.

"Lois, she is in there right now playing Chopin."

"Today is my father's birthday," he went on, "and my wife wanted Molly to help decorate her grandfather's cake. And you know what she said? 'Mom, I can't. Don't you understand? I need to play the piano.' "

Sleep Talk brought balance to Molly's life. Her withdrawal from her piano playing was the result of a damaged self-image. When she did not win first place in her piano competition, she estimated her personal worth according to her performance, and for five months she lived with the image of herself as a failure. Her father's reminder that, much as he values her talent, his love for her is not conditional on her performance made a crucial difference in the way she values herself.

Today, not only is Molly doing brilliantly with her piano playing, but she also has expanded her creative endeavors to include writing and scoring a musical play.

At the same time I prepared the script for Molly, I also wrote one for Jack's six-year-old daughter on bonding with a parent:

« *Gracie, this is your father.*
I want to let you know how much I love you.
I want you to know how proud I am that you are my
daughter.

I want you to know how proud I am even when we are not
   together.
You are my daughter, and I love you very much.
When I go to work and I am away from you, I still think
   of you.
It is such a pleasure to spend time being with you.
You are my treasure.
I love you.
Sweet dreams. »

Later, during a phone conversation with Jack, I asked, "How's your little one?"

"Right now she's under the weather," he said. "Sniffles, a touch of flu. So, I haven't been using her program."

We hung up. But after thinking about this for about ten seconds, I called him back.

"Change the program," I told him. "Rewrite it. Tell her you love her. Tell her you're proud that she's your daughter. Tell her you know that she knows how to activate her immune system. Tell her to use whatever it takes to let her body activate her immune system so that she has a healthy, strong body. End with 'I love you' and 'Sweet dreams!'" (See Chapter 13 for this script.)

Even though we may not know exactly how to activate our immune system, we can give our body permission to do so, and children, having no "programming" that tells them they can't do this, are especially adept at it.

Jack called me back the next morning.

"Lois, she is symptom free!"

This kind of success story is so common among parents who have used Sleep Talk with their kids that I'm wondering these days if there are any limits at all to the effectiveness of these techniques. But I suppose the real question is: *Are there any limits to the power of love?* Because love is the fuel behind all the changes I've been describing.

Is Sleep Talk Manipulation?

People unfamiliar with the way Sleep Talk works sometimes ask me whether it isn't simply a form of manipulation. How can I justify encouraging parents to manipulate their children? The first time I heard the question, I burst out laughing.

"I would call it *influencing*," I said. "Isn't it a parent's responsibility to guide a child in the direction of civilizing and educating him? That's what parenting is about."

Lisa, when she was trying to control Kevin's unruly behavior, first tried to manipulate him by yelling at him and sending him to his room. Not surprisingly, that didn't work. But when she enlisted his cooperation by expressing her love and pride in him and acknowledging his ability to participate in making choices that would improve his life, the change in him was rapid and astonishing.

So, to my mind, the question is not whether we parents try to manipulate our children, but whether we choose effective or ineffective methods of achieving results.

The biggest bonus of all is that when you become caught up in the benevolent cycle that Sleep Talk initiates, you are as likely to be influenced by your child's response as she is by the words you read as she lies sleeping.

Parents today, caught up in the multiple pressures of modern life, often worry about spending enough "quality" time with their kids. Believe me, the two minutes you spend at night reading a Sleep Talk script to your child are the highest-quality moments you can possibly spend.

And the benefits last a lifetime.

2

HOW
SLEEP TALK
WORKS

Lewis Thomas, a physician known for his insightful philosophical essays on medical subjects, once wrote: "The only solid piece of scientific truth about which I feel totally confident is that we are profoundly ignorant about nature."

A lack of knowledge about why certain drugs are effective does not prevent doctors from routinely using them. Even though no one understands exactly how aspirin works, it is essential to the practice of modern medicine.

Likewise, many aspects of Sleep Talk have yet to be thoroughly studied, and I believe that, as the technique becomes more widely used, scientists will be stimulated to design research projects that can give us greater understanding of the process.

Stages of Sleep

To understand the reasons for the timing of Sleep Talk sessions, it's helpful to know something about the different kinds and stages of sleep. In both children and adults, there are two basic kinds of sleep: REM sleep (characterized by rapid eye movements under closed lids), in which we dream, and NREM (non-REM) sleep, which is dreamless. The four stages of NREM sleep are characterized by different kinds of brain wave activity, with stage 1 being the closest to waking (faster brain waves) and stage 4 the deepest sleep (the slowest brain waves).

When I counsel parents about using Sleep Talk, I suggest that they read the script to their child one or two hours after his bedtime. At this point, most children are firmly established in the deepest stages of sleep and are difficult to rouse, even with the most intense noise.

Awareness of Sounds During Sleep

Physiological studies tell us that the brain is continuously active during all states of sleep, even though it processes information differently from the way it does in the waking state. Of all the senses, changes in sensitivity to auditory information have been studied the most thoroughly, and this research has particular relevance to Sleep Talk.

Early sleep experiments examined auditory arousal thresholds (AATs)—how loud a tone was required to awaken someone from each sleep stage.

Scientists used a series of tones of increasing loudness to detect awakening thresholds, and they found that sensitivity to sounds was equal in stage 2 and REM sleep, whereas louder tones were necessary to arouse a person from slow-wave sleep. Generally, people became more sensitive to sounds as the night progressed, regardless of their stage of sleep.[1]

---

1. A. Reichschaffen, P. Hauri, and M. Zeitlin, "Auditory Awakening Thresholds in REM and NREM Sleep Stages," *Perceptual and Motor Skills* (1966) 22: 927–42.

The meaningfulness of stimuli has a clear effect on how readily a person awakens. In two different studies, researchers used the sleeper's name as a stimulus. In 1960, a group of scientists found that a greater number of fist-clench responses and K-complexes (a distinctive EEG waveform) occurred in response to the subject's name than to the subject's name read backward or the names of others.[2]

In a study done fourteen years later, another group of researchers predicted that stimuli that were personally significant to the subject would be processed more accurately during REM sleep than during other sleep stages. These scientists adapted the same forward and backward own-name procedure, and their prediction that responses would be faster in REM than in stage 2 sleep was confirmed. Forward own-name responses were more effectively perceived than backward own-names in both stages.[3]

Both these studies confirm the importance of getting the sleeping child's attention through speaking his name at the beginning of each Sleep Talk session. The possibility of learning to respond to certain stimuli while paying less attention to others has been confirmed in other sleep studies. For example, a group of researchers examined people's ability to make simple discriminative responses during sleep. They instructed subjects to turn off tones by pressing a switch taped to the subject's hand. Then they presented the same tones during sleep and recorded the switch-pressing responses. Switch presses were always most frequent in stage 1 and least frequent in stages 3 and 4. Response frequencies were intermediate in stage 2 and REM sleep. However, if subjects were threatened with punishment (very loud sounds and electric shock) for failures to respond, response frequencies were increased in all stages.[4]

The increased responsiveness under threat of punishment (negative reinforcement) is significant. But love is also a powerful (and positive) form of reinforcement. I believe that further experiments

---

2. I. Oswald, A. M. Taylor, and M. Treisman, "Discriminative Responses to Stimulation During Human Sleep," *Brain* (1960) 83: 440–53.

3. G. W. Langford, R. Meddis, and A. J. D. Pearson, "Awakening Latency from Sleep for Meaningful and Nonmeaningful Stimuli," *Psychophysiology* (1974) 11: 1–5.

4. H. L. Williams, H. C. Morlock, and J. V. Morlock, "Instrumental Behavior During Sleep," *Psychophysiology* (1966) 2: 208–16.

might well show that subjects also increase their responsiveness under *positive* reinforcement, such as the message of parental love and pride that is an essential part of all Sleep Talk scripts.

As the research indicates, meaningful sounds such as the child's name are likely to get her attention even in the sleep state. I predict that when studies of Sleep Talk are made in a sleep laboratory, they will show that the parent's speaking of the child's name brings her out of REM sleep or the deeper stages of NREM sleep to stage I sleep. This sleep stage is characterized by a mixture of brain waves, most of which are alpha waves. Alpha waves also predominate in the relaxed waking state, and a parent who has had time to unwind after the stresses of the day is likely to be in this state. So, parent and child at this moment will tend to be literally "in sync," in terms of their brain waves, in a relaxed state in which negativism and criticality are suspended. The bonding between parent and child is powerfully supported by this mirroring of each other's EEG patterns, with the physical rhythm being inseparable from the emotional connection.

Learning During Sleep

In general, the research on factual learning during sleep has not been encouraging about the possibility of perceiving new complex concepts while asleep and remembering them on waking.[5] However, it is important to remember that studies of sleep learning have concentrated on the accumulation of factual information (such as language vocabulary) rather than the shifts in mind-set and attitude that Sleep Talk encourages.

The information that Sleep Talk presents to the child is different both in kind and in context from the factual sleep learning that has been studied in sleep labs. Most important, *the content of Sleep Talk is not new; the problems being addressed in the scripts are familiar to the child*, having been previously discussed with the parent during the waking state.

---

5. E. Eich, "Learning During Sleep," in R. R. Bootzin, J. F. Kihlstrom, and D. L. Schachter, eds., *Sleep and Cognition* (Washington, D.C.: American Psychological Association, 1990), 88–108.

We know that people are able to process information during sleep—that while sleeping, we can respond to sensory events in our environment (such as the sound of one's own name) and retrieve material that we learned and stored in our memory while awake (such as possible alternative behaviors).[6]

The goal in Sleep Talk, unlike that in sleep learning, is not to have conscious memory of the content of the session. Rather, it is to offer the child alternatives to his present behavior that may result in greater success, even though the content of the scripts is not accessible to consciousness. In the context of presentation through Sleep Talk, a child is less likely to resist considering these alternatives to established behavior.

The effectiveness of Sleep Talk is well known to parents who have used the technique with their children, and I look forward to the time when researchers design studies to confirm its power by testing it under laboratory conditions.

Memory During General Anesthesia

In the meantime, it may be useful, in searching for analogues to the Sleep Talk process, to examine studies of patients overhearing and remembering conversations in the operating room while under anesthesia. Even when drugs are given that prevent conscious recall of such conversations, patients may take in information on an unconscious or preconscious level, and their postoperative healing may be affected by what they hear. Ernest Lawrence Rossi, Ph.D., and David B. Cheek, M.D., in their book *Mind-Body Therapy* describe many cases in which patients' misunderstanding of a surgeon's words has interfered with healing until, under hypnosis, the misapprehension was revealed and corrected.[7]

What is clear from these cases is that patients do hear, and remember what they hear, when under anesthesia, even though this

---

6. Pietro Badia, "Learning," in *Encyclopedia of Sleep and Dreaming*, Mara A. Carskadon, editor in chief (New York: Macmillan, 1993), 328.

7. Ernest Lawrence Rossi and David B. Cheek, *Mind-Body Therapy* (New York: Norton, 1988), 151–2.

information is not accessible to their conscious mind except through the aid of hypnosis. Since anesthesia presents no obstacle to mental processing of verbal information, it stands to reason that such processing would also occur during the natural sleep state.

The effects described by these researchers are similar to those that parents observe in their children with Sleep Talk. Although the children often give evidence of having heard the Sleep Talk message (such as repeating certain phrases verbatim in waking conversations), I know of no case in which the child has consciously remembered details of a Sleep Talk session.

Research overwhelmingly supports the theory that consciousness may not be necessary for memory and learning. Studies done by H. Bennett have demonstrated that patients are able to understand and respond to a verbal message given under anesthesia, even though they have no conscious awareness of that message.[8]

There are, of course, distinct differences between natural sleep and anesthetically induced unconsciousness. An anesthetized person will not make any spontaneous movements, while a sleeping person makes many large shifts of position during the night. The EEG of a sleeping person will predictably and spontaneously change patterns throughout the night, while the EEG of a person under anesthesia has distinct patterns that depend upon which anesthetic agents and which dosages are being used.

In natural sleep, heart rate, blood pressure, and respiration become slow and regular during NREM sleep and rapid and irregular during REM sleep, with all these changes being controlled by the sleeper's brain. These same physiological variables are profoundly affected by anesthetics and may become rapid and irregular as the patient emerges from anesthesia. Many anesthetic drugs that eliminate pain also severely depress heart rate and respiration.

Although anesthetics are widely used, the mechanisms of their action remain unknown. Brain mechanisms that generate natural states of consciousness are also incompletely understood, and much research remains to be done in both these areas.

---

8. H. Bennett, "Perception and Memory for Events During Adequate General Anesthesia for Surgical Operations," in H. Pettinati, ed., *Hypnosis and Memory* (New York: Guilford, 1988). Quoted in *Mind-Body Therapy*, 153.

However, one clear common factor in both sleep and anesthesia is the person's ability to hear and understand what is said.

Mind-Body Connections

Since many of the Sleep Talk scripts in this book relate to issues of health and healing, it is important to be aware that research about this area has established a clear connection between mind and body. Further work needs to be done to determine how specific mind and body components interact in the healing process, and researchers are currently at work on this question.[9]

This type of research is also likely to throw considerable light on what makes Sleep Talk work. What is already clear is that the emotions expressed by the parent and the responses of the child play an enormous role in creating the possibility of changes in the child's behavior.

Candace Pert, one of the most distinguished researchers in the area of mind-body connections, writes eloquently about the connections between mind and emotions:

> In the beginning of my work, I matter-of-factly presumed that emotions were in the head or the brain. Now I would say they are really in the body as well. They are expressed in the body and are part of the body. I can no longer make a strong distinction between the brain and the body.[10]

The Sleep Talk Process

The Sleep Talk situation, in which parent and child share a common rhythm, serves not only to strengthen the basic bond between them but also to provide a strong basis for change and growth. As every parent knows, the pattern of growth in childhood often involves tak-

---

9. *Mind-Body Therapy*, 202–3.
10. C. Pert, "Neuropeptides: The Emotions and Bodymind," *Noetic Sciences Review*, 2, p. 16. Quoted in *Mind-Body Therapy*, 219.

ing two steps forward, then one step back (in order to consolidate gains and establish a solid base from which to take the next step forward). In order to risk trying out new behavior, a child needs to feel safe, and the sense of unity with a parent (on a physical/emotional level) offers a solid platform from which to jump to the next stage of maturation.

In this moment of physical/emotional unity, the parent's assurance of love and pride in the child further strengthens the solid base under the child, so that she feels supported in attempting whatever change of attitude or action the parent is offering as a possibility. She also feels supported in situations in which healing of physical or psychological trauma is needed, and the body/emotion connection with the parent is especially significant in helping the child activate her immune system or shore up fragile psychological structures.

The more a parent uses Sleep Talk with a child, the more solid the child's base of self-confidence and trust becomes, and the more inclined she will be to try out the options the parent is offering. Thus, success builds upon success, as the bond between parent and child becomes ever stronger.

The next chapter presents seven simple, specific steps you can take to help ensure an effective use of Sleep Talk with your child.

3

SEVEN STEPS TO SUCCESS WITH SLEEP TALK

As profound as the effects of Sleep Talk are, the process of doing it is simple. Here, in a nutshell, are the seven steps you need to follow for successful results with your child:

1. Identify your child's needs.
2. Prepare and record the script.
3. Approach your sleeping child and identify yourself.
4. Read the Sleep Talk card word-for-word.
5. Read for a minimum of five nights; break for one or two nights, then repeat the process.
6. Avoid discussing Sleep Talk with your child.
7. Expect results.

1. Identify your child's needs.

The most important thing to recognize, first of all, is that what requires attention is *your child's needs, not your own.* Your responsibility as a parent is to assist your child at each stage of life in achieving the tasks appropriate to that stage. In order to do this, you need to pay attention to what she is struggling to do and offer her tools that will help her accomplish those tasks.

It's important to recognize at the outset that the Sleep Talk scripts in this book are not designed to produce a "perfect" child (whatever that is). Rather, the scripts are geared toward helping you help your child deal with particular areas of stress at her present stage of life. They cannot substitute for your close attention to your child and her personal problems.

I'll be discussing in the next chapter the major tasks of each life stage and how the scripts in this book are geared to communicate effectively with children of different ages. But I want to emphasize here that realistic expectations about your child's capacities at each stage are vital to the success of the Sleep Talk program.

For example, it would not be realistic to expect a two-year-old to eat neatly with a knife and fork and with no spills or mishaps. But it might be realistic to use Sleep Talk to help your toddler be more open to eating a variety of foods (if you've noticed that she's a picky eater).

Now, there may be more than one area where your child is experiencing difficulties. The best course is to decide what seems to be troubling her the most, what her own attention is focused on, and choose a script that addresses that.

2. Prepare and record the script.

The following chapters include scripts appropriate to all ages and to a variety of problems. At the end of the book, you will find a Master Index to Sleep Talk scripts. It is likely that one of these scripts will be right for your child.

If you do not find what you want here, you can easily adapt one of my scripts that seems close to your child's particular needs. Before you do this, be sure to read the rest of this chapter for important guidelines.

Once you have decided which script to use, write it on a three-by-five card. The reason for writing it out is so that you will remember what it says. This may sound simple, but I found that by the end of the day (especially when my children were young), I was so exhausted that I would go into a child's bedroom, say the opening lines (which are the same in all the scripts), and then go blank; I would end up stumbling and mumbling, sometimes not addressing the important issue at all. That little three-by-five card kept me on track and allowed me to focus on the connection with my child rather than on remembering the script.

You may want to use a small flashlight or night-light, or simply leave the hall light on, to help you read the card. If your child is young enough to take lengthy naps during the day and you are at home together, you might want to experiment with reading scripts to your child during nap time.

Even if you feel sleepy yourself, even if you feel unable to focus on the content of what you're reading, realize that as you read, you are making space for an important interaction with your child, just as the child is making space while listening to you. Even if on some nights you feel as though you're just reading words, realize that there is a level at which you have prepared *these* words for *this* child, and that preparation and intention fill the moment with power even if you're not "in the mood."

Realize, too, that your care in choosing and preparing this script and participating in this nightly ritual serves as a powerful reminder to you of the loving bond between you and your child. I know that my own Sleep Talk readings to my kids were as beneficial to me as to them.

3. Approach your sleeping child and identify yourself.

After your child has been asleep for an hour or two, he is ready for Sleep Talk. The brain has a protective mechanism, and your child's mind will not let you in unless you approach him in a specific way. Your addressing the child by name and identifying yourself by the name he calls you opens the safety gate so that he can hear you. So, for example, when I have a script to read to my son T.J., I would start by saying: "T.J., this is your mom."

Our conscious processes are not turned off during sleep. Even if your child is in a deep sleep—a delta or theta brain wave level— your speaking his name and identifying yourself brings him up to the alpha level, where dreams and creative thinking take place.

If you have two or more children sleeping in the same room, you need to address them separately (even if you are using the same script for both). The way the brain works, the child who is being addressed takes in the message, while the other one hears it as just so much background noise. Once the second child's name is mentioned, she tunes in to the message meant for her.

Tara and Briana, my two daughters, shared a room when they were little, and one morning Tara said to me, "Were you talking to Briana last night?" When I said I was, she said, "Oh, I thought so," but never mentioned being aware that I had read a script to *her* just before I read one to Briana. Even though Tara realized that I was talking to her sister, she had no interest in the content of what I was saying, since the message was not addressed to her.

4. Read the Sleep Talk card word-for-word.

After addressing your child by name and identifying yourself, you say the most cherished words any of us can hear from a parent: "I want to let you know how much I love you. I want to let you know how proud I am that you are my son/daughter."

Don't give in to the temptation to edit these sentences in an effort to make them more concise. It is less effective to say: "I love you. I'm proud that you are my son/daughter." The phrase "I want to let you know" puts you in the picture and adds emphasis to this all-important message. Not only do you express your feelings for the child, but you also make a point of expressing *your desire to communicate your love and pride.*

Once your child hears that you love him and feel proud of him, he is likely to be receptive to whatever you have to say next. And you as a parent, having made a heart connection with your child, are likely to offer him the help he needs in the spirit of your love and pride. You are not telling him what to do, not setting goals for him, but rather offering information and confidence in his success.

In our culture, we are rarely taught how to learn from our successes. I sometimes hear people asking an individual who has just achieved something splendid: "How did you do that?" And the most common answer is: "I don't know—just lucky, I guess."

One of the important things the Sleep Talk scripts in this book are designed to do is to offer information about what a child needs to do to succeed in certain areas. The scripts also include an assumption that the child is capable of doing whatever is required for the success. In fact, the scripts offer approval for the child's accomplishment before it is manifested in life—while it is still in potential. (It is no less real for this.)

Am I suggesting that you offer your child untruthful feedback? Not at all. What the Sleep Talk program offers is an opportunity for you as a parent (or grandparent or other caretaker) to see the child through the eyes of love and pride and positive expectations— and for the child to be aware of being seen in this way. All of us perform better under these circumstances.

Scientific studies confirm this. For example, when teachers are told at the beginning of a school year that certain students are gifted (even though the students are average), the children's achievements by the end of the year are greater than those of other average students who the teachers believe have learning disabilities.

So, positive expectations have a demonstrable effect, and when love, pride, and crucial pieces of information necessary for making good choices are added to the mix, the result is a booster shot to your child's self-esteem and achievement. Note that you are not making choices for your child, you are simply offering him choices he may not be aware of and expressing confidence that he will make good ones (possibly better ones than you could have thought of).

The wording of the scripts is designed to offer your child possibilities and tools. Your support and love assist him in making changes he already wants to make (this is where your choice of scripts is so important). And the child's response in this positive atmosphere is likely to be: "Yes, I can do that."

Your closing words again express love and appreciation:

"I love you so much. Thank you for being in my life. I love you. Sweet dreams."

This ending, which is used (with slight variations) in all Sleep Talk scripts, leaves the child with a positive feeling about himself and a signal that this particular message is concluded.

5. *Read for a minimum of five nights; break for one or two
   nights, then repeat the process.*

Different scripts require different amounts of time before effects
become apparent.

Sometimes, as with the script Dr. Jack Gutman read to his
daughter Molly about her piano playing (discussed in Chapter 1),
changes can happen literally overnight, but even with this kind of
quick success, it's important to continue reading the same script for
at least five nights.

With a script about schoolwork, it would be best to read to your
child on "school nights"—Sunday through Thursday—taking a break
on Friday and Saturday nights.

Chapter 1 described the way Barbara used a script on health
when her daughter Maureen was suffering from grand mal seizures.
In this case, Barbara read the script to Maureen for three months
without a break, until finally the seizures stopped. So, in some situations, nightly readings over a lengthy period may be valuable.

You as a parent, being aware of your child's particular problems
and able to assess the effectiveness of a particular script, are the best
judge of how long to continue. In general, I recommend reading for
at least five nights, then breaking for one or two nights before
repeating the process with the same or a different script.

6. *Avoid discussing Sleep Talk with your child.*

It is best not to discuss Sleep Talk with your child.

If she wakes up while you are reading a script, do not explain
what is on the card. Simply say, "I was just telling you good night,
and I love you and sweet dreams." (In other words, say just the last
few phrases on the card, but do not discuss the script's content.)

If your child asks the following morning, "Were you in my
room talking to me last night?" *never deny it.* Say, "Yes, I was
there—just telling you how much I love you, wishing you sweet
dreams." If she is going to remember anything, she will remember
that. Even if she was awake and heard your voice reading earlier
portions of the script, that will make no difference, because she will
not remember the content. But in order to maintain a level of trust

with your child, it's important that, if asked, you tell her the truth about being there.

The reason for limiting your discussion of Sleep Talk is that your child in the waking state can negate anything positive you say about her. She probably won't negate it by denying that it is so. She's more likely to say, "Well, if I'm so wonderful, why did I have to take out the trash?" or "If you love me so much, why wouldn't you let me have the car Saturday night?" Sleep Talk bypasses that kind of negativism, and the message of love and pride and new possibilities gets through without interference.

One night, I was reading my daughter Tara a script about making friends. This was during a troubled time for her—she felt that nobody liked her, nobody wanted to be around her. When I finished reading the script, she turned over and said, "Is there anything else, Mom?" And I said, "No, I think I got it all. I love you." And I walked out of the room.

She never brought up the subject again, and I don't think she meant to reject what I was saying; she knew this was an area she was struggling with. I think she just needed to let me know she wasn't asleep.

The point is, there is no reason to get upset if your child wakes up and asks what you're doing in her room. You're there to tell her you love her and are proud of her. To kiss her goodnight and tuck her in and wish her sweet dreams. Who could object to that?

7. Expect results.

Understand that you cannot set goals for another person, not even your child. But you can support your child, assist him, encourage him. When you see him struggling, you can provide positive information that will allow him to create more satisfying outcomes for himself. In the end, we as parents have to give up our need to control, and trust that our child—given love and sufficient information—will ultimately make good and responsible choices.

Paying close attention to what is going on in your child's life is essential in choosing a script that addresses his needs. But even if you choose an inappropriate script, there are still benefits, since all the scripts strengthen the bond between parent and child.

Suppose the script you have chosen addresses a specific problem—say, your child's shyness—and after five nights, nothing seems to be happening. Then one day you go to a conference at his school, and his teacher says, "I think you need to have your son's eyes tested." You do this and discover that he needs glasses. Now you realize that the problem was not your son's shyness, but rather his blurred vision. You saw his symptoms clearly but misunderstood the cause. So, you shift to another script, one that helps him adjust to wearing the glasses.

Be aware that your first efforts with Sleep Talk may simply lead you to realize that you are using an inappropriate script. That is valuable information, since it helps you rethink your child's primary problem and try a different script. There is no formula for choosing the right Sleep Talk script. Painting by numbers doesn't work when we're dealing with human beings. It's essential to keep looking at your child's behavior, keep tuning in to his particular problems. There is no substitute for paying attention.

When you do find the script that is appropriate for your child's needs at this particular moment, the results will be clear. There will be changes in his behavior and attitude. You may see these for yourself, or you may hear about them from others, such as your child's teachers.

There will be times when a child's behavior and attitudes show marked improvement after working with a particular script. It's fine to stop reading at that point, but be aware that with some problems, it may be helpful to return to the script later. For example, in the Introduction, I discussed the problems of ten-year-old Kevin, whose perfectionism and anger made family life difficult. After his mother read him a script on attitude adjustment, his behavior improved greatly. Some months later, when a stressful situation at school triggered his old problems, his mother went back to reading the same script, with good results.

It's important to understand that in cases like Kevin's, you are not going to be able to change the child's basic character structure, but you can give him tools that will help him use his natural qualities in more effective ways. His skill in using these tools is likely to develop gradually over time, and your patience and persistence in

returning at appropriate times to certain key scripts will pay big dividends in his increased effectiveness and self-esteem as well as in your
relationship with him. Building on success, step by step, is the name
of the game here.

When a script is working for your child, you may get verbal feedback that lets you know he is getting the message. For example, one
day I was driving my son T.J.—who was then in the sixth grade—
home from school. I asked him how school had been that day, and
he said, "Fine." Then he reached over and patted my knee, saying,
"You're proud of me, aren't you, Mom?" Now, that particular phrase
happens to be one I specifically use in Sleep Talk, and his quoting
it confirmed for me that he was hearing the script I was using. Time
and again, my clients and students have reported similar experiences.

Obviously, T.J. feels good about my pride in him, and when he
comes to make decisions about how to handle particular situations
in his life, I believe he's aware that certain choices might help sustain my pride, while others might not. I hope this helps tip the balance for him in picking more positive alternatives. It seems to me
that's an appropriate role for a parent—not to force a child to do
anything, but to encourage him in certain directions.

I like the way a client of mine put it: "My grandmother used to
say, 'You'll catch more flies with honey than with vinegar,' and
that's exactly what your Sleep Talk does!"

4

SCRIPTS FOR
DIFFERENT AGES
AND STAGES

You can begin using Sleep Talk at any stage of your child's life. The only prerequisite is your love and desire to deepen your communication with your son or daughter.

The two-minute nightly script reading provides information that can help your child take the appropriate next step toward maturity. This chapter offers some guidelines about what tasks children are ready to accomplish at different ages.

It's important to understand that *the agenda for growth is set by your child, not by you.* Your job is to pay attention to the child's efforts and do your best to help him use his energies more effectively to achieve the goals of his particular stage of life.

Building Skills by Stages

Sleep Talk scripts vary according to the age of the child and the complexity of the tasks she is ready to take on. For example, children of all ages are able to take on some degree of responsibility. But the responsibility of a newborn (which is simply to sleep and eat and grow and begin to communicate her needs to adults) is less complex than that of a school-age child.

Helping your child learn to take responsibility appropriate to her age is a way of helping her keep herself safe. You want to give her information she can take in and use at each stage. But once you give her this information, the next step in her growth is for you to get out of the way and let her practice using the information within the framework of her present abilities. This allows your child to assimilate the information and gain confidence that will allow her to move to the next level. In this uncertain and dangerous world, it is difficult for parents to trust that the essential lessons will be learned, but it's essential that parents take that leap of faith and trust the child to do her part. Even for the most loving and concerned parents, it's just not possible to control a child's life from infancy to the teenage years and then expect her to go out into the world and make good decisions and good choices on her own.

Mistakes as Information

One of the most important gifts you can give your child, from birth right through the teenage years, is an environment where he is allowed to make mistakes. As we stumble on our way to learning how to do something, mistakes provide us with information. Nobody is immune to making mistakes. I've made a lot of them on my way to learning how to be a parent, and my kids have been wonderful about forgiving me and loving me anyway.

I think of this whenever I'm tempted to be critical of *their* mistakes.

Messages Beyond Words

The level of vocabulary and sophistication of the ideas expressed in Sleep Talk scripts will of course vary with different ages. The most important communication between you and your child—especially at younger ages—takes place through your tone of voice, the way you hold your child, and other subtle factors that science has not yet found ways to measure. Even before your child exhibits language skills, your reading of Sleep Talk scripts sets up a two-way energy flow between you. Be aware that the words are designed not only as a verbal message for your child, but also as a powerful trigger for your own feelings.

The essential aspect that all the scripts in this book have in common is the love and pride they express. This is the key to establishing the flow of communication between you and your child.

The Purpose of Parenting

There is a purpose to this whole process of parenting—but nobody tells you what it is when you receive in your arms that little bundle wrapped in the pink or blue blanket. When you look at that little face that's been entrusted to you—and the thrill and terror of your new responsibilities suddenly hit you—nobody tells you that if you live long enough and if you survive the inevitable stresses and mistakes, the best part of parenting is having your children in your life as adults. So, your ultimate purpose is to get through the child-development years to savor the pleasure of having in your life a magnificent adult with whom you have an excellent relationship. What you're aiming for is to have your kids become self-sufficient, independent adults who like themselves, treasure their childhood memories, and enjoy interacting with you. If you're aware at the beginning how this process works, you can make better choices about the kind of memories you want to end up with.

Prenatal Bonding

Communication between parent and child begins earlier than you may realize. Scientific studies show that the fetus is strongly influenced by the mother's feelings toward her pregnancy and also by the quality of her relationship with her partner. The father's attitude toward the child is also extremely important.

There are certain techniques both parents can use to connect
with the unborn child, and these preparations frequently influence
what happens in the delivery room. In Chapter 5, "Sleep Talk Before
Birth," I offer scripts that can help both mothers and fathers achieve
an uncomplicated delivery and rapid bonding with their baby after
birth. I also offer a script that can help you prepare your children
for the birth of a sibling.

Infancy

In the first year of life, the baby learns an immense amount. He learns
to breathe in the first moments after birth, makes a connection with
his mother, learns to eat. Soon he learns to trust that he will be fed
when he is hungry and that his needs will be attended to. Establishing a strong bond of trust with parents is the most important task
of this stage of life, and the basic Sleep Talk bonding script is designed
to facilitate this process for both parent and child.

The parental message to the child is simple: I love you, I'm proud
of you, you are a wonderful baby, and I'm so happy that you are
my son/daughter. Through hearing this message repeatedly, the child
develops a feeling of being welcome in the world. Despite occasional
frustrations caused by hunger or the discomfort of wet diapers, he
is reassured that others value him and can be relied on to help him
get what he needs.

From the parents' perspective, the Sleep Talk script offers important benefits also. Through repeated readings of this message, parents come to appreciate more fully their role in the baby's life.
Affirming the love and pride they feel helps to nurture those feelings. At a time when sleep deprivation is a special hazard, new parents may need this periodic reminder of how important their child
is in their lives.

Toddlerhood

In the second year of life, children begin to be aware of issues
around exploration, separation from parents, and self-control. The

toddler's ability to walk allows her a new freedom and self-confidence to make discoveries about her world. This urge toward independence inevitably brings her up against boundaries and limits as she discovers that her own desires may conflict with those of her parents.

At this age, the child is able to understand many words, and her speaking vocabulary is also expanding. Through hearing her parents say "no" to various activities she wants to pursue, she realizes that she, too, has the power to say this magic word, and it becomes a refrain in her life. Because of the dance that parents and toddlers frequently do around this word, I have tried to avoid using it with my kids whenever possible. Instead of saying, "No, don't touch that," I say, "You may touch that with one finger." Phrasing communications in a positive way has the advantage of keeping the "nos" for the big issues.

Parents often talk about the "terrible twos," but this is in many ways a wonderful age. The child's development is proceeding by leaps and bounds, and he is eager to learn and explore and grow. He's learning to feed himself, learning to control his body functions (toilet training), learning to relate to others in the family.

Your appreciation of his boundless energy, adventurousness, and excitement about the world can help him succeed in the tasks of this age level. Chapter 6 includes scripts you can use to support your child through the major challenges of this age: bonding with a parent, bonding with a working parent, bonding with sister/brother, toilet training, trying new foods, and sleeping.

Preschool Age

From age three to age five, children make huge advances in physical growth, language abilities, and learning. They learn to interact with other children, enjoy using their imagination, and take significant steps toward establishing a self-concept.

At this age, the child is especially sensitive to praise and blame, so using Sleep Talk scripts can be especially helpful in building a positive self-image. Children of this age need to learn how to focus their energies, and they are eager to help with household tasks.

Along with all the new explorations the child is involved with at this stage, she is also beset by many fears and phobias. Such issues as sibling rivalry, excessive thumb sucking, bed-wetting, safety, and respect for property may need attention from parents, and I provide scripts on these issues in Chapter 7.

Many children at this age become involved in day care arrangements for the first time, and Sleep Talk can help your child to do well in school, learn to listen, get along with others, take turns, pay attention, participate on the playground, maintain health, and exhibit self-control. Chapter 8 offers scripts on all these subjects.

School Age

Between the ages of five and twelve, children make the enormous transition to the wider world through their attendance at school, involvement with formal learning, and expanding relationships with peers and adults.

From age five to age nine, they learn the pleasure of work and find stimulation in new ideas and new activities. At this stage, they come to understand the connection between their value in the world and the things they produce (for example, their grades for schoolwork and their participation in sports). They come to see themselves as "competent" or "incompetent" based on their achievements.

From age ten to age twelve, their major task is to get a sense of their own core identity, and their relationships to their peers help them define themselves. Also at this age, consciousness of sexuality develops, and children begin to focus on relationships with the opposite sex.

Throughout this period, issues arise about self-confidence, self-control at school, participation in class, being on time for school, listening, staying on task, keeping one's room clean, homework, fingernail biting, injuries, attitude adjustment, shyness, teamwork, relationships with family, safety, and sleeping habits. Chapter 9 offers scripts you can use to help your child deal successfully with these areas as well as with those relating to various aspects of academic schoolwork.

Adolescence

Relationships with the opposite sex take on even greater importance from age thirteen on, and personal identity and image become a major focus. At this age, ties with the family begin to loosen, and peer pressure becomes a more powerful force.

Particularly pressing issues for adolescents include self-confidence, caring, perseverance, homework, common sense, leadership, initiative, choices about time and money, making friends, organizational skills, and sexuality. Chapter 10 presents Sleep Talk scripts that parents can use to offer significant help in these areas.

Responsibility and ethics become increasingly important as teenagers "try on" adult roles in interactions with friends, family, and employers. Chapter 11 offers special scripts related to values and responsible behavior in such areas as manners, using effort for inner direction, protection of property, stealing, telling the truth, honesty, exchanging and sharing property, improving performance, dealing with anger, and being assertive.

Because one of the major tasks for children at this stage of life is to achieve self-sufficiency and independence, teenagers may resist a parent's attempts to be helpful. For example, Sean at age seventeen was on the brink of serious trouble. Caught with a group of friends speeding in a stolen car, he already had a felony conviction on his record. Donna, his mother, came to me because of her concern about his heavy smoking, his drinking, and his choice of friends. Together we worked out the following script for her to read to him:

《 *Sean, this is your mother.*
 I want to let you know how much I love you.
 It makes me happy when you don't drink or smoke, but take care of your body.
 I appreciate it when you surround yourself with trustworthy friends.
 I enjoy seeing you happy, healthy, and having fun.
 You pick and keep good people to have fun with.
 Sometimes things may not be easy in the beginning.
 I am proud of your effort to move beyond barriers to a place of achievement.

Thank you for your effort to achieve.
Thank you for being my son.
I love you.
Sweet dreams. 》

After she had read this script to him for three or four nights, she found he had placed a chair under the doorknob inside his room to prevent her entering. The next day, she called to ask me what she should do about this. Usually, as I indicated in Chapter 3, I recommend that parents avoid discussing Sleep Talk with their child, but in this instance I suggested mother and son come in for a talk with me.

During our session, Sean admitted that he was not happy about the results that his behavior was producing. Even though he knew that he needed to do things differently, he had fallen in with a particular group of kids, and most of the time he just went along with their agenda with no particular desire to change.

I described to him the process of Sleep Talk and explained that his mother was trying to help him. I asked him to give her permission to continue reading to him, with the understanding that he would be the one to make the ultimate decisions about his own life. He did give her permission and stopped putting the chair under the doorknob at night.

Six months later, he graduated from high school with his class (an outcome that had been seriously in doubt), brought home a new group of friends, got a full-time job, and stopped smoking and drinking. The last I heard, three years later, everything was going well for him.

With teenagers like Sean, discussing Sleep Talk may be necessary to secure their cooperation.

Adulthood

If you are considering using a Sleep Talk script with adult children who are living at home, the kind of discussion Donna and I had with Sean would probably be essential. It might also be helpful to show the adult child this book as a way of letting him know how the technique works.

My own grown children often request that I help them with various problems in their lives through reading scripts to them, and it's possible that this pattern will emerge in your family also. For example, when my daughter Briana was getting ready to take the bar exam, she requested that I prepare a script to help her. (She passed the exam on her first try.)

Crisis Periods and Special Needs

Sleep Talk's power becomes especially evident at times of crisis. When families experience major health problems, divorce, or death, this technique can help children cope with these profound stresses. In adoption situations, special scripts can facilitate the child's bonding with the new family.

When children are struggling to succeed in arts or sports activities, scripts can offer timely information and encouragement. And when physical or mental disabilities come into the picture, timely Sleep Talk can help both child and parents make the most of available resources.

Chapters 12 and 13 discuss all of these areas and offer scripts tailored to a variety of specific problems.

Script Readers

At my classes and seminars, I am frequently asked who should read the Sleep Talk script to the child. The reader could be any caring person: a parent, a grandparent, an aunt or uncle, a caretaker. I have known situations in which an older sibling takes on the role of parent for a much younger brother or sister, and in cases like this, having the older child read Sleep Talk scripts might be extremely helpful. The scripts in this book could easily be adapted for use by people in any of these categories.

Foster parents might also use Sleep Talk, but I would insert a note of caution here. If you are providing foster care for a child, it's important not to make promises you may not be able to keep. It would be best to avoid bonding the child tightly to your family if the connection might be temporary. Of course in a case like this, there would be nothing wrong with telling the child how wonderful he is, how much you appreciate whatever he is doing, and how pleased you are to have him in your life.

Medical Applications of Sleep Talk

Another area my students often ask about is medical applications. My nursing experience suggests that Sleep Talk can be a powerful force for healing in a hospital situation as well as at home. I know a pediatric nurse who uses the following script with her patients:

> « *Carol, this is your nurse, Kathy.*
> *I want to let you know how wonderful I think you are.*
> *I appreciate your willingness to do what it takes to get well.*
> *You are a good team player with the medical staff.*
> *Thank you for opening yourself up to heal.*
> *Do what it takes to activate your immune system.*
> *Let your body do what it knows how to do.*
> *Thank you for being who you are.*
> *I love you.*
> *Sweet dreams.* »

I suspect that medical uses of Sleep Talk techniques could be effective with adults as well as with children, and I am currently developing applications in this area.

Sleep Talk for Adults

The techniques I describe in this book might very well be expanded to allow spouses or domestic partners to help each other through Sleep Talk. The basic principle of expressing love, pride, and support is applicable to any close relationship in which people share living space. The underlying question, of course, is one of trust, with both parties being responsible for themselves and each other. I can envision a variety of scenarios through which significant help might be requested or offered—and given.

Another possible application is for adult children to offer love and acceptance to infirm parents in home, nursing home, or hospital situations. When the mother-in-law of my coauthor Patty underwent open-heart surgery, Patty prepared several scripts to read. The first was simply supportive—expressing love and appreciation on behalf of her husband and herself for his mother's being in their life. Later, when her mother-in-law was unconscious and near death, Patty read a second script expressing their appreciation for her and her life, telling her they loved her so much that they never wanted her to suffer. Whatever decision she made about living or dying, Patty said, they would accept, but they did not want her to go without knowing that she was loved. For two days, every time Patty went into her mother-in-law's hospital room, she read this script. At the end, her mother-in-law regained consciousness, told everyone in the room she loved them, closed her eyes, and died.

As I mentioned, I am currently developing techniques that can be used with adults in various areas, and I will have more to say about this subject in a subsequent book.

5

SLEEP TALK

BEFORE

BIRTH

Medical research confirms what many pregnant women already sense: that there is powerful two-way communication between mother and child during gestation. Sleep Talk is one technique you can use to let your unborn child know that he or she is loved and welcomed. The scripts I have used with pregnant women and their husbands have had powerful effects both physically (in the smoothness of pregnancy and delivery) and emotionally (in establishing the bonding process between parent and child through an atmosphere of love and trust).

In order to appreciate the value of Sleep Talk during pregnancy, you need to know something about the research that has been done in recent years on fetal-maternal communication. You might also find it helpful to have some information about my personal experiences with pregnancy and birth.

I went through my three pregnancies during the '60s, a time that looks to me now like the dark ages. Birthing rooms and ultrasound

were unknown, husbands were definitely not welcome in the delivery room, and women in their first pregnancies generally knew far
less about the process than they do today. My medical training gave
me some background, of course; I at least knew what was happening to me physiologically. But knowledge and experience offer very
different perspectives, and I had the usual insecurities.

The most helpful advice I got from anyone at this crucial time
came from my mother. "Remember," she said, "pregnancy is not a
disease." (Many obstetricians treated it that way in those days, and
some still do.) What I was going through was a natural process. I
might be uncomfortable, I might be throwing up, but this was a normal part of the process, and I needed to stay focused on the ultimate goal: a healthy baby.

Many factors are involved in a woman's experience of pregnancy, but studies have shown that her relationship with her
own mother is an important predictor of her comfort level during that period and her avoidance of complications in delivery. I
can well believe this is true, given the easy time I had with all
of my pregnancies.

In fact, I felt so good during my first one that I lied about how
far along I was so that I wouldn't have to quit my nursing job when
the rules said I was supposed to. George and I had recently moved
from Florida to Southern California, where neither of us had any
family, and I didn't know many people. The prospect of sitting at
home all day after six and a half months sounded awfully boring,
especially when I was enjoying my job so much. In the end, I kept
working until I was eight months pregnant. My labor lasted only
four and a half hours (the average for a first pregnancy is eighteen
hours), and I stayed in the hospital the usual three days (quite a contrast to the revolving-door arrangement that's common now).

In my pregnancy with Tara, our second child, I sensed right away
that this baby would be a girl, just as I'd sensed that the first would
be a boy. My feeling toward all three children as I was preparing to
give birth to them was one of tremendous respect, and I suppose
that reflected my own parents' attitudes toward me. I felt very loved
and respected by my mother and father, who always honored my

brother and me as individuals. I think this, more than anything, made me aware that there needs to be some understanding beyond simply loving a child—some acceptance of her as a separate and distinct person.

Later, in a psychiatry class I took at Johns Hopkins, the professor made the point that our goal for our children should be to help them reach their maximum potential, as defined by the child. She put into words the essence of my own parents' attitude toward my brother and me, and this is something I've instinctively brought to my parenting of my own children. The point is not to try to compensate for the frustrations and regrets of your own life by making a plan for your child to fulfill, but to support the child in realizing his or her own dreams.

Factors That Influence Pregnancy and Birth Experiences

Now that my younger daughter, Briana, is pregnant with her first child, I'm more aware than ever of the ways the world has changed since my own pregnancies. When I had my children, the accepted pattern was for a mother to stay home with her kids; nowadays the norm is for her to go back to work soon after giving birth. I'm not convinced this situation is ideal, but it is the world we live in.

When I was pregnant, there was no understanding of the consciousness of the fetus and its ability to see, hear, taste, feel, and learn while still in the womb. The common view then was that at birth, a child is a blank slate whose personality and abilities are shaped by the parenting that he or she receives.

We now know that a child's feelings and perceptions in utero have a strong influence not only on the way he later sees himself (happy or sad, outgoing or shy, confident or anxious) but even on his IQ. Research on this subject clearly indicates that the chief source of the messages the child gets about himself in the womb is his mother. Her attitudes toward herself, her husband, and her pregnancy have a powerful influence not only on the presence or absence of complications in her pregnancy and delivery but also on her child's subsequent health and development.

This does not mean that every minor worry on a mother's part is likely to damage her child. But it does mean that deep, chronic anxieties or serious conflicts about motherhood can have powerful negative effects on her unborn child's personality. It also means that such positive emotions as love and happy anticipation can contribute to the development of an emotionally and physically healthy child.

Research has also made clear that the father's role, far from being that of a mere bystander (as it was commonly seen when I was pregnant), is crucial. Studies have shown that the way a man feels about his wife and unborn child is one of the most important factors in the success of the pregnancy.

Obstetrician Thomas Verny, in his informative book *The Secret Life of the Unborn Child*, summarizes the research in physiology, neurology, biochemistry, and psychology. Studies in all these areas confirm that, from the sixth month in utero onward, the child can remember, hear, and even learn.

Since about 1980, organized programs for parents have demonstrated the benefits of carefully planned prenatal stimulation. The largest experiment in prenatal stimulation took place in Caracas, Venezuela, under the direction of psychologist Beatriz Manrique, involving six hundred families (divided into experimental and control groups) in an experiment that tested the babies for six years following their prenatal program.

Test results revealed the advantages of prenatal stimulation in virtually every category over the entire time period. Babies who received prenatal stimulation showed superior auditory and speech development, motor skills, memory, and intelligence. In addition, mothers who participated in the program had greater confidence in approaching birth, were more active in labor, and had greater success in breast-feeding. Fathers were more strongly attached to the children and remained committed to the family after birth, a significant improvement in family cohesion in comparison with the control group fathers. Because of such positive results, the government of Venezuela has decided to make the program available throughout the country.[1]

Studies have demonstrated that babies are involved in learning their native language before birth. Hearing develops in the fetus as early as sixteen weeks of gestational age, and a mother's voice reaches the uterus with very little distortion, since the sound waves pass directly through her body. Acoustic spectroscopy, which makes possible elaborately detailed portraits of sound similar to fingerprints, has documented prenatal learning of the mother tongue. By twenty-seven weeks of gestation, the cry of a baby already contains some of the speech features, rhythms, and voice characteristics of its mother. Newborns react to language in ways that confirm that learning has taken place in utero: French babies prefer to look at people speaking French, while Russian babies prefer to watch those speaking Russian.[2]

The close psychological connection between a pregnant woman and her fetus was demonstrated in a remarkable experiment by Dr. Michael Lieberman that showed that the unborn child becomes emotionally agitated (as measured by the increasing rate of his heartbeat) whenever his mother thinks of smoking a cigarette. There was no need for her to actually smoke; her merely thinking about having a cigarette was enough to upset him. The fetus of course has no way of knowing whether his mother is actually smoking—or thinking about it—but he is able to associate her smoking with the distressing experience it creates in him. Physiologically, her smoking lowers the oxygen content of the maternal blood passing through the placenta, and this drop in his oxygen supply puts him into a chronic state of anxiety that begins shaping his personality even before birth.[3]

---

1. B. Manrique, "Prenatal, Neonatal, and Early Childhood Intervention in Six Hundred Families: A Study in Progress," *Pre- & Perinatal Psychology Journal* (1989) 4 (2): 73–82

2. B. G. Blount, "Parental Speech and Language Acquisition: An Anthropological Perspective," *Pre- & Perinatal Psychology Journal* (1990) 4 (4): 319–38

3. Michael Lieberman, quoted by L. W. Sontag in "Parental Determinants of Postnatal Behavior," in Harry A. Weisman and George R. Kerr, *Fetal Growth and Development* (New York: McGraw-Hill, 1970), 265.

The work of Dr. Dennis Stott has demonstrated that, by the sixth or seventh month in the womb, an unborn baby is strongly influenced by his mother's emotional state. Dr. Stott reasoned that a child's physical and psychological health at birth and during the first years of life would offer evidence as to the kinds of messages he received from his mother before birth and how clearly he understood those messages.

What emerged from Dr. Stott's research was that the unborn child is capable of discriminating between serious, deep-seated stresses experienced by his mother in the course of her pregnancy and stresses that, while intense, do not threaten her basic emotional security. The data showed that the stresses that counted were personal, usually involving tension with the woman's husband. These stresses "tended to be continuous or liable to erupt at any time and they were incapable of resolution."

Of the fourteen women in Dr. Stott's study who were subjected to these chronic, unresolvable personal stresses, ten gave birth to children with physical or emotional problems. Children born to women who had other types of intense, long-term stresses (such as the illness of a family member) did not have these problems. All of which offers compelling evidence that the unborn child is able to discriminate between stresses that pose a significant threat to his mother or himself and those that do not.[4]

Studies of a thousand babies whose mothers had experienced various degrees of depression during pregnancy showed that the babies themselves displayed depression at birth in proportion to the depression scores of their mothers.[5]

Psychologist Monika Lukesch, after following two thousand German women through pregnancy and birth, concluded in her study that the mother's attitude was the single most important factor in her child's physical and emotional health. Dr. Lukesch's subjects all had similar economic backgrounds and levels of intelligence,

4. Dennis Stott, "Follow-Up Study from Birth of the Effects of Prenatal Stresses," *Developmental Medicine and Child Neurology* (1973) 15: 770–87.

5. V. Lussier, H. David, J-F. Saucier, and F. Borgeat, "Self-Rating Assessment of Postnatal Depression: A Comparison of the Beck Depression Inventory and the Edinburgh Postnatal Depression Scale," *Pre- & Perinatal Psychology Journal* (1996) 11 (2): 81–91.

and all had the same amount and quality of prenatal care. The only major difference among them was their attitudes toward their unborn children, and this made a crucial difference. The children of accepting mothers, who looked forward to having a family, were much healthier, both at birth and afterward, than the children of rejecting mothers.

Another factor that was extremely important in determining whether the child would be healthy was the quality of a woman's relationship with her spouse. Dr. Lukesch rated this the second most important factor in determining the way the child turned out.[6]

Thomas Verny tells a story that vividly illustrates the communication between a mother and her unborn child:

> A child whom I'll call Kristina provides an . . . example of intrauterine bonding. I learned about her from Dr. Peter Fedor-Freybergh, a boyhood friend of mine who is now a professor of obstetrics and gynecology at the University of Uppsala in Sweden and one of Europe's leading obstetricians.
>
> . . . At birth, Kristina was robust and healthy. Then something strange happened. Bonding babies invariably move toward the maternal breast, but inexplicably, Kristina didn't. Each time her mother's breast was offered, she turned her head away. At first, Peter thought she might be ill, but when Kristina devoured a bottle of formula milk in the nursery later, he decided her reaction was a temporary aberration. It wasn't. The next day, when Kristina was brought to her mother's room, she refused her breast again; the same thing happened for several days thereafter.
>
> Concerned, but also curious, Peter devised a clever experiment. He told another patient of his about Kristina's baffling behavior, and that woman agreed to try breast-feeding the child. When a sleepy Kristina was placed in her arms by a nurse, instead of spurning the woman's breast as she had her mother's, Kristina grasped it and began sucking for all she was worth. Surprised by her reaction, Peter visited with Kristina's

---

6. Monika Lukesch, "Psychologie Faktoren der Schewangerschaft," dissertation, University of Salzburg, 1975.

mother the next day and told her what had happened. "Why do you suppose the child reacted that way?" he asked. The woman said she didn't know. "Was there an illness during her pregnancy, perhaps?" he suggested. "No, none," she replied. Peter then asked, point-blank, "Well, did you want to get pregnant then?" The woman looked up at him and said, "No, I didn't; I wanted an abortion. My husband wanted the child. That's why I had her."

That was news to Peter but, obviously, not to Kristina. She had been painfully aware of her mother's rejection for a long time. She refused to bond with her mother after birth because her mother had refused to bond with her before it. Kristina had been shut out emotionally in the womb, and now, though barely four days old, she was determined to protect herself from her mother in any way she could.[7]

All is not hopeless in a case like this. If Kristina's mother were willing to change her attitude, Sleep Talk scripts could be a big help in bonding with her child. But how much better to begin using this powerful technique before the child is born, rather than seeking to repair the damage later.

Communication Channels Between Mother and Unborn Child

Dr. Verny suggests that there are three separate communication channels between a mother and her unborn child:

- the physiological connection (through which nutrients are supplied to the child)

- the behavioral connection (in which the child communicates discomfort by kicking, and the mother communicates reassurance by rubbing her stomach)

---

7. Thomas Verny, with John Kelly, *The Secret Life of the Unborn Child* (New York: Dell, 1981), 76–8.

- the sympathetic communication that lets even a six-month-old fetus know that he is loved (or, as in the case of Kristina, unloved)

It is this last channel through which Sleep Talk communicates, and I believe that the connection these scripts establish during pregnancy can contribute to an uncomplicated delivery of a healthy child and a strong bond between parent and child after birth.

Mental health professionals know that certain women are at especially high risk when they become pregnant:

- a woman who is extremely worried about the effects of pregnancy on her physical attractiveness

- a woman who has a bad relationship with her own mother

- a woman in a troubled marriage

While Sleep Talk scripts are not a panacea, I believe they can make a huge difference in mitigating the effects of stress in situations like these.

Women whose salaries are essential to the support of their families are also at considerable risk, and nowadays such women are far more numerous than their stay-at-home sisters. My daughter Briana is a lawyer, and it is unlikely that she will give up her profession after her baby is born. Both she and her husband are using Sleep Talk scripts to communicate with their unborn child, and I feel confident that she will continue feeling good through the rest of her pregnancy and that her delivery will be smooth and uncomplicated.

The Child's Role

The sense of mutual responsibility of mother and child for each other's well-being may seem fanciful, but I can assure you that it is based on sound medical evidence. Until a few decades ago, it was assumed that the burden of physiologically sustaining a pregnancy fell entirely on the mother. But it is now clear that the child's role is also significant.

It is the fetus who triggers many of the physical changes his mother's body must undergo to sustain and nourish him. The placenta, which is an organ of the unborn child, produces various hormones that maintain the pregnancy. By producing these substances, the fetus participates in his own survival. If a child senses himself in a hostile environment, in some instances he may withdraw this physiological support. The result could be a so-called spontaneous abortion.

Using Sleep Talk can help the unborn child sense that he is loved and wanted, and so offer important encouragement for him to do everything possible to come into the world whole and healthy.

Memories of Birth

My studies with Dr. David Cheek in the early '70s gave me many insights into our abilities to remember the details of our birth and even the time before it. One of the hormones (oxytocin) present in the mother's bloodstream during the normal birth process (and shared with her child via the placenta) has a side effect of obliterating direct memories of birth, but Dr. Cheek suspected that under hypnosis these memories might become accessible. (The same is true of people under a general anesthetic; through hypnosis, many are able to remember minute details of what went on in the operating room.)

Dr. Cheek performed a stunning experiment in which he put under hypnosis four young men and women he had delivered during his years as an obstetrician and asked each to describe how his or her head and shoulders were positioned at birth. He was certain there was no way his subjects could know this, since the information had been in a locked file in his office for more than two decades.

In every case, what the hypnotized person told Dr. Cheek was later confirmed by his records. Each man and woman accurately described how his or her head had been turned at birth and which arm emerged first, as well as the way he or she was delivered (head first or breech).

If a person can remember a detail as minor as how his head was turned at birth, it seems likely he will also have a memory of more unsettling events, such as the struggle through the birth canal, the panic at being unable to breathe for a few seconds, the trauma of being born prematurely. And if these common experiences are complicated by his mother's fear or resentment, the effect must surely be profound.

Insights Through Rebirthing

In several private sessions with Dr. Cheek, I learned the techniques of rebirthing that he had developed to help people handle the effects of their traumatic birth experiences. Even when the birth experience has been less than traumatic, there are often ghosts from the past that need to be laid to rest.

My own birth experience is a case in point. I discovered during my sessions with Dr. Cheek how frightened my mother was about her pregnancy with me and how unprepared she felt to take care of me (her first child). This was not a case of her not wanting me, but simply of her fearing that she might unintentionally harm me in some way through her ignorance. I've heard her say to people, "Lois nearly starved to death because she was allergic to my milk." But the problem was that she was so anxious about doing everything right that her body simply shut down, and she didn't have enough milk for me. Obviously, I was never in any danger of starving. When I talked with her later about my session with Dr. Cheek, she confirmed that these were indeed her feelings, and she was amazed that I had any way of knowing about them. Typical of my mother, she was completely open to this new perspective. "Oh," she said, "so that's the reason I did that!"

One of the things Dr. Cheek and I discussed during my studies with him was the problem many people have in differentiating between an unwanted pregnancy and an unwanted child. For an individual who has carried from birth the belief that he was unwanted, it can be extremely helpful to examine the possibility that, even though his mother's pregnancy with him might have been inconvenient (because of finances or being unmarried, for example), by the time he was born, he *was* loved and wanted.

It is so easy for any of us to assume: *It's all my fault*. In the case of a child sensing his mother's anxiety around her pregnancy, it would be a small step to assume he was unwanted. But again, an unwanted pregnancy does not necessarily mean that the child, once he was born, was unwanted. The techniques Dr. Cheek developed offer a powerful tool for reimagining our birth the way we want it to have been, including feeling loved and wanted. Experiencing this process can make a difference in the way we perceive ourselves from that moment on.

My experience of Dr. Cheek's work made me aware, above all, of how important it is to find a way to dump the garbage of our past. The Sleep Talk scripts I have since developed are geared to helping parents and children do that not only after birth but even before. In order for all of us to grow and flower (in the womb or outside it), we need to feel safe. We need to trust our parents and ourselves. The scripts I have used with pregnant women and their husbands have had powerful effects both physically (in the smoothness of pregnancy and delivery) and emotionally (in establishing the bonding process between parent and child through an atmosphere of love and trust).

Using Sleep Talk to Change Negative Patterns

When a woman has a difficult time in labor, she tends to repeat this pattern with subsequent pregnancies. Barbara (whose use of Sleep Talk scripts with her daughters is described in Chapter 1) took my class after she had experienced a difficult delivery with her first daughter and was pregnant with her second. I suggested she use the following script (the same one my daughter Briana is now using):

《 *Baby, this is your mother.*
 I want to let you know how much I love you.
 I want to let you know how much I am looking forward to holding you and having you in my life.

Thank you for helping me keep healthy during this
  pregnancy.
I look forward to taking care of you.
Thank you for taking care of me.
When it is time for your birth, move toward the light.
When it is time for your birth, move through the birth canal
  smoothly and quickly.
Move toward the light.
Regardless of the circumstance, we will be OK.
I love you.
Sweet dreams. »

Barbara's delivery of her second daughter was much smoother, and with her third daughter, her labor lasted just over an hour. Part of the value of these scripts is that they reassure the mother as well as the child that, no matter what happens, "we will be OK." So, even if there are unexpected complications in the delivery room, the sense of confidence on the part of both mother and baby will bring a positive attitude to the situation.

I have used this script with a variety of women, some in their first pregnancies, others—like Barbara—with a history of difficulties associated with pregnancy. It has had impressive results in every case.

Chapter 1 discussed the case of Jennifer, whose guilt over her son Devlin's premature delivery and her long separation from him after his birth was still troubling her when he was six years old. Had she used the above script before his birth, I believe it might have prevented a great deal of suffering.

Studies have demonstrated a correlation between maternal stress and premature birth. Dr. Cheek, after a lifetime of experience as an obstetrician, concluded that the baby triggers premature labor when it is afraid. He found that if mothers verbally reassured the babies that they were safe and should remain inside the mother, the premature labor would stop.[8]

---

8. D. B. Cheek, "Use of the Telephone and Hypnosis in Reversing True Preterm Labor at 26 Weeks: The Value of Ideomotor Questioning in a Crisis," *Pre- & Perinatal Psychology Journal* (1996) 10 (4): 271–84.

Much has been learned in recent years about the hazards of neonate intensive care units (NICUs). Not only do children grow more slowly when isolated in these units, but also separating the baby from his parents at this critical stage is likely to interfere with bonding. When Stanford University experimented with allowing parents into its NICU, researchers discovered that infection rates did not increase, and the premature babies who had been visited and touched regularly had significantly higher IQs than those kept in isolation.[9]

More NICUs now allow parents to visit and touch their infants, but this practice is by no means universal. If I were expecting a baby today, I would certainly discuss with my doctor early in the pregnancy what facility my child would be placed in, in the event of a premature birth—and make sure it is one that allows visitation. If my baby had to spend time in one of these units, I would make sure to visit often and to read the script from Chapter 6 on bonding with a parent.

Understanding the Birth Process

The more you know about your body and the process of pregnancy and birth, the more easily you'll be able to visualize the kind of experience you would like to have with your baby's birth and the more confident you'll feel about trusting your own instincts. There are many good books available today to help you understand what is happening. Of course, you need to be open to whatever arises; your experience probably won't be exactly the way you imagined it, but it could be even better. Whatever information you can get from books and from women who have had successful pregnancies can help you "program" yourself for a smooth delivery.

All these efforts will enhance the value of the Sleep Talk scripts you use to talk to your baby beforehand.

---

9. Marshall H. Klaus and John H. Kennell, *Maternal-Infant Bonding* (St. Louis: C. B. Mosby, 1976), 104.

It's also important to feel confident about the team who will be assisting at your delivery. Nowadays, birth-preparation classes, birthing rooms, and the presence of the baby's father as part of the team can offer wonderful psychological support for women. As more and more mothers work outside the home, more and more fathers are taking an active role in nurturing and caring for their babies and sharing household tasks.

The Father's Role

One young man I know, a representative of one of the pharmaceutical companies who regularly visits my husband's medical office, was telling me one day how excited he was about his wife's being pregnant. He said he wished there were more he could do. Of course that was a natural cue for me to say, "I know something else you can do." I explained how Sleep Talk works and gave him the following script:

《 *Baby, this is your father.*
I want to let you know how much I love you.
I want to let you know how much I am looking forward to having you in my life.
Thank you for coming into my life.
I am so excited thinking about you.
We will see you when the time is appropriate.
Remember to move toward the light.
And take care of your mother.
I love you.
Sweet dreams. 》

He told me later that he had used the script regularly and that it seemed to give his wife more confidence. This isn't surprising, considering that this script includes a powerful expression of his love for his wife. It makes clear that he cares deeply about the health of both mother and child, and that's a welcome reassurance for a woman in the midst of a pregnancy. As we've seen in the studies I described, the woman's sense of trust and safety in her relationship with her husband helps her create a sense of trust and safety for the child in her womb.

The Role of Siblings

When a family is expecting a new child, it's important to include older children in the process. A script that offers love and appreciation to brothers and sisters for their care of the baby is likely to go a long way toward defusing sibling rivalry.

When Barbara became pregnant for the third time, she asked me for a script that would help prepare her two daughters for the arrival of a baby sister. Here's the one I gave her:

《 *Georgia, this is your mom.*
I want to let you know how much I love you.
I want to let you know how proud I am that you are my daughter.
This is an exciting time for all of us.
We are going to have a baby, and you are an important part of it all.
Thank you for being this baby's big sister.
This baby needs you to teach her how to be as wonderful as you.
I appreciate all the wonderful things you are.
I love you so very much.
Sweet dreams. 》

This script allows the older children to feel loved and secure, and it reassures them that their relationship with their parents isn't going to be endangered by the presence of the newcomer. That makes it safe for them to allow new people into their lives, in general. It sets a pattern for seeing new people as part of an adventure, not a threat, and this attitude will become especially valuable when the child becomes old enough to move out into the world.

One time, my youngest, T.J., said to me, "Mom, who do you love best?" I said, "I love you with all my mind and all my heart and all my life." He said, "Oh, then you love me best." I said, "No, I love you with all my mind and all my heart and all my life, and I love Trey with all my mind and all my heart and all my life, and I love Tara with all my mind and all my heart and all my life, and I love Briana with all my mind and all my heart and all my life." He said, "Then you don't love me best." I said, "T.J., you are so lucky to have a mother that loves as much as I do."

I think he finally got the idea that *the more people you love, the more love there is.*

When a new baby comes into the family, it's important for the older kids to realize that love is not the same as attention. The baby may need the same type of attention that the older children had when they were infants. And so, you attend to the baby when she cries or when she needs to be changed. An older child may go to the bathroom by himself, but he still needs to be fed and wants to be held, and you do those things for him. Even though the attention may sometimes be uneven, the love is not, and scripts like the one I gave Barbara for her older daughters help both parent and older children realize this.

This kind of script sets up in the mind of everybody in the family the sense that we are a family unit, that we need to help each other as best we can, and that love is a given. Even if one child gets more attention for the moment, that doesn't mean the others are loved any less.

Pregnancy Is Temporary, Parenting Is Forever

It's important for expectant parents to keep in mind that *the name of the game is not pregnancy; it's parenting.* Pregnancy is simply a step on the way to the main event, which is creating a family unit in which love, trust, shared values, and mutual support are the essential foundation. This is established right at the beginning, with the commitment of the mother and father to each other and their child.

The scripts in this chapter, simple as they seem, are in a sense the most important in this book. If parents can create a connection with the child before birth, they will be rewarded in innumerable ways later on. Once love and trust are established and communicated, once that essential bond is established, the problems that arise later are much more easily resolved.

We all become our best selves when we feel loved and valued. One of the great joys of parenting is to see the children you have raised with love and respect grow into adults who love and respect themselves, each other, and you. I have had this experience with my own children, and I know you can have it also.

6

SLEEP TALK AND
YOUR INFANT
OR TODDLER

"A family can bring up a baby only by being brought up by him," wrote pioneering child psychologist Erik Erikson.[1]

This comment seems not only common sense, but also a fundamental principle that's easy for parents to miss in their preoccupation with doing everything according to some book or other. It's important to recognize that at the same time your child is learning how to be a human being, *you* are learning how to be a mother or a father.

In the first two years of life, a child learns and grows a staggering amount. Respecting the changes that go with each new stage—being aware of both the limitations and the possibilities—is essential to parenting today, as it has always been. For the child, learning to trust is the essential task of the first year, as it has always been.

---

1. Erik H. Erikson, *Identity and the Life Cycle* (New York: Norton, 1980), 57.

What is different today, for many families, is the context in which the child learns this fundamental bonding. When I became a mother, most women in my position were expected to stay at home during the first few years of the child's life. Today, far more common is the mother who goes back to work before her baby is a year old.

Some books on parenting have been realistic about this societal shift, but others have made mothers feel guilty about the decision to return to work. I don't see how this serves anyone—the child least of all. In a world where my daughter Briana, pregnant with her first child, is planning to resume her law career after she gives birth, families need to make alternative arrangements that will still allow children to have a solid bond of trust with their families.

Maybe part of the reason so many "authorities" have insisted a mother must stay home with her child in the early years or risk causing irremediable damage is that no one has come up with an alternative that makes sense.

Sleep Talk offers parents such an alternative.

No matter how many caretakers are involved in looking after a baby, Sleep Talk can keep the central bond strong in the lives of both child and parent. Even when a nanny or baby-sitter or day care provider has charge of the child for a significant part of the day, a Sleep Talk script on bonding can strengthen the parent-child connection.

In the larger scheme of things, continual rebonding at night with the parent offers the child a secure foundation. I don't believe that it matters who changes the child's diapers during the day or feeds him, so long as these caretakers are sensitive and affectionate. The child will identify with the spirit of love that is present in all the people who care for him and will still learn the trust that is his most important first-year lesson. It doesn't matter which person brings in that spirit of love, and a child is not harmed by being supported by a series of people rather than by his mother alone.

Bonding with a Parent

Even if you are fortunate enough to be able to stay home with your child during the early years, a bonding script provides a way of dumping whatever emotional garbage may have accumulated in the course of a day and reaffirming the love and pride you feel for your child. Here is the script I used with Briana when she was a baby:

《 *Briana, this is your mother.*
I want to let you know how much I love you.
I want to let you know how proud I am that you are my daughter.
I am so lucky to have such a beautiful, wonderful baby in my life.
I enjoy watching you grow.
You are strong and healthy.
I am proud of you.
I am so happy to see your smiling face.
I love you. ⸺
Sweet dreams. 》

This script would be appropriate for either parent to use with any child during the first year. Its simplicity of both language and message makes it clear, even to a baby. Remembering from the previous chapter how clear communication is between mother and child even before birth, we should not be surprised that even children in their first year of life can understand the essence of this message.

My coauthor Judith Searle remembers hearing her mother and her pediatrician discussing her in his office as she sat on the examining table during her first year. Judith's mother was complaining about her baby's continual rapping on the window with a spoon, and the doctor was offering advice about how to put a stop to this potentially dangerous behavior. ("Swat her on the bottom the next time she does it; with those rubber pants she's wearing, it will make a lot of noise. It won't hurt her, but it will scare her.") What went through Judith's mind as she listened was this: *They think I'm a baby; they think I don't understand.* She never rapped on the window again.

The Sleep Talk script on bonding has the double function of reassuring the child and helping the parent stay focused on what is most important. No matter how frustrated you may feel at the chaos the new baby has brought into your household, your love for her is fundamental. Reaffirming that love during peaceful moments strengthens this all-important bridge of communication.

Communication, of course, is a two-way street. While you are continually trying to be sensitive to your child's needs, she is struggling to make her needs clear to you. Is she crying because she's hungry? Does she need a sweater? In an atmosphere of love, the answers to questions like these become more apparent. As your child becomes aware of your concern for her (and of herself as a person *worthy* of concern), she comes to trust that her basic needs will be met, even though you may not always be physically on the scene.

The Father's Role

Studies of infants' bonding with their fathers have exposed the error behind the notion that a mother's presence is more important to a child than a father's. Even though a man does not experience pregnancy, is incapable of breast-feeding his child, and generally spends less time with the baby than his wife does, his bond with his offspring can be just as strong as hers.

Thomas Verny's study of children's mealtimes offers impressive evidence for this. Knowing that eating is as much an emotional act for an infant as a physical one, Verny reasoned that if the child was "uncomfortable or wary" he wouldn't eat. Therefore, if a baby drank as much while his father was holding the bottle as he did when his mother was holding it, that would strongly suggest he valued both parents equally. And this is the way it turned out to be. The amount the child drank remained the same, whichever parent was doing the feeding.[2]

But what about the father himself? Is he as capable of nurturing a child as the mother is? One of the most positive developments in our society in recent years has been the increasing role of fathers

---

2. Thomas Verny, with John Kelly, *The Secret Life of the Unborn Child* (New York: Dell, 1981), 160–1.

in their children's lives—and the increasing confidence of fathers about their nurturing abilities.

Researchers have found that a father seeing his newborn baby responds the same way the child's mother does: he coos and stares and talks to the baby just as often and just as enthusiastically. Some years ago, Dr. Ross Parke and his team of psychologists made observations in the maternity ward of a small Wisconsin hospital and reported that, when visiting times were adjusted to the fathers' schedules, the fathers touched, held, rocked, hugged, and kissed their newborns as much as their wives did.[3]

Another group of researchers discovered that what produces this engagement of fathers with their babies is the same thing that produces it in mothers—early contact with their infants. The sooner fathers in this study were able to see their newborns, the more absorbed they were, and the more avid to touch and hold and play with the babies. What's more, if the father was present at the birth, he was able to distinguish his child from others in the hospital nursery (which fathers absent from the delivery did not report being able to do).[4]

From the moment of a child's birth, the amount of attention she receives from both parents makes a crucial difference in the kind of person she becomes. After genetic inheritance, the quality of parenting is the single most important factor in shaping a child's intelligence. The kinds of play to which she is exposed, the way she is treated, and the sense of connection with both father and mother all play an important role in the process.

My conclusion from all this is that having the father read the Sleep Talk bonding script to his child is just as important as having the mother read it. There is every reason for both parents to have their separate moments of bonding with their sleeping child in the course of an evening.

---

3. Ross Parke, at symposium on "Maternal Attachment and Mothering Disorders" sponsored by Johnson & Johnson, October 18–19, 1974, p. 61.

4. M. Greenberg and N. Morris, "Engrossment: The Newborn's Impact on the Father," *American Journal of Orthopsychiatry* (1974) 44: 520–31.

Bonding with an Adopted Child

When George and I adopted our son T.J., he was eighteen months old and had been in six homes during the previous five months. Just like any birth child, he needed to feel loved and secure.

Parents often say to an adopted child, "We chose you because you're special." But this message is double-edged. It carries the implication: *If I can choose you, I can also send you back.* Of course, anyone who has ever been a parent knows that, no matter how wonderful any kid is, there are times when you'd like to send him back. But with an adopted child, it's important to be especially careful about the implications of what you say, since he is likely to be especially sensitive on the subject.

Even if a child hasn't learned to trust early in his life, I believe there is no stage at which he cannot learn trust. All he wants is to be loved, and you need to reassure him that he is a lovable child. The other important fact that needs to be recognized is that he is an *addition* to the family—a valid addition.

Here's the script I used with T.J. right after he became part of our family:

《 *T.J., this is your mother.*
I just want to let you know how much I love you.
I just want to let you know how proud I am that you are my son.
You are so special and important in my life.
You are a lovable child, worthy of being cared for and a valid addition to our family.
I am so excited to have you in our family.
Thank you for being in my life.
I love you.
Sweet dreams. 》

When parents adopt a child, often the family is somewhat cautious about rallying around and accepting the new addition. Frequently there is a sense that the child is on probation, with people waiting to see how he turns out before *really* including him in. So, the script is designed to counteract this emotional hedging and bond the child to the parent by reassuring him that he's valuable. As with all the other scripts in this book, supporting the child's self-respect is a basic underlying theme.

In Chapter 13, I'll be discussing in more detail issues and scripts related to adoption.

Bonding of Brothers and Sisters with a New Baby

When a new baby comes into the home, older brothers and sisters are likely to feel left out, as all attention focuses on the newcomer. But if parents are sensitive, they can use Sleep Talk to help their older children bond with the new son or daughter.

When Joan brought her newborn, Lisa, home from the hospital, her older daughter, Nell, was four. A few days after the baby came home, Joan found Nell in the baby's room staring at Lisa in her crib. "How do you like your baby sister?" she asked Nell. "Oh, she's just wonderful," Nell replied, "and do you know that her fingers bend way back?"

Joan called me the next day to ask if I had a script that could help Nell bond with her baby sister. Here's the one I gave her:

« *Nell, this is your mom.*
I want to let you know how much I love you.
I want to let you know how proud I am that you are my daughter.
I am proud to be the mother of such wonderful children.
I feel so happy.
Thank you for all of your help.
I appreciate it when you take good care of the baby and me.
I am so proud of you.
Thank you for being my daughter.
I love you so much.
Sweet dreams. »

Joan noticed that Nell was much more affectionate with the baby after that, and after a few weeks, she stopped reading the script.

When Lisa was two months old, Nell started talking about wanting to hold the baby. Joan put Lisa, who weighed about ten pounds at that point, on the carpeted floor and let Nell hold her there. Then Joan left the room to answer the doorbell. Hearing the baby crying, she rushed back. "What happened?" she asked Nell. "Well," Nell said, "she tried to walk, but she fell." Obviously Nell had tried to stand Lisa up on her feet, and of course she fell over. Since they were on the carpet, there wasn't much damage done, but the event set off a warning bell in Joan's head.

"I know I shouldn't have left Nell alone with the baby," Joan told me on the phone. "But sometimes so much is happening, you get distracted." She asked if I could provide a script that could nip in the bud any resentment Nell might build up toward the baby.

Here's the second script I wrote for Joan to read to Nell:

« *Nell, this is your mother.*
I want to let you know how much I love you.
I want to let you know how proud I am that you are my
  daughter.
I admire the care you give your sister.
I appreciate the love you show.
Thank you for taking care of your sister.
You are a big help to me.
I appreciate your help.
Thank you for being my daughter.
I love you so much, and sweet dreams. »

It's important for older children to be made part of the care-taking process. If they're going to be part of the team, they need to know what their functions and duties are. The biggest mistake Joan could have made would have been to berate Nell for being mean to Lisa. Scolding Nell would only have fed her resentment. But thanking her for taking care of the baby and expressing appreciation for her help encouraged her to make a pattern of those behaviors. Nell became a model big sister to Lisa, and the two girls, now grown, remain close.

Two-Year-Old Bonding with a Parent

The phrase "terrible twos" has a universal meaning for parents. This is the stage at which the child becomes more active and begins to assert his autonomy in the world. The parent can support his tentative efforts at independence by helping him to explore his options.

The importance of the word "no" in his vocabulary at this point indicates that he's becoming aware of his power to choose or reject things in his world. He keeps using the "no" as a way of exploring the limits of his power. He may periodically test those limits by checking out his parents' responses to kicking, screaming temper tantrums. A wise parent will understand that, however maddening this stage may be, the child needs to go through it if he's ever to become an independent, confident human being. For a mother or father to become engaged in a contest of wills with a willful two-year-old is a serious mistake.

Obviously, there are going to be times when a parental "no" is the only appropriate response. Sometimes you will have to say, "No, you may not sit on top of the china cabinet." But I try to say "yes" as much as possible, keeping "no" for the really serious issues (such as the child's being in danger). If you say "no" too often, the child stops hearing it, and it ceases to have any effect at all. I've seen parents in a supermarket with a kid this age, continually saying "no," with the child paying no attention, a whirlwind of activity, cutting a swath behind him.

It's important for a parent to acknowledge that the child now has alternatives and to encourage him to explore them fully. For example, if he wants to eat only peanut butter and jelly sandwiches, it's helpful to remind him that there are other delicious things to eat as well. Parents can be a real world-opener at this point, offering the child new, fun ways to do things and continually reminding him that he doesn't have to limit himself.

When the daughter of a friend and nursing associate of mine had to go into the hospital for a lengthy stay, her husband, Luke, had to take full charge of their son Dennis, who was almost two years old. Luke felt overwhelmed by the antics of this normal, active boy, and

my friend suggested he call me for some help. I explained the way
Sleep Talk works and gave Luke this script to read to Dennis:

« *Dennis, this is your dad.*
    I just want to let you know how much I love you.
    I just want to let you know how proud I am that you are my
        son.
    You are so energetic and enthusiastic.
    You can do so many things now.
    I appreciate it when you become quiet and calm.
    You are very strong.
    You are gentle.
    I know you like doing the same things over and over.
    I get excited when you try new things.
    You are so wonderful.
    Thank you for being my son.
    I love you so much.
    Sweet dreams. »

Luke called me back four days later to say that "Dennis the Men-
ace" had "settled down by half." He was still an active child but
able with his father's encouragement to explore new ways of doing
things. I think reading this script also gave Luke an appreciation of
how exciting the world is for a child Dennis's age and made him
able to see the value in the boy's activities. Rather than feeling
besieged, the father became delighted with his son's curiosity and
intelligence. Thus, the bonding was strengthened on both sides.

Two-Year-Old Bonding with a Working Parent

Chapter 1 described how Dr. Jack Gutman, the sports medicine spe-
cialist, used a script on bonding with his six-year-old daughter
Molly. This same script is appropriate for children from about age
two on. It's a tool both mothers and fathers with demanding work
lives can use to keep lines of communication open with their young
children. No matter who is taking care of the child during the day,

reading this script at night or during a child's nap time reaffirms the parent as the "anchor" of the child's security.

I don't mean to suggest, of course, that a mere reading of this (or any) script can make up for neglect or mistreatment. But in a normal loving family, when adults' careers make it impossible for them to be full-time caretakers, Sleep Talk can serve as a powerful rebonding technique for both parents and child.

Shirley, a student in one of my Sleep Talk seminars, took almost two years off from her job as a flight attendant after her daughter Marsee was born. Shirley's husband, Trevor, was a pilot, and cutbacks in his hours due to the merger of his employer with another airline made it necessary for Shirley to go back to work. They took a lot of care in making an arrangement for Marsee that could accommodate their erratic schedules, and Shirley began reading this script to her daughter:

« *Marsee, this is your mother.*
I want to let you know how much I love you.
I want you to know how proud I am that you are my
daughter.
I want you to know how proud I am even when we are not
together.
You are my daughter, and I love you very much.
When I go to work and I am away from you, I still think of
you.
It is such a pleasure to spend time being with you.
You are my treasure.
I love you.
Sweet dreams. »

One day when I was on my way to Florida to visit my family, I found Shirley working my flight. Since the plane wasn't full, she was able to sit with me for part of the journey and tell me about her experience of using the "Bonding with a Working Parent" script with her daughter.

She confided that she had felt depressed at the prospect of going back to work and really hated to leave the little girl. Then she added, "But you know what, Lois? I think this little problem has actually brought us closer together. I appreciate my time with her more than I ever did." I asked if Marsee had a hard time adjusting to the irregular schedule. "No," Shirley said, "she really likes the woman who's taking care of her, and she seems pretty comfortable with the whole arrangement. At first I felt a little jealous, but I can see that it's a great experience for her."

Without a doubt, Shirley's mature attitude about going back to work was a factor in Marsee's easy adjustment, and the solid bond that had already been established between mother and daughter allowed them both to handle the necessary changes. The underlying love was never in question, and the Sleep Talk script simply helped make the transition smoother for everybody.

The Two-Year-Old Picky Eater

Food often becomes a major problem between parent and child at this age. It's understandable that when the child is dealing with so much that is new in his life he needs some things he can depend on to stay the same. Actually, we all fall back on certain "comfort" foods when we're feeling stressed, and kids are no different from adults in this basic pattern. But with gentle encouragement, a child can gradually expand his range of acceptable food alternatives.

I've observed that in families that treat new foods as an exciting adventure, kids eventually get into the spirit of this approach. But whatever the family's eating habits, a parent can offer a child support in exploring new possibilities.

Patty's grandson Jimmy (whose whirlwind activities were tempered by scripts his grandfather read to him, as she described in Chapter 1) is a classic example of a child whose restless energy continually pushes him to the limits of his ability to cope with new experiences. In contrast to his adventurousness in the rest of his life, his eating habits were conservative in the extreme. The only foods he was willing to eat were peanut butter and jelly sandwiches, French fries, and milk with dry cereal. His mother, Wendy, was concerned that his diet was too limited for his rapidly growing body and expansive spirit.

Here's the script Patty wrote for Wendy to read to Jimmy:

« *Jimmy, this is your mom.*
I want to let you know how much I love you.
I want to let you know how pleased and happy I am when
  you eat your food at mealtime.
You are a good eater.
You keep your body healthy and strong by eating good foods.
I am proud of you when you try new foods.
I appreciate your taking "one bite" of new foods.
It is like an adventure.
Your taste buds are growing up.
Thank you for being my son.
I love you so much.
Sweet dreams. »

Even though Jimmy's repertoire of acceptable foods expanded within the first week that Wendy read him this script, she continued these sessions for several more weeks. The boy's picky attitudes about food disappeared almost completely (he continued to resist spinach), and Wendy reported that he became willing to try at least one bite of anything she put on his plate.

Children at this age are learning to feed themselves, and coping with getting spoon to mouth while keeping some food in it is a major challenge. The resulting mess can be acutely painful to a parent who is compulsive about maintaining a spotless kitchen. After watching four children explore the delights and mishaps of self-feeding, I would advise parents simply to accept the mess and not make an issue of it.

Imagine how awkward you would feel if an injury suddenly forced you to use your nondominant hand to eat your meals. For your child the problem is many times more complicated than that. Remember that he is doing his best and that, given your unwavering love and support for his efforts, he will learn. A sense of humor and a philosophical attitude toward spilled milk can go a long way toward maintaining your sanity during this period of trial and error.

Toilet Training

Parents' patience with messes gets tried even further in the area of toileting habits. Once children become physically able to control their bowels, they need to have a parent show them what to do. My own experience is that the best way to do this is to show them the potty (and perhaps their own roll of toilet paper) in the bathroom. Explain what it's for, but don't push them to control their bowels until they're ready. Let them come into the bathroom and watch while the parent uses the toilet, to see how it's done. The little girl goes to watch her mother, and the boy watches his father.

If the boy's mother is a single parent, she should let him watch her sitting on the toilet but should not try to teach him how to stand and urinate. He'll pick that up from a family member, or at a friend's house, or in nursery school.

As with all new areas of learning, the parent's encouragement is crucial here. If a parent is straightforward about explaining and modeling the appropriate way to use the toilet, the child will be equally straightforward about assimilating this information and taking a healthy attitude toward the process.

Here's a typical script that I offer as part of my Sleep Talk seminars:

《 *Jeremy, this is your mom.*
I want to let you know how much I love you.
I want to let you know how proud I am that you are my son.
You are growing up to be so big.
I appreciate it when you need to go to the bathroom. You ask for help.
Sometimes you may not need help and go to the potty by yourself.
I am proud of you when you go to the pot and keep your clothes and pants dry.
Thank you for keeping your underpants clean and dry.
Thank you for peeing and pooping in the pot.
I am proud of you because I know you are proud of yourself.

Thank you for being my son.
I love you so much.
Sweet dreams. »

There will be mishaps, to be sure, but eventually your child will consistently get it right. The more you support and praise your child's efforts, the sooner that is likely to happen.

Many authorities on child development have pointed out that when infants and toddlers fail to learn, this is rarely because they lack adequate intelligence. Most often, it is because they have not been shown the proper way to do things.

Timing is a key element, and parents need to be alert to the child's readiness for particular kinds of learning. Reading a dozen books on child development will be of little help if a parent fails to recognize the limitations that a child's physical development imposes. Since children vary widely in their readiness for such tasks as using the toilet, parents who can maintain a loving and patient attitude are likely to survive this difficult period with the least psychological wear and tear.

Sleeping

It's important for parents to understand that some children need less sleep than others. One-year-olds generally sleep around fourteen to sixteen hours a night; two-year-olds range from twelve to fourteen hours; and three-year-olds spend between ten and fourteen hours sleeping. Children at these ages also need one or two naps during the day.

Healthy, contented children may not always be delighted to go to bed. However, once they are settled for the night, they usually fall asleep quickly. Sometimes a child will resist going to bed because he hasn't had enough attention, and sleep looks like further isolation. Or he may be overstimulated by scary television programs; it's a good idea to be aware of what he is watching just before bedtime. If a child is slightly anxious, he may become more frightened in the dark.

Judith, my coauthor, remembers being frightened of the dark around this age. She generally resisted going to bed and insisted that her parents leave her bedroom door partly open, with a light on in the hallway. When her parents had company, she frequently would get out of bed and join the adults in the living room. Threats of spanking were ineffectual; as testimony, her mother cites one occasion when Judith climbed up on the sofa in her pajamas and walked up and down on the cushions saying, "Well, make up your mind. Are you going to spank me or not?"

If I had been working with Judith's mother, I would have suggested a script like this:

《 *Judith, this is your mom.*
I want to let you know how much I love you.
I want to let you know how proud I am that you are my daughter.
I appreciate it when you are ready to go to bed after a busy day.
I love you so much.
You become relaxed and rested as you sleep.
If you wake up during the night, it is easy for you to go back into a natural normal sleep.
I love seeing your happy, smiling face in the morning.
Thank you for being my daughter.
I love you.
Sweet dreams. 》

It's up to the parent to make "bed" and "sleep time" safe places for a child. In the Haddad household, stories and back rubs were part of a nightly ritual that made bedtime a pleasant, calm, and loving time. I didn't sing lullabies to my kids, but there were certain folk-type songs they always enjoyed at bedtime, such as "Lavender Blue." T.J.'s favorite was a song that begins: "There's a great big beautiful tomorrow just a dream away. . . ."

I especially like that song because it offers reassurance that tomorrow will arrive and that the child will be safe in the meantime. Parents who send a child to bed as punishment are inviting trouble, it seems to me.

A Strong Foundation

The Sleep Talk scripts I've presented in this chapter—and through-out this book—all have certain themes in common:

- Love for your child

- Respect for your child's individuality

- Pride in your child's accomplishments

- An awareness of appropriate limits and expectations at different stages of your child's development

- A sense that you as a parent are entitled to needs and feelings of your own

The way you treat your child during the first two years of life profoundly affects the more complex stages and communications that come later. No parent gets through this period without making mistakes, but the general pattern of love and delight in your child can override any momentary glitches. The child's basic tasks during this period are to learn *trust* in the parents and *confidence* in his or her ability to be an independent presence in the world.

My message for parents helping their child to accomplish these crucial tasks is similar to the message they are giving the child: use Sleep Talk scripts to strengthen your bond with your child, *trust* your child to communicate his or her needs, and have *confidence* that you are exactly the right parents for this child.

7

SLEEP TALK AND YOUR PRESCHOOL CHILD

I started baby-sitting for Brittany when she was a toddler, partly because I wanted to give T.J., our youngest, the experience of having a "little sister" to care for, and for a year and a half, she was with us five days a week, eight hours a day. After that, she continued to visit on a regular basis.

At age four, she came back for a visit with her mom, a new baby sister, and her grandmother. When I opened the front door, Brittany greeted me with hugs and kisses. Once inside, she checked to see if everything was where she had left it. Then she started up the stairs.

"Brittany," her grandmother said, "you can't go up there. You don't live here."

Slowly Brittany started back down the stairs. When she reached the landing, she stuck her little head through the railing posts and looked at us sitting in the living room.

"It's OK," she said, "I know where everything is. You don't need to worry." And back up the stairs to the playroom she marched.

Brittany remembered where her "fences" were in our home. Having helped build acceptable boundaries herself, she knew how to use them. From the beginning of our time together, I had made it clear that it was OK for her to touch anything in the house with one finger, and I knew I could trust her to take care of my things and of herself.

Respecting Boundaries

In many households with preschool children, the continual refrain is: "Don't touch that," "Leave that alone," "No, don't." Most people talk to their kids this way in the early years of their lives. They do this because this is the way their own parents talked to *them*.

There is a better way, one that's easier on both parent and child.

Learning to show respect for other people's property—for appropriate fences and boundaries—is a major hurdle for children age two to five. One of the essential tasks for parents at this stage is to *enlist the child's help in learning to manage her own impulses*. If parents show sufficient love and respect, the child will respect herself and will take pride in trying out new behaviors that her trusted parents are already giving her credit for.

In order to teach a child responsibility, it's important to actually give her some responsibility, trusting her to observe certain limits relating to valuable and breakable objects. Touching with one finger allows the child to participate with objects in her world. The rule is that *everything is available to her, if she takes care of it*. A lot of times, the child doesn't want to play with an object or even pick it up; if it's beautiful, she just wants to touch it to see what it feels like. So, you give her permission to participate in the relationship by taking care of everything, and you let her touch things with one finger.

Touching with One Finger

My Sleep Talk script for touching with one finger has been extremely effective in helping children learn this kind of responsibility. Here is a script I wrote for Joan, a mother who was exhausted from trying to keep three-year-old Nell from cutting a destructive swath through the family home:

《 *Nell, this is your mommy.*
   I want to let you know how much I love you.
   I want to let you know how proud I am that you are my daughter.
   I want to let you know how much I appreciate it when you take care of your things.
   You are so careful.
   You are careful when you touch pretty things.
   You know when to touch and when not to.
   You know how to touch with one finger.
   I am so proud of you because I know you are proud of yourself.
   I trust you to look after things.
   Thank you for looking after our things.
   Thank you for your care.
   I love you so much.
   Sweet dreams. 》

In just four days, Nell understood the concept of touching with one finger, and from then on, she participated in building the fences that helped keep her family's possessions safe. What makes this technique especially powerful is the underlying message. Joan was, in effect, saying to her daughter: *It's important for all of us to have respect for things, and I have respect for you in trusting you to do that.* Joan was modeling the attitude of respect for Nell, showing her how to claim that quality for herself. Rather than insisting on dominating her child, this mother helped the girl claim a measure of power for herself and practice using it responsibly.

One of the nicest compliments I've ever received was from my daughter Briana: "Mom, one of the great things about you is that when you enter into a relationship, even with a baby, you don't disempower them. You expect them to have a share in the responsibility for the relationship."

This is what allowing the child to touch with one finger accomplishes. This shared responsibility builds on the basic trust established between parent and child in the first two years of a child's life. The question of boundaries is involved with the child's growing sense of himself as a separate person with an independent will, a person able to take the initiative and assert himself in the world with increasing confidence. Throughout the preschool years, a child's self-concept is strengthened when parents praise his accomplishments.

From my observation, parents who take a do-as-I-say-not-as-I-do attitude generally fail in their attempts to instill positive qualities in their children. Usually these parents are simply following the same pattern of parenting that was practiced on them. In order to break this vicious cycle, they need information about a better way, and the Sleep Talk scripts here and throughout this book can offer real help.

Sleep Talk and Language Abilities

As we saw in the last chapter, parents can use these scripts to communicate the love and pride they feel, even to babies and toddlers. A parent's tone of voice has immense power even before the child has any significant language abilities, and it's important to remember that children understand many things that they do not yet have the skill to express themselves.

Between the ages of two and five, language learning takes a series of great leaps forward. At age two, most children have a vocabulary of fewer than fifty words, and they commonly use two-word phrases to communicate, but even at this early stage, they are able to imitate their parents' tone of voice. Between their second and third birthdays, most can use nine hundred words, respond to simple directions, and feel confident about expressing themselves verbally. By age four and a half, most have a vocabulary of nineteen hundred words and form five- or six-word sentences.

Arguing

Toward the end of the preschool period, children become experienced enough with language to begin arguing with their parents and with each other. At this stage, no matter what you tell the child to do, he always has some reason he can't do it. If you ask him to pick up his toy, his response is likely to be that he'll do it in a minute, or he doesn't need to do it, or it's not his toy.

When your four- or five-year-old argues, he's creating a smoke screen so that he won't have to follow through with behavior, and children of this age can be extremely good at this game. When a child discovers his power to use arguments as a way of resisting having others' will imposed on him, he'll commonly extend this behavior to his relationships with other children and dominate them too forcefully.

I wrote the following script on arguing for a mother whose four-year-old son was continually picking arguments with other children in his play group:

« *Ivan, this is your mommy.*
I just want to let you know how much I love you.
I just want you to know how proud I am that you are my son.
You have so much good energy.
It's fun to see you work and play with other children.
You play well with other children and take care of them.
They feel safe when you take care of them.
You have many friends and family that love you very much.
I'm proud to be your mother, and I'm proud that you are my son.
I love you.
Sweet dreams. »

Although there was a definite improvement in Ivan's behavior the week after his mother read him this script, I think his gains might have been even greater had his father—a trial lawyer on whom Ivan seemed to be modeling his behavior—been the one to read the script to him. When a child argues a lot, I've noticed that frequently, one of the parents is in the habit of doing the same thing. I've often seen a Sleep Talk script break up unproductive behavior in both the parent and the child.

Bonding Between Child and Parent

Bonding with a parent, discussed at length in the last chapter, remains all-important, and scripts addressing this issue can strengthen basic trust between child and parent at any age. Inevitably, in the course of an average day with young children, any parent is likely to be over-loaded, distracted, and neglectful. Juggling all the demands, keeping all those balls in the air, is nearly impossible.

Once the kids are finally asleep, you may go into their room and stand there thinking about all the things you didn't say, the hugs you didn't give, all the times you turned them down or yelled at them or sent them to their room.

But now it's time to dump the garbage of the day—all the unfin-ished business—and say what's really important, which is how much you love them and treasure them.

This script on bonding with a parent allows you to reestablish that all-important bond of love and trust:

> 《 *Jerry, this is your mom.*
> *I want to let you know how much I love you.*
> *I want to let you know how proud I am that you are my son.*
> *I love to see your smiling face.*
> *I am happy that you are in my life.*
> *You are my friend.*
> *You are my wonderful son.*
> *Thank you for being my son.*
> *I love you.*
> *Sweet dreams.* 》

Bonding with a Working Parent

It's important to realize that any of these scripts is likely to have as powerful an effect on you as on your child. I wrote a version of the "Bonding with a Working Parent" script for Evelyn, a woman who had two small children and who wanted to go back to school. After she'd been reading it to her kids for about a week and a half, she called me and said, "Lois, this is working so well."

"In what way?" I asked.

"I really work at being a good mother," she said. "Even though there are other things I want in my life, I love my children and would do anything for them. But before I started the Sleep Talk, I never knew I could love as much as I do now. This has been a new experience—finding out how much I can love."

Many other parents who have used my Sleep Talk scripts on bonding respond as Evelyn did. In the push-pull of priorities that parents—and especially working mothers—endlessly juggle, it's easy to forget that the love between you and your child is the highest priority of all, the one that drives all the others. The bonding script serves as a powerful reminder of the commitment you have to your kids. Reestablishing the circle of loving energy between you and your child has the wonderful side effect of replenishing the energies that jobs, schedules, and impossible demands deplete in your daily life.

Helping Others

When we love someone, we want to be helpful, and children, beginning at about age two, increasingly enjoy helping their parents. This impulse to help becomes extended to other family members, and a parent who encourages a child's early efforts is likely to see the helpfulness expanded further to include a baby-sitter or playmate.

Larry is a widower whose wife died giving birth to his younger daughter, Mariel, now one and a half years old. Mariel's three-year-old sister, Trudy, seemed unwilling to have anything to do with her little sister, possibly because she associated the baby's appearance on the scene with the loss of her mother. Here is a script on helping others that I wrote for Larry to read to Trudy:

《 *Trudy, this is your dad.*
I want to let you know how much I love you.
I want you to know how proud I am that you are my daughter.
I want you to know how proud I am of you when you see someone to help.
I appreciate it when you help me.

I appreciate it when you help your little sister.
Thank you for being helpful, kind, and considerate.
Thank you for being my wonderful daughter.
I love you.
Sweet dreams. »

After Larry had read this script to his daughter for five nights, Trudy's behavior underwent a distinct change. When she saw her father feeding Mariel, she reached for the spoon and said, "Me feed baby." Despite the considerable mess involved, Larry was wise enough to let Trudy make the attempt. Eventually he arranged for Trudy to give Mariel her bottle regularly every evening. The relationship between the two girls has continued to develop, with Trudy now playing regularly with her little sister and Mariel responding with delight to this attention.

Focusing Energy

Chapter 1 included a script that Patty's husband, Chuck, read to his four-year-old hyperactive grandson, Jimmy. It combined the "helping others" theme with the idea of focusing energy. In that script, Chuck expressed his love for and pride in Jimmy and thanked the boy for his help in specific areas (in the house, in the car, with his little brother). Then Chuck added the line, "Your calm, relaxed manner and energy makes me smile."

What we're seeing here is a grandfather helping a child with one of his major tasks for this stage of life: establishing boundaries for his behavior. Jimmy was naturally a dynamo—an outgoing child who was blissfully unaware of the havoc he was creating as he charged through the household knocking the tape recorder off the table, flipping the picture sideways, kicking the cat on his way down the hall. He needed to be made aware that his impulses had an effect on others and that others appreciated his controlling his behavior.

Unlike Nell, whose energies were those of a normal child, Jimmy's hyperactivity was so extreme that his doctor had prescribed Ritalin. A script such as the one I wrote for Nell on touching with one finger would probably have asked for changes beyond Jimmy's capacities. But the script that Chuck read about controlling energies had a dramatic effect on the boy's behavior.

After Jimmy's visit with his grandparents, his parents continued reading him a version of the "Focusing Energy" script. Eventually his behavior became so much less frenetic that his dosage of Ritalin could be reduced. But when his parents stopped reading him the script, the medication again had to be increased.

Through trial and error, Jimmy's parents arrived at a cycle of alternating various scripts with occasional periods of no reading. Since Jimmy's rampages sometimes included overly rough play with the family cat, one of the alternative scripts was about taking care of animals, a subject I'll be discussing later in this chapter.

The point I want to make here is that there is a lot of variation among children at this age. Some, like Nell and Brittany, are better able to control their energies, and for them a script like "Touching with One Finger" may be appropriate. Others, like Jimmy, have an extremely difficult time with control of any kind and sorely try the patience of their parents, grandparents, and other relatives.

Whatever the situation with your child, it's important keep in mind that the whole idea of control is brand-new to a child of this age. He wants to do the best he can, and he needs continual confirmation that his struggles are being understood and appreciated.

Thumb Sucking

Children of this age often suck their thumbs, and many parents find this behavior embarrassing. Thumb sucking is basically a form of self-comforting, akin to rocking behavior we often see in preschoolers, and if parents can ignore it, it will disappear in time. There may be a number of reasons a child sucks her thumb. She may be hungry and her parent hasn't acknowledged that information. Or perhaps her bottle was taken away too soon.

It's important for parents to make a distinction between their disapproval of the child's behavior and their love for and pride in who the child is, her essence.

So, a Sleep Talk script may serve not only to create awareness for a parent of the difference between an activity and who the child is but also to let the child know that there is a different way to behave. Here's the "Thumb Sucking" script I wrote for my client Ruth to read to three-year-old Lizzie:

《 *Lizzie, this is your mom.*
   I just want to let you know how much I love you.
   I just want you to know how proud I am to be your mom
      and how proud I am that you are my daughter.
   I want to let you know how proud of you I am when you do
      not suck your thumb.
   When you feel uptight, you can take a deep breath and relax.
   You can feel that warm feeling inside and keep your hand
      away from your mouth.
   You are calm and confident.
   You are wonderful.
   I am so proud of you because I know you are proud of
      yourself.
   Thank you for being my daughter.
   I love you so very much.
   Sweet dreams. 》

Chapter 3 discussed the Sleep Talk principle of staying with positive aspects, rather than suggesting that a child *not* do something, and this script is one of the few exceptions. But in the interest of letting Lizzie know exactly what Ruth wanted, the wording was necessary.

Lizzie's thumb sucking stopped after Ruth read the script to her for four nights. For this little girl, the thumb sucking seemed like a garment she was able to take off and never put on again. Maybe all she needed was to be reminded that her mother loved her, and that reassurance did away with her anxiety and her need for self-comforting.

Bed-Wetting

Thumb sucking and bed-wetting—another behavior of preschoolers that is especially stressful for parents—may both be used as forms of control. A child may deliberately suck his thumb in public, knowing it will embarrass his parents. A child who chronically wets his bed is effectively controlling the family agenda in the morning. The schedule is tight at the beginning of the day in many households, with Mom struggling to get the kids off to preschool so she can get to her job on time. Under this kind of pressure, she may not have time to give the kid a hug, but she'll have to make time to take those wet sheets off his bed.

Occasionally there are physical problems that cause children to wet the bed, but they are rare. Especially when the bed-wetting takes place over a period of time, it is most often a control issue, and the control is being asserted by the child. But if the love and respect the child is seeking through this action are offered freely, there will be no need for him to continue wetting his bed.

The sad thing is that, in their frantic search for something that will put an end to the bed-wetting, parents often resort to embarrassing the child: "I want you to meet my son Johnny. He's the bedwetter." Talk about disempowering! When the parent mistakes the child's behavior for who he is, the child feels totally rejected. You can guess what effect this escalation of the conflict is likely to have on his sheets tomorrow morning.

It's important to recognize that what is involved here is a contest of wills. As with thumb sucking, the fundamental question is: *Who is going to control my body? Whose will is going to prevail?* What the child needs to know (that he doesn't know) is that Mom really loves him and is proud of him, that she respects him as a separate human being with a will of his own who can decide not to wet his bed. His lack of confidence that she honors his right to choose is most likely a major cause of his wetting the bed in the first place.

Fortunately, a Sleep Talk script can usually break this vicious cycle. An example is Damon—a boy in Florida who was a cousin of Mike, the child I described in the Introduction who was terrified of the water. Damon's mother, Laura, seeing the way my script had helped Mike lose his fear of swimming, asked me to write one for her son, who at five and a half was still wetting his bed. This is the script I gave her:

《 *Damon, this is your mom.*
I just want to let you know how much I love you.

*I just want you to know how proud I am that you are my
     son.*
*I want to let you know how proud of you I am when you
     wake up in the morning and your pajamas are dry.*
*When you wake up, you have plenty of time to get to the
     toilet.*
I appreciate it when your bedsheets and you are dry.
*I am proud of you because I know that you are proud of
     yourself.*
*It does not matter where you spend the night—you wake up
     in a dry bed.*
Thank you for being my son.
I love you so very much.
Sweet dreams. »

Laura read the script for five nights, and on the morning of the
sixth day, Damon's sheets were dry. Elated, she stopped the readings, and in a few weeks he began wetting the bed again. So, she
resumed the Sleep Talk, staying with it this time for several weeks
after he stopped the behavior. He never wet his bed again.

It seems to me that Damon's need was not so much information
as attention and love, and when he'd gotten enough, he decided that
the bed-wetting behavior no longer served him.

Being Brave When It Hurts

When children age three to five begin exploring their environment
and moving out into the wider world, it's natural for them to feel a
little scared about hurting themselves. Because parents love their kids
and are more aware than ever these days of the possible dangers, they
sometimes communicate their own anxieties in such a way that the
child becomes terrified of physical injuries. Not surprisingly, when
such children skin a knee or cut a finger, they go into hysterics.

The story I told in the Introduction about Briana's friend who
broke her arm on the playground is an example of this. Thanks to
Briana's confidence in her own ability to control pain and heal herself, she was able to calm her friend in this situation and teach her

the skills she needed. When the friend's mother called me later to express her thanks for Briana's help, she told me that her daughter was usually hysterical over any injury. I sensed that the underlying message from this mother to her daughter might have been: *"You're not going to be safe unless you do it my way, stick close to me, and avoid taking any chances."*

I believe that some children are inherently more inclined to fearfulness than others, but parents can offer valuable information to any child about his ability to heal himself. This reassurance is especially important when the child is wondering how far he dares go in exploring the unknown.

Here is a Sleep Talk script I wrote for Helen, mother of five-year-old Ed. Helen's ex-husband, Leon, liked to take the boy on challenging physical activities such as waterskiing, and Ed, who had little experience of sports, was apprehensive about getting injured. This script on being brave when it hurts can reassure a child about exploring activities that might result in cuts or bruises or falling:

« *Ed, this is your mother.*
I want to let you know how much I love you.
I want you to know how proud I am that you are my son.
I want you to know how proud I am of you when you are brave.
When you have cuts, bleeding, or "owies," you are brave.
You quiet yourself.
You take a deep breath, relax, and begin to heal yourself.
Your body is good at healing itself.
Let your body do what it knows how to do.
I am so proud of you.
You are my treasure.
I love you.
Sweet dreams. »

This script helped Ed see the new experiences with his father as more of an adventure than an ordeal, and after the next weekend of waterskiing, he told his mother, "I got a cut on my leg from the rope, but my body is good at healing itself." One more example of a child's feedback letting us know that he has heard the Sleep Talk message.

Being Brave When Scary Things Happen

Children at this age are experiencing a lot of "firsts," and they need
to know what to do when something new and scary happens. In
1994, when we had a big earthquake in Southern California, four
of my students called me for a script because their kids were scared
of sleeping by themselves.

Four-year-old Sophia, for example, would resist going to sleep.
Even her mother's reading of her favorite bedtime story didn't seem
to help, and the girl would be rigid with fear as her mother tucked
her in. She'd continually get up and come into the living room during the evening, asking if there was going to be another earthquake
tonight. Her parents got used to Sophia's crawling in with them in
the middle of the night, and they usually didn't have the heart to
send the terrified child back to her own bed.

Sophia's mother, Ellen, was one of my students, and I discussed
with the group at some length the special problems the earthquake
had created for their kids. In a situation like this, it's not enough
simply to help your child relax; she also needs to be ready to take
some action.

Here's the script I gave Ellen:

《 *Sophia, this is your mother.*
I want to let you know how much I love you.
I want you to know how proud I am that you are my
    daughter.
I want you to know how proud I am of you when scary
    things happen and you know what to do.
When there are loud sounds or events like an earthquake, a
    rainstorm, an electrical storm, or a thunderstorm, you
    become quiet.
You take a deep breath and relax.
This still means you can take action if you need to.
If you need to take action, you can do it quickly.
You are very brave.
I am so proud of you.
Thank you for being my capable daughter.

I love you.
Sweet dreams. »

In just four nights, Sophia was sleeping through the night in her own bed, but I suggested that Ellen keep reading her the script for another two weeks. Even after experiencing a few aftershocks, Sophia continued to be fine about sleeping alone.

In dealing with fears of any kind, it's important to acknowledge the child's anxiety. Parents who respond to their child's terror by saying, "Oh, don't feel that way" or "There's nothing to be afraid of" or "You're being a sissy" are simply reinforcing the child's feeling of vulnerability. Not only is the child still scared, his trust in the validity of his own feelings is undermined. When you give your child the compliment of acknowledging his fear and praising him for his courage, he comes to realize that fear doesn't need to escalate to panic, that he himself has the power to bring some control to the situation and calm himself. Once again, your acknowledgment of his ability to shape his own responses, even in extreme situations, helps him form habits of coping that will become lifetime strengths.

Fears of New Experiences

When a mother decides to go back to school and puts her three-year-old son in preschool, as Evelyn did, a lot of fears often come up for the child. He may have never heard a siren, never heard the sounds of big trucks, a vacuum cleaner, bells, horns, heavy rain. Here's a script on fears that I wrote for Evelyn to read to Scott:

« *Scott, this is your mother.*
I want to let you know how much I love you.
I want you to know how proud I am that you are my son.
I want you to know how proud I am of you when you see
and hear new things.
You get excited about the sound of trucks, the vacuum
cleaner, bells, horns, the rain.
You can take a deep breath and relax.

You listen to hear and see new and exciting sights and
   sounds.
Thank you for being my wonderful child.
I love you.
Sweet dreams. »

When Evelyn picked up Scott from nursery school after reading this script to him for five nights, the teacher told her there had been a big fire just down the block from the school that morning. With some trepidation, Evelyn asked her son as they drove home, "So, what was it like, having that big fire right near you with all the sirens and everything?"

Even before he spoke, Scott's smile said it all. "Exciting!"

As in so many other Sleep Talk cases, the boy's feedback of actual words used in the nighttime readings was striking. Even though I've been teaching these techniques to parents for twenty-eight years, I'm still stunned when I hear stories like this.

Nowhere is the truth of the biblical words "Perfect love casts out fear" more clearly demonstrated than in the effectiveness of Sleep Talk in dealing with children's fears. What is really happening is that your love for your child is acting as an antidote to the poison that fear instills.

I believe that we learn to love through *being* loved. You are, in effect, teaching your child how to love by expressing your love for him. I believe that all parents love their children; the problem is not with love itself, but simply with *communicating it.* Sleep Talk offers a way of clearing the channels for this loving communication between you and your child. During these crucial first five years, you nourish your child's ability to establish loving relationships throughout life.

Fears of Bugs and Insects

There may be areas where parents have irrational fears that they want to avoid passing on to their children. One of my students confessed that she was terrified of bugs and insects and asked me how she could avoid infecting her four-year-old daughter with her own anxieties. I suggested the following script:

« *Torry, this is your mom.*
I want to let you know how much I love you.
I want you to know how proud I am that you are my
      daughter.
I want you to know how proud I am when you watch
      nature's wonders with fascination.
Bugs, insects, and spiders put on a wonderful show of nature.
You look and watch.
You keep yourself safe.
You are careful.
You watch and learn.
Thank you for being my inquisitive, interested child.
I love you.
Sweet dreams. »

Notice that nowhere in the script does Torry's mother deny her own fear of insects. But she encourages her daughter's healthy impulses. In a situation like this, the child is likely to be aware of her mom's fear, so she may proceed carefully in exploring insect life. But if Dad isn't afraid and her best friend isn't afraid, she might risk a little more. She might also be aware that Mom's working on her fear, trying to get over it, and this is a wonderful model for a child.

Animals

My daughter Tara was a Pied Piper, continually bringing home animals. She could walk to the neighbor's house, two houses down from ours, and come back with somebody's pet. If it had a tag on it, of course we had to give it back, but we always had animals. George and I never knew what would be in our bed when we woke up. Tara is now a veterinarian, and we still have four dogs in our backyard, a cat in the house, and twenty-eight horses.

Many children have a strong affinity for animals, and having a pet can be a wonderful opportunity for a child to experience unconditional love as well as learn how to protect an animal and keep it safe. The principle of "touching with one finger" applies also to the care of pets. Children learn to respect an animal's independence and

needs and are able to model their behavior with the pet on the
respect their parents have shown for them. Keeping an animal safe,
of course, involves keeping oneself safe, too.

Here's a script I wrote for a friend whose young son was almost
as much of a Pied Piper as Tara:

> « *David, this is your mother.*
> *I want to let you know how much I love you.*
> *I want you to know how proud I am that you are my son.*
> *I want you to know how proud I am of you when you are*
>   *around animals.*
> *You are quiet and calm.*
> *You watch and learn.*
> *If it is a strange or new animal, you don't touch it.*
> *You wait quietly to learn about it first.*
> *I am so proud of you.*
> *I love you.*
> *Sweet dreams.* »

Did this script change David's behavior with animals? Not notice-
ably. The most important effect of reading it was to give his parents
confidence that his natural love for animals would not put him at
risk. Once again, by treating the child *as if he has already taken
responsibility* for keeping himself and the animal safe, they actually
helped make him safer.

Safety: Talking to Strangers

As parents watch their preschooler move further out into the world,
the question arises: What is the best way to approach the child's relationships with strangers who may or may not be a threat? All parents want to keep their children safe. The problem is that by keeping
them too safe, we may prevent them from learning to take care of
themselves and so leave them more vulnerable than they need to be.
They need to learn how to keep themselves safe, and one of the most
important resources for keeping yourself safe is the awareness that
you have effective tools even when you're out there all alone.

Preschoolers are taught not to talk to strangers or to get in a car with anyone they don't know, and that is the beginning of important safety awareness. But I would hate the idea of raising my kids to be so fearful that they couldn't be open and friendly to new people.

The truth is that none of us can be perfectly safe in this world. But we need to have the courage not to cripple our children with fear in a misguided effort to protect them. When we tell a child, "Don't talk to strangers," we forget that there might be a situation in which talking to a stranger could get her out of serious trouble. So, she needs to trust her gut feelings about when it's safe and when it's not.

Mandy's mother, Zoë, asked me to write a script for her daughter after the five-year-old had a frightening experience while playing outside with two other children near her suburban home. A car pulled up and stopped near the three little girls, and the driver opened the passenger-side door and asked if one of them could give him directions to a school nearby. Mandy's playmates refused to answer him and ran away, but Mandy approached the car, wanting to help. The man said he couldn't hear what she was saying and asked her to get into the car with him. At this point, she ran home and told her mother what had happened.

Here is the script I wrote for Zoë to read to Mandy:

« *Mandy, this is your mother.*
I want to let you know how much I love you.
I want to let you know how proud I am that you are my daughter.
I want to let you know how proud I am of you when you meet strangers.
You are friendly.
You are careful.
You keep yourself safe.
You follow your hunches about whom to trust.
Thank you for keeping yourself safe.
Thank you for telling me where you will be.
You are a special person and deserve to feel safe.
I love you.
Sweet dreams. »

It's important for parents to be aware that a child of this age is capable of following her instincts about people. The more a parent respects her opinions and hunches, the more the child is going to trust her own feelings.

And a script like this can offer protection not only against strangers but also against others who might take advantage of a child. These days, we hear some disturbing reports of the sexual abuse of children in stepfamilies—by stepfathers, step-siblings, and other relatives. If children are taught to follow their gut feelings and feel confident about expressing them, I believe that many of these abuses could be nipped in the bud, simply because the abusers would fail in their attempts to intimidate children through threats or to persuade them that they themselves were to blame for the behavior.

Sleeping

As we saw in the last chapter, the problem most parents have with toddlers concerning sleeping is getting them to go to bed. With three- or four-year olds, the problem is that they are up at the crack of dawn and don't understand why everybody else isn't eager to get up with them. When this becomes a pattern, parents get irritated, and some even resort to locking the child out of their bedroom, which is likely to bring up other behavior problems. So, the object is to keep the child in his bed playing with his toys or looking at his books until the rest of the household is up.

Here's a Sleep Talk script that worked well for four-year-old Tony:

《 *Tony, this is your dad.*
  I want to let you know how much I love you.
  I want to let you know how proud I am that you are my son.
  I appreciate it when you get a good night's sleep.
  *If you wake up in the night or in the early morning, you read
      your books or play quietly in your bed.*
  You drift back to sleep and wake up feeling happy.
  I love seeing your happy, smiling face.
  Thank you for being my son.

I love you.
Sweet dreams. »

The common element in all the scripts in this chapter—and indeed all the scripts in this book—is that they help establish situations in which both parents and children become winners. The strongest influence on your child is likely to be the way you model the qualities you are praising in her. In a sense, your child is like a tuning fork, echoing the feeling tone that you are emitting. When your own vibration is one of love, the child's answering tone will also be love, and in this process your child learns to feel and express love. Love is the magic catalyst in the alchemy through which all of us are transformed from uncivilized little animals to mature human beings. Sleep Talk helps foster the atmosphere of love and pride in which this growth and change become possible.

At this stage of a child's life, where gathering the courage to take the initiative is the essential task, encouragement from a trusted parent can make all the difference. Nowhere is this more evident than in the transition between home and day care or nursery school, as we'll see in the next chapter.

8

SLEEP TALK
AND YOUR CHILD
IN DAY CARE

My oldest child, Trey, started Montessori school when he was two years and two days old, and continued there until he was five. Tara, who is younger, was very aware of how much her brother enjoyed school. Every day when I would pack a lunch for him, she insisted that I pack one for her, too. One day when Tara and I drove Trey to school, the teacher said, "Why don't you let her stay today."

I said, "Tara, you can go with Trey if you want to." Even though Tara was just nineteen months old at that point, she grabbed her lunch box and never looked back.

A child's eagerness for the school or day care experience is obviously the best possible scenario. But every child is different, and parents need to be sensitive both to the child's readiness and to their own anxieties about the separation. It's important to be flexible about this kind of decision and to recognize that both you and your child have needs that deserve to be considered. If, after her first day at the school, Tara had decided that she didn't want to go back, I would have accepted that and waited until she was ready for the experience.

I was fortunate in being able to stay home with my children until my third child, Briana, was two and a half (I went back to work the day after she started Montessori school), but many mothers feel compelled—mostly for economic or career reasons—to go back to work earlier. There are situations in which a parent needs to find reliable day care, either in the home or elsewhere, for children who are even younger, and it's important that a parent not feel guilty about making these choices.

British psychologist Penelope Leach made many parents anxious when she wrote that a mother's working outside the home weakens the child's bond with her, and that women should therefore stay home until their children are at least eight years old.

But studies contradict this. In 1996, a major federal study of infant day care (involving ten sites and 1,200 children) reported that day care did no harm to the mother-child bond. These babies remained securely attached to their mothers. When psychologist Lois Hoffman examined fifty years of studies, she found no significant differences in any measure of child development between the children of working mothers and mothers who stayed home.[1]

Getting Ready to Go

In a world where all of us, sooner or later, need to become independent, the child's move out into the world of day care or nursery school inevitably brings up powerful emotions about separation, and these may be as charged for the parent as for the child. My own decision to keep Briana with me past the age when her older brother and sister had gone off to Montessori school is a case in point. I simply wanted the pleasure of having my youngest child at home with me a little longer, and she was content to stay. When she did start school, she quickly made up for lost time.

1. Caryl Rivers, "Parenthood Is Common Sense, Not Quantum Physics," *Los Angeles Times*, November 12, 1997, B7.

But there are situations in which both parent and child feel conflicted—for a variety of reasons—about the child's moving into the wider world.

Olivia, who was three and a half, was very rebellious when her mother, Claudia, tried to put her in nursery school. The head of the school, who is a friend of mine, referred the mother to me, and I sensed after talking to her that a significant part of the problem was Claudia's own unwillingness to let go of Olivia. So, I wrote this script on "getting ready to go" partly to help Olivia take the plunge and partly to help Claudia feel more comfortable about supporting her daughter in this new level of independence:

« *Olivia, this is your mom.*
I want to let you know how much I love you.
I want to let you know how proud I am that you are my
daughter.
Soon you will be ready to go to school.
This is an important time for all of us.
You will meet new friends, learn many things, and have fun
playing.
I love being with you, and I am proud to have such a big girl.
Thank you for being my "school-going girl."
I love you.
Sweet dreams. »

After Claudia read this script to Olivia for a week, she brought up the subject of the school again, and the child was willing to try. Olivia turned out to be quite a gregarious young lady and very happy in the school. I later learned that Claudia's problem was related to a conflict with her husband over her going back to work. She had been in a retail sales job for a large department store, and her husband had been in graduate school. After Olivia's arrival on the scene, he quit school and got a job that allowed him to support the family. It seems Claudia was afraid that if she went back to work, he might quit his job and go back to school, and the whole burden of support would again be on her shoulders. She didn't want to confront him about this, so sending a subliminal message to Olivia that her mother needed her at home effectively postponed the day the parents would have to come to grips with the problem.

Parents are human, too, and sometimes our personal agendas impact in less than positive ways on our children. In this case, Claudia's reading the Sleep Talk script to Olivia at least got the issue clarified in her own mind.

In general, I think the scripts on bonding (presented in Chapter 7) are especially valuable for helping parents establish a loving, supportive relationship with their preschool child. The script on getting ready to go is designed more for the child, letting her know what's out there for her. Invariably, a child who is between two and five knows somebody who's already in school, either an older sibling or a neighbor or a relative, so she has some idea of what school is about. The script serves as reassurance that by taking the next step, she's not going to lose anything (the parent will be back); she's simply going to get more.

The problem of moving out and trying something new is a perennial problem for all of us—parents as well as children. Every time a parent supports a child in taking one of these giant steps, the child grows in self-confidence, which makes further risks possible at the next stage and throughout life.

Alternatives for Day Care

When a family needs day care, it's essential to find the best possible situation for a particular child, and parents need to use common sense about this. If a family can afford an au pair, a nanny, or a regular baby-sitter in the child's home, this may be a good choice when the child is an infant.

However, finding affordable care for babies is a major problem for many American families, some of whom make excellent informal arrangements with a relative, friend, or neighbor. It's especially important for parents to create a support group for themselves, which might mean working out an exchange for baby-sitting or arranging a car pool with other parents.

When Trey was a baby, we were living in California, and I missed my friends and family in the South. But among the couples George and I got to know were a number of wives who also had roots in the South, and my friendship with these women who shared my values and culture was an important support for me as a young mother. For example, Patty Wilson and I developed a "child exchange" during the summer months that offered our kids a special version of summer camp. Patty lived on a farm in Fallbrook, and my kids looked forward to a few weeks there each summer, gathering eggs from the hens and weeding the vegetable garden. Her kids were just as thrilled with the urban cultural experience at my house, such as visiting Disneyland and going to children's theater. Our exchange enriched the experience of the children in both families.

Choosing a Day Care Facility for Your Child

In choosing a day care or nursery school arrangement for your child, you need to be aware of your alternatives and consider both your own needs and your child's. For example, home care might be available for your child two doors down from your house. Now, that's very convenient if you're going off to work every day, so you might be inclined to choose that. On the other hand, if your child is three years old and the woman is taking care of three babies and no older children, that situation might not fit his needs. Since it's important for a three-year-old to interact with kids his own age, you might decide it was better to put him in a school, even if that means driving a mile and a half out of your way.

The most important thing to consider in choosing a facility is the person taking care of your child and the psychological energy flow. Much more important than the physical surroundings is whether the person is caring and honest and kind. Assess how well those in charge have organized the place for dealing with the children, how well the caretaker sets priorities in meeting children's needs, how alert and flexible the person is.

A Good Home-Care Facility

My friend Betsy provides day care in her home five days a week, and I especially admire the way she handles it. She takes up to six kids, generally between the ages of two and five. She has two daughters of her own, one seventeen and one twelve, and when the girls come home from school, they help out by playing with the little ones.

Betsy's house generally looks cluttered, but the kids are busy with various activities. They do finger painting, for example, and she directs it in a skillful way that makes it both fun and educational. One day I was there visiting, and one of the older kids looked around and said, "Hey, is it cleanup time yet?" Betsy has made a game of "cleanup time" in which everything goes back into its "home." The toys have a home in the toy box, and the crayons have a home in the crayon box. Everything comes out at the appointed time to visit with the kids; then when the kids have finished with that activity, they have a cleanup, and the things go back to their homes.

Betsy has little picnic tables, and all the children have their assigned seats, with their names on the seats so they'll know where to sit. Everybody likes to go there and play. Her own daughters' friends come, and the expectation is that the older kids will take care of the younger ones. The kids like it so much that they never want to leave. Not surprisingly, she has a waiting list.

Good home-care arrangements and professionally run schools both have as their top priority *serving the needs of the child*.

Learning from Successes

The principle of having children learn from their successes is basic to all effective learning situations and is a fundamental principle of my Sleep Talk scripts. Giving a child credit for doing something right and expressing pride in her achievement frees the growth process to continue unencumbered.

One of the things I particularly like about Dr. Montessori's program is her awareness of the importance of parental influence at crucial times in a child's life. Dr. Montessori's mind was wide-ranging, and her observations of birds gave her insights into the maturation process in children. She observed that members of a certain bird species were capable of singing two octaves if they stayed with their parents continuously until adulthood. But if a bird was taken away from them at puberty (the human equivalent of age twelve), then returned to the nest later, it would be able to sing only one octave. And if taken away again and not returned until fully grown, the bird could never sing octaves at all; it could only chirp. Dr. Montessori noted that there seems to be a sensitive period during which having adult models is especially important for development of the bird's full potential, and she extended this idea to her educational system for children.

Throughout this book, the Sleep Talk scripts I'm offering for each stage of life take account of particular levels of maturation and the way parents can support their child in the natural next step in growth. In the two-to-five age group, autonomy and independence are crucial, as we have seen. As philosopher Joseph Chilton Pearce points out, "Intelligence can only grow by moving from that which is known into that which is not yet known. . . . When the physical environment is unvaried . . . when there is no bodily contact with a stable caretaker (for example, verbal approval for each achievement), a child does not grow intellectually."[2]

Surviving in the world means interacting with people. Obviously, the first interaction is at the home level, and once the child feels safe there, the parent's responsibility is to expand that circle. So, the parent who resists allowing a preschool child to try her wings in the wider world at this age is doing her no favors. Getting along in preschool has a direct effect on how she's going to get along in the workforce twenty years from now.

Possessions and Learning to Exchange

One problem that frequently comes up with preschool children is hoarding of possessions, and I think the Montessori method of han-

---

2. Joseph Chilton Pearce, *Magical Child: Rediscovering Nature's Plan for Our Children* (New York: Dutton, 1977).

dling this is sensible. After all, how is a child going to learn responsibility for possessions if he never *has* any? Using the piece of equipment that he himself *chose* to work on is excellent practice for learning responsibility.

In the home, I think parents also have an opportunity to teach children respect for property by seeing to it that children have their own space and their own toys. One of the ways we define who we are is through knowing what is ours (as opposed to someone else's). Forcing a child to share his possessions with others seems to me a violation of his integrity, and I believe there are more effective ways to encourage a generous spirit.

Defining boundaries, as discussed in previous chapters, is at the heart of this question. The infant needs to define where "I" begins and Mommy ends. The child at age two and a half can learn to define the boundary between "mine" and "yours." If something is "mine," I need to take care of it if I want to keep on enjoying it. This is easily extended to things in the child's environment that are not hers but that she is allowed to interact with.

Little children are very good at accepting this kind of responsibility. When Brittany came over to stay at our house, one of her favorite things to play with was the Tupperware drawer in the kitchen. She could take out all the containers, scatter them around, put on the lids, rattle a small container inside a larger one, whatever she wanted to do. When she was finished, she knew that it was her responsibility to put everything back in the drawer. It was my Tupperware, but as long as she took care of it, she was welcome to play with it. She had no desire for Tupperware of her own, so this arrangement was fine with her. It's really an extension of the "touching with one finger" idea discussed in Chapter 7. Children enjoy this kind of structure because it makes them feel secure.

The next step, sharing possessions with others, is a tricky area for children at this age. I personally would never demand that any child share his possessions with another child. But learning to exchange—to allow Johnny to play with my toy now because when he brings over his toy, he'll do the same for me—makes sense. I prefer to see the basic idea as one of exchange rather than sharing because exchanging implies mutual benefit, a win-win situation.

Sharing, on the other hand, implies that the child has to give up something without necessarily getting anything in return.

Learning about transactions between people is basic to a child's understanding of what interacting means and, ultimately, what love means. If I love you, I'm kind to you, and if I get kindness from you in return, then I've made a good choice. If we teach a child to exchange and trade, we're teaching a useful tool for living. In my view, simply insisting that a child share, without a mutual exchange, often has undesirable long-range consequences.

Doing Well in Nursery School

This kind of awareness of others' needs is crucial to a child's nursery school performance. Children who are unable to sit still and who disrupt other kids' learning because they're unable to channel their energies in a positive way may need some help. In previous chapters, I've discussed Patty's grandson, Jimmy, who showed a lot of improvement in school after his grandfather (and later his mother) read him a script on focusing energy.

As he became more able to control his hyperactivity, I helped his mother write another script to help him use other students as a model for his own behavior and sit still for extended periods when that was appropriate:

《 *Jimmy, this is your mother.*
I want to let you know how much I love you.
I want to let you know how proud I am that you are my son.
I want to let you know how proud I am when you do well in school.
When you get along with people in school, I am proud of you because I know that you are proud of yourself.
Thank you for sitting still in class.
Thank you for doing well.
Thank you for being my son.
I love you.
Sweet dreams. 》

Some children fail to do well in school not because of uncontrolled energy like Jimmy's but because of shyness. Chapter 1 discussed a script I wrote for Kelly to help her be more assertive and raise her hand in class when she knew the answers. We all know that it's generally the squeaky wheel that gets the oil, but it's important for parents to be equally sensitive to the child who is *too* well behaved. Using appropriate Sleep Talk scripts can be just as important in helping a timid or withdrawn child risk more activity and visibility. Remember that the script I wrote for Kelly was so successful that her mother later asked me to do a course correction with a script encouraging her to listen.

Listening

Here's another script about listening that I wrote for the grandson of my client Sarah, whose daughter Maura had five children. Maura's youngest son, Kyle, at four and a half, had talked almost constantly ever since he was two. Nobody ever got a chance to say anything when visiting Maura's household because this kid literally never stopped talking. Kyle had a fantastic vocabulary, but his constant babbling was very manipulative, very controlling. The way Sarah described the situation, it sounded as though Kyle was using talking as a way of asserting his identity in the world and so preventing himself from being overlooked.

I wrote the following script for both the grandmother and the mother to use with Kyle:

《 *Kyle, this is your mother [grandmother].*
I want to let you know how much I love you.
I want you to know how proud I am that you are my son
    [grandson].
I want you to know how proud I am of you when you are
    quiet and listen.
You listen to what is being said.
When you listen, you know what to do.
When you listen, you gather information you can use.
Thank you for being a good listener.

You are a big help.
Thank you for the quiet times.
I love you.
Sweet dreams. 》

About six months later, I asked Sarah how things were going with her grandson, and she told me she was able to enjoy being with Kyle for the first time since he was a baby. The fact that the inter-action between Kyle and his grandmother improved is a good sign.

In the opposite situation, one in which a child never talks, obvi-ously this script could be adapted to include lines such as "I feel proud of you when you talk with others as well as when you lis-ten" and "Thank you for being a good conversationalist" and "Thank you for letting people know what you think."

Getting Along with Others

There have been some children for whom I've written a series of scripts as they've moved to different stages of their lives. Patty's grandson is a case in point. With Jimmy's history of hyperactivity, getting him to slow down enough to connect with others and show consideration for them was the next important step, one that I knew would be crucial for his relationships throughout his life. Here's the script we prepared for Jimmy's mother to read to him:

《*Jimmy, this is your mother.*
I just want to let you know how much I love you.
I just want you to know how proud I am that you are my
    son.
I want to let you know how proud I am when you get along
    well with others.
When you get along with people in school, I am proud of you
    because I know that you are proud of yourself.
When you love me, you are tender.
When you are with others, in school or on the playground,
    you are considerate.
You are a tender and gentle person.

Thank you for being my son.
I love you.
Sweet dreams. »

Once again, expressing pride in the child's already having achieved the thing he needs to achieve has the effect of making him feel good about himself and want to make that behavior (and the positive responses it elicits from others) part of his pattern. Learning that one's own behavior toward others is a big factor in determining their responses is essential to making basic property exchanges. A well-developed sense of empathy—the ability to see situations through another person's eyes—is an extension of this, and a crucial skill both in the workplace and in intimate relationships. This Sleep Talk script encourages the child to value compassion and develop it in himself. The more he explores using it, the more adept he will become, and the more encouraged he is likely to be by the responses he gets from others.

Positive reinforcement—from parents, peers, and teachers—once again proves the most powerful learning tool of all.

Taking Turns

Part of getting along with others, of course, is learning to take turns. Three-and-a-half-year-old Diane was referred to me by her teacher because of her roughness with other children on the playground. She would elbow her way to the front of the line for the slide, push others out of her way, and generally behave in an extremely confrontational way. The other kids felt that this wasn't fair, and there were a lot of complaints about her. The teacher suggested that Diane's mother, Judy, call me and make an appointment. During our consultation, Judy was not very receptive to my suggestons, and I got the impression that the kind of aggressive behavior Diane was exhibiting toward the other kids wasn't all that uncommon in her home environment. However, Judy said she would read Diane the Sleep Talk script I wrote:

« *Diane, this is your mother.*
I want to let you know how much I love you.

> *I want to let you know how proud I am that you are my*
>   *daughter.*
> *I want to let you know how much I appreciate it when you*
>   *take turns.*
> *You are so full of life and have such a good time.*
> *You can wait or stand in line until it is your turn.*
> *Others enjoy playing with you because you know how to be*
>   *fair.*
> *I am so proud of you and love you so much.*
> *Sweet dreams.* »

I don't know whether Judy actually read this script to Diane, but the girl continued to be aggressive, and eventually she was asked to leave the school. My feeling is that Judy was under pressure to follow my suggestions, and that this script may have challenged her own pattern of behavior in a way she wasn't prepared to deal with. As I've discussed in connection with other examples, these scripts often have as much effect on the parent as on the child; if a parent's values are at odds with those the script expresses, there may need to be some serious self-examination.

Even though this case is not one of my success stories, I'm including it here because I think it could be useful to a child whose parents see the value of helping her learn to get along with others.

On the Playground

I wrote a slightly different script, also on the theme of getting along with others, for Tony (the boy in Chapter 7 whose early rising in the morning drove his dad crazy). Tony wasn't aggressive like Diane. He was a very bright four-year-old who was good at playing by himself but simply didn't know how to connect with other kids. He needed to be introduced to the idea of kindness and consideration for others, and also to the idea that playing with others can be fun.

> « *Tony, this is your dad.*
> *I want to let you know how much I love you.*
> *I want to let you know how proud I am that you are my son.*

I want you to know how proud I am of you when you have
    fun on the playground at school.
You are kind and considerate.
You like to play with all of your friends, and they like to play
    with you.
You are a wonderful son.
You have fun.
I like to play with you.
Thank you for being the wonderful person you are.
I love you.
Sweet dreams. »

After Joe, Tony's dad, had read him this script for a week, Tony spontaneously told Joe that he'd "had fun" playing tag with the other kids at school. A nice side-benefit of this script was that it led Joe (who is something of a workaholic) to introduce the idea of tossing a ball back and forth with his son, something he'd never done before. Both father and son in this case learned how much fun it can be to explore the give-and-take of play.

Paying Attention

There are some children for whom paying attention is a problem. Unlike Jimmy, the boy whose hyperactivity made it difficult for him to focus, my son T.J., when he was almost five, had an attention deficit, a difficulty with following through on things. For example, he might complete a task and then neglect to put the equipment away. But if his teacher said, "T.J., put the equipment away," he'd immediately cooperate and put it away.

I noticed his problem at home, too, and my husband came down pretty hard on him about it, which I didn't think was the best way to handle this situation. But I was certainly aware of the attention deficit with T.J. I'd go to him and say, "T.J., pick up your books, put your shoes away, make your bed, and hang up your clothes." When I came back thirty minutes later, nothing would be done. The natural reaction is: *You're defying me; you're not paying attention.*

But getting angry about this pattern was not accomplishing any change, and I realized I needed to take a closer look at what was really going on with this boy. What I finally realized was that the attention deficit is really a "left brain" condition—one that affects the analytical reasoning part of the brain, which my other three kids had no problem with. But T.J. operates primarily on the right side of his brain. I finally realized that in my presentation of so many details, I was overwhelming him with demands he couldn't process.

When I said to him, "Do what you need to do to make this room look good," the books would be put away, the bed would be made, and the clothes would be hung up. If I could find the way to give him the big picture, he knew exactly what to do and did it. There was never a problem with his *willingness*, only with his inability to process a request that was too complex for him.

In conjunction with my own adjustment in the ways I asked T.J. to help me, the following script was extremely effective:

« *T.J., this is your mom.*
I want you to know how much I love you.
I want you to know how proud I am that you are my son.
I want you to know how proud I am of you when you pay
    attention to what is going on. It helps me.
You are a big help to me, and I appreciate it. When you pay
    attention at school or while playing, I know you are OK.
Thank you for being my wonderful son.
Thank you for being in my life.
Thank you for paying attention to the things around you.
I love you.
Sweet dreams. »

The big thing I learned from this situation was *to pay attention myself in a different way*, through extending my empathy to a child whose brain is simply wired in a different way from my own. It's important that you pay attention to your child's distinctive traits, such as processing information differently from the way your other kids do or differently from the way your book on child rearing describes.

Health

One inevitable side effect as kids in this age group come into more and more contact with other kids is that they pick up colds and flu and pass them around the family. Once they start spending time with other kids, whether it's in day care or a preschool or a home, they're going to be exposed. Now is when the immune system comes into play. Obviously there's no way of banishing sickness from a household with young children, but there are things you can do to help your kids stay healthy most of the time.

My awareness of needing to do some kind of script on this subject came out of pure desperation. I discovered that when I sent my kids to school, they'd get sick, and then I'd get sick, and then I'd give it to the youngest child, and we'd all be sick. There had to be some way to break this vicious cycle. As I discussed in the Introduction, I had become aware early in my work on the UCLA pediatrics ward that giving my burn patient an awareness of the way his body was working to heal itself seemed to have an effect on his progress.

I realized I needed to develop a script that could help my kids resist the illnesses that were going around at school. And this age, between two and five, is a good time to introduce the idea that we all have tools in our own bodies to keep ourselves healthy. Here's the version I've used successfully both with my own children and with my clients' children:

《 *Briana, this is your mom.*
I want to let you know how much I love you.
I want you to know how proud I am that you are my daughter.
I want you to know how proud I am of you when you keep your body strong and healthy.
Even when others around you are sick or have colds, you stay healthy most of the time.
Thank you for being my healthy daughter.
I appreciate your ability to do this.
Thank you for knowing how to keep your body healthy.
I love you.
Sweet dreams. 》

Notice that in this script I say, "you stay healthy *most of the time.*" This is to avoid setting up a situation in which contracting a cold is seen as a failure. Whenever I've used this script, my kids have had fewer episodes of colds and flu, and I've been much healthier myself. This kind of enlightened self-interest is, in a way, a model for nearly all the cases I describe in this book. When your kids' lives are working well, your own life works a lot better on every level.

Now, the truth is, I don't know how to activate my immune system. I don't know anybody who does know how. But if I were going to trust somebody to activate an immune system, it would be a kid, because he wouldn't know there was anything complicated about the task and so wouldn't stand in his own way. More likely, he would think, "Mom usually tells me the truth, and she told me to activate my immune system, so I'll do that." And he does. This ability comes out of the love and trust between parent and child that is the foundation for every one of my Sleep Talk scripts.

Action Control: Biting

Mel, a psychotherapist for whose daughter I had previously written several scripts, called me a few days ago for help with a new problem. It seems that three-year-old Melvina gets so excited when she's hugging her parents or her friends that she sometimes loses control and bites them. Most of the biting problems I've dealt with were with kids who bit out of aggression, when they were upset and tired, but this version of the problem was a new one for me. Here's the script I wrote for Mel to read to his daughter:

《 *Melvina, this is your dad.*
I want to let you know how much I love you.
I want to let you know how proud I am that you're such a loving girl.
When you get excited about being close to people, you can take a deep breath and relax.
I am happy when you do not bite others.
I appreciate it when you do not bite me.
I love you and feel sad when you hurt me.

Thanks for taking care of me.
I love you.
Sweet dreams. »

At this age, control is a key concern, and this script offers some information to Melvina about ways to get control of her impulses. Taking a deep breath and relaxing is good advice for a person of any age who is on the verge of losing control, and it's a tool Melvina will be able to use throughout her life.

After I talked with Mel, I started thinking about what could be the reason for this kind of biting behavior. Sometimes when parents are changing their child's diaper or dressing her they'll say, "Oh, I love you so much, I could just eat you up!" And it could be that something like this made the association for Melvina between being loving and biting.

In the case of a child whose biting comes out of aggressiveness or fear (or a combination of the two, as we see in dogs that are "fear biters"), I'd alter the script slightly. One time, our son Trey bit my husband, and George bit him back. In this case, I think Trey's biting came out of a playmate's having bitten *him*, and his trying out the behavior for himself. George's biting him back made it clear that the bite hurt, and Trey never did it again. In a case like this, I think a better response would have been to use a script such as the following:

« *Trey, this is your father.*
I want to let you know how much I love you.
I want you to know how proud I am even when you become
    upset and tired.
When you are upset and tired, you can take a deep breath
    and relax.
I am happy when you do not bite others.
I appreciate it when you do not bite me.
I love you and feel sad when you hurt me.
Thanks for taking care of me.
I love you.
Sweet dreams. »

Action Control—Hitting

The same problem with impulse control sometimes results in a child's hitting others, lashing out at them because he doesn't know what else to do with his fear and anger. Take the case of four-year-old Allen. Norma, his mother, who was a student of mine, said complaints came from Allen's caregiver that hitting had become his solution to any conflict with other children in the group. Here's the script I wrote for Norma to read to him:

> « *Allen, this is your mommy.*
> *I want to let you know how much I love you.*
> *I want you to know how proud I am of you.*
> *When you are upset, take a deep breath and relax.*
> *You can take a deep breath and relax.*
> *I am happy you do not hit others.*
> *I appreciate it when you do not hit me.*
> *You express "action control."*
> *You know how to talk and express yourself.*
> *You know how to be a gentleman.*
> *Thank you for being my son.*
> *I love you.*
> *Sweet dreams.* »

Norma called me less than a week later to say that when she'd gone to pick up Allen that day, the woman who had been taking care of him said he hadn't resorted to hitting other kids at all that day. Riding home in the car, Allen said to Norma, "I'm a gentleman." "Yes, you are," she said, "and I'm very proud of you."

Pain Management and Control

I've taught my own kids at this age to use techniques of deep breathing and refocusing or relaxation to manage difficult moments in their lives, and I had a dramatic demonstration of the effectiveness of these tools one day when Briana was five. We started skiing as a family when she was four, and by the time she was five, she was on a ski slope higher than we were, and she broke her leg. I was just coming out of my ski lesson when a man from the ski patrol came up to me and said, "Lois Haddad?"

I took a deep breath. "Which kid?"

"It's Briana," he said, "but I don't think her leg's broken because she isn't crying."

It turned out she had a spiral fracture of her leg, and we took her to the hospital to get a cast on it.

Afterward I said to her, "The ski patrol guy didn't think you'd broken your leg because you didn't cry."

"Mom," she said, "that *hurt*. I wasn't going to just lie there and hurt, so I did my deep breathing and relaxing, deep breathing and relaxing—because I knew you and Dad would come."

This is ample evidence for me that it's not necessary to wait until kids are older to begin working on this kind of control.

Encouraging self-confidence in a child about her ability to control her own feelings and to connect with the feelings of others pays big dividends when the child goes on to elementary school, as we'll see in the next chapter.

9

SLEEP TALK AND YOUR SCHOOL-AGE CHILD

Age five to age twelve is a busy and crucial period in a child's life. The beliefs, habits, attitudes, and values formed at this stage underlie the complex tasks of adolescence and adulthood.

Our essential responsibility as parents during these years is to teach our children the basic rules of life, and Sleep Talk can offer invaluable help in this effort. So much is going on in a child's life during this time that it's easy to lose track of the fundamentals, especially when both parents are working (which is the case in most households today).

All the scripts in this chapter—in fact, in all the chapters—are related to the rules of life. As in every game, from Monopoly to Dungeons & Dragons, we need to know the rules before we can begin playing, and at this stage, it's appropriate for parents to help their children learn and understand the rules of life. No doubt you have your own set of rules, even though you may not have made an actual list, and I imagine that at least some of them may be similar to mine.

Here are Haddad's Five Rules of Life (learned from A. Arrien):

1. Show up. Sounds simple, but I know a lot of adults who have yet to show up in their own lives, and I'll bet you do, too. This rule implies a willingness to be present, a willingness to be seen, and a willingness to take responsibility for where you are in your life. The scripts on self-confidence that I offer in this chapter and elsewhere can help a child understand and follow this rule (and they might even inspire a few parents to start showing up).

2. Pay attention. I've never had much trouble with showing up, but paying attention is harder for me. People want you to pay attention to what they think is important. However, a parent, a math teacher, and a kid's best friend may have radically different ideas of what is important. When everybody wants a piece of you, how do you keep from becoming fragmented? The basic guideline here is learning to pay attention to what has heart and meaning for you. As children come to understand this rule, they are able to make choices and become responsible for them. Among the many scripts in this chapter that help the child (and parent) connect with this rule are the ones on listening, staying on task, and safety.

3. Whoever appears in your life is exactly who is supposed to be there. This also means that whoever is not in your life is not supposed to be there. I have not always been delighted with this rule, but it has helped me learn to deal with people in compassionate and practical ways. When we learn to tell the truth without blame or judgment, we can accept into our lives people who may be difficult but who offer important life lessons for us. Scripts in this chapter that address this rule include making friends, helping one another as a family, and relationships with grandparents.

4. Whatever happens is exactly what is supposed to happen. This is another rule I'm not in love with. When I got breast cancer, I was not exactly thrilled, yet it got my attention and put me back on my path. What happens in our lives offers a signpost as to where we are at that particular moment. You can't get to San Jose unless you know where you're starting from, and you can't get anywhere in your life unless you have clearly in mind where you are right now. When bad stuff keeps showing up in your life, you can be pretty sure it's trying to make you take a look at where you are. Because until you do that, you have no way of knowing how to get where you want to go (or maybe even of deciding where you want to go). Some scripts I'll be discussing in relation to this rule are attitude adjustment, negotiating solutions, and approaching adults as a resource.

5. **When it's over, it's over.** This rule offers a reminder of the finite quantity of life, but it also shows us how to dump the garbage of our relationships and focus on what is good and nourishing about them. It allows us to avoid crying over spilled milk (or brooding interminably about who spilled it) and to get on with cleaning it up and getting another glass. There's no need to take all the garbage of one day or situation or relationship into the next one; we're capable of learning from our mistakes and carrying with us only what is life-enhancing. Scripts on parent rebonding, attitude adjustment, and test-taking apply this rule in important areas.

We all get a chance to cycle through these five rules many times in the course of a day. We learn from our mistakes and get on with the fun and the challenge of living our lives. If we're playing Monopoly, when we get to Park Place and Boardwalk we don't pick up our money and quit. We pass Go, collect our $200, and show up again. And again. The Sleep Talk scripts in this chapter are designed to teach our children these rules, simply and lovingly.

Self-Confidence

In order to show up in our own lives, we need self-confidence, and a parent can make a great contribution to a child's life by expressing love and pride in him.

Jason was eight when his father, Nick, came to me for help. An only child, the boy had a background of early-childhood illnesses. Though he absolutely loved his dad and was obviously trying to find his way, he appeared uncertain that he'd ever be able to measure up. He was extremely quiet, couldn't speak very well, and seemed always

to be waiting for people to take care of him. Here's the Sleep Talk
script I gave Nick to read to Jason:

《 *Jason, this is your dad.*
I want to let you know how much I love you.
I want to let you know how proud I am to be your dad, and
    how proud I am that you are my son.
I am so proud of you when you feel good about who you are.
I appreciate it when you share your feelings and thoughts
    with me and whoever is appropriate.
When you talk, your voice is beautiful, strong and clear.
You make eye contact with other people.
You are calm and confident.
You feel good about who you are, and that makes me happy.
Thank you for being my son.
I love you so much.
Sweet dreams. 》

The results were impressive. Jason began showing up as Jason,
not the sickly baby who needed to have things done for him. His
voice got stronger, and he looked people in the eye. Nick said it was
like watching a flower open. Of course, once Jason started showing
up as himself, the feedback he got from his parents, his friends, and
his teacher reinforced the information his father had given him
about the first Rule of Life. By showing up, he got the ball rolling
in the right direction.

Parent Rebonding

Parents too may need a little booster shot of confidence at this stage.
When my son T.J. was in first grade, I needed to send everybody
off to school in the morning, deal with the car pool if it was my
turn that day, then get myself to work at George's office. At the end
of the day, I needed to come home, make dinner, and put the kids
to bed. Things reached the point where I realized I would have to
do my menus and grocery shopping for the whole week during the

weekend, because when I arrived home at night after work, I was just too tired to do anything but cook the same meal we'd had the night before, unless I'd written down what we were having. I could cook or I could think, but there was no possibility of doing both on the same night.

I was aware of a lot of stress, to put it mildly, and I realized that I needed a script to use with T.J. that would strengthen the bond between us. Here's the script I read to him:

> « *T.J., this is your mother.*
> *I want to let you know how much I love you.*
> *I want to let you know how proud I am that you are my son.*
> *My life is so full and wonderful because you are a part of my every day.*
> *I like the way you treat me and love me so much.*
> *Thank you for your love.*
> *Thank you for being my son.*
> *I love you.*
> *Sweet dreams.* »

You've probably already figured out that this script was really more for me than for T.J. I like hugs, and I like my family to tell me they love me, and during this stressful time, I was feeling the lack of that. So, by reading this script, I helped create a circle of loving arms around me and a sense that I was loved in return.

It's important for any parent to be able to ask for what she needs and recognize that her own needs are important, too. I got a lot of love from T.J., and it helped me through this difficult period.

Morning Preparation for School

Many children also experience a great deal of stress as they try to cope with the task of getting themselves ready for school in the morning. Melody's mother came to me in despair over her loving, gregarious, unfocused eight-year-old daughter. This was an intelligent, unconventional child who was active and interested in the world but highly distractable. She had no interest in her own clothes and generally looked like an unmade bed. Melody was continually getting yelled at in the morning for not being ready for school on time. Here's the script I wrote for Melody's mother to read:

《 *Melody, this is your mother.*
I want to let you know how much I love you.
I want you to know how proud I am that you are my
    daughter.
I want to let you know how much I appreciate it when you
    get ready for school on time.
You make appropriate choices and pick clothes that look
    good on you.
Your hair is clean and brushed shiny.
Your teeth are brushed and clean.
Your body is clean.
I am so proud of you.
I am proud and appreciate it when you use your time wisely
    getting ready for school.
Thank you for being such a help to me.
I love you.
Sweet dreams. 》

What Melody needed was a script that would give her information about exactly what she had to do to get herself ready to go, and this script provided a checklist. After about five days, there was clear improvement, and the girl was able to get herself together to get to school on time.

Listening

But this was by no means the end of Melody's story. Once she got to school, her distractedness made it difficult for her to listen in class. This spirited little girl needed to understand the rules that would allow her to function effectively in a school situation. Here's the second script I wrote for her mother to read to her:

《 *Melody, this is your mother.*
I want to let you know how much I love you.
I want you to know how proud I am that you are my
daughter.
I want you to know how proud I am of you when you are
quiet and listen.
You listen to what is being said.
When you listen, you know what to do.
When you listen, you gather information you can use.
Thank you for being a good listener.
You are a big help.
Thank you for the quiet times.
I love you.
Sweet dreams. 》

This script gave Melody an alternative to her unfocused, self-generated behavior. It allowed her to recognize that the classroom (like all other social situations) requires give and take. She simply needed to have the rules explained to her several times. When it came to creativity, Melody showed enormous gifts; her art projects were always the best in the class. But if a child like this is not given help in focusing her attention, she is likely to have difficulty in moving into social groups later. Melody got the message, and her classroom behavior became appropriately modulated.

Staying on Task

By the time Melody was ten, it was clear that she needed help in staying on task. Creative and energetic as she was, she would continually start a task, become interested in something else, and fail to finish her first project. Her quick, distractible mind would move on to the next thing, and she rarely followed through on anything. Here is the script I wrote for her mother to read to her:

《 *Melody, this is your mother.*
I want to let you know how much I love you.

I want you to know how proud I am that you are my
daughter.
I am so proud of you when you see a job that needs to be
done and you do it.
You stay with a job or task until it is completed.
You know how to get things done.
You are at your best when you follow through with your
tasks.
Thank you for being my daughter.
I love you so much.
Sweet dreams. »

After listening to this script, Melody showed signs of becoming more self-controlled. The Sleep Talk scripts helped her understand that she had the power to control not only the rate at which her ideas generate but also the follow-through.

Now, eighteen years later, she works as a television producer, a job that uses her creativity and her gift for keeping many balls in the air at one time. Her relationship with her parents is a good one.

Today a child like Melody might very well be diagnosed with attention deficit disorder and put on drugs. While I recognize that there are situations in which drugs such as Ritalin may be appropriate, I think the kind of Sleep Talk scripts that I wrote for Melody would be worth a try before pursuing medication. Some children who have ADD do need medication, but all can benefit from parents' support for their efforts.

Keeping Room Clean

With so many demands impinging on the child at this age, it's not surprising that keeping her room clean might be low on her list of priorities. I'm in favor of parents' being fairly tolerant about this kind of thing, but there are limits, and I found myself right up against them with Tara, my older daughter, when she was twelve. The problem was twofold: (1) the disorder was so extreme that you could not even walk into her bedroom, and (2) she could never find anything. I was continually hearing, "Mom, have you seen my bookbag?" or "Mom, have you seen my other shoe?" Occasionally I would wade in and try to find whatever it was, but my frustration was mounting. Finally, in desperation, I tried the following script:

« *Tara, this is your mother.*
  I want to let you know how much I love you.
  I want you to know how proud I am that you are my daughter.
  I want to let you know how much I appreciate it when you keep your room neat and clean.
  It helps me when you keep your room neat and clean. You can find your things.
  I am proud of you because I know that you are proud of yourself.
  Thank you for being my daughter.
  I love you.
  Sweet dreams. »

Much as I would like to report a complete about-face, I have to admit that Tara is never going to win any medals for the neatness of her room. But she was smart enough to understand the usefulness of the information I was giving her in this script, and her room went from hopeless to what I would call "organized-cluttered." You could actually walk into it, and she was able to find her things.

We employed a woman to come in once a week to do the heavy cleaning and keep the house in shape. The house rule was that if your room was picked up, Carmen would go in and change your bed linens and dust and vacuum. But if your room was too messy for her to work in, it would be your responsibility to change your bed and do the dusting and vacuuming yourself. So, the kids had an incentive to keep things in some kind of order.

The Bell

The saga of the chaos in Tara's room reminds me of a time when Tara and Briana were both home from college and T.J. was about seven. I walked down the hallway in our house and saw at least one wet towel on every bed—maybe two wet towels if the person had washed her hair.

I got out my big ceramic bell and started ringing it. The three kids gathered in the hallway, and Tara asked, "What's wrong?" I said, "It's time for the towel-hanging demonstration and lecture." Tara looked at T.J.: "Is she still doing that?" "Yeah," he said, "and it's a lot longer and a lot more boring now."

And so I began: "You bend over. You pick up the towel. You spread it out, and then you walk toward the hook in the bathroom. You lift your arm up and you put the towel over the hook, and then you step back. You survey the job you have done and consider it good. . . ."

That bell is a loud one, and I've used it over the years whenever I needed to get my kids' attention. When they were out playing in the neighborhood, it was a signal for them to come home. Everybody knew what it meant—not just Tara and Briana, but also the other kids. "I've got to stop playing with you now," they would say, "because your mother wants you to come home." Standing in front of our house and yelling for them wasn't nearly as effective; I could yell my head off, and no one would come. But the bell always worked. I used it from the time they were very young, and whenever I rang it, they knew they needed to show up.

Making Friends

Every parent of a kid this age knows what it's like to see your kid come home crying. "Nobody likes me; nobody wants to play with me." Kids at this age are trying things out, trying to figure out what works. They make mistakes, and people's feelings get hurt. Sometimes children will gang up on one kid; then later the child will be accepted into the circle, and they'll all gang up on another kid. There are children who have an especially hard time making friends, but all kids go through a period of feeling they don't have any friends and nobody wants to be with them.

The script I'm offering here is one I've used with my kids and given to parents of many other kids in this age group to help them make the connection between "showing up" as a friend and having friends:

> 《 *Don, this is your mom.*
> *I want to let you know how much I love you.*
> *I want to let you know how proud I am that you are my son.*
> *Thank you for being my friend.*
> *You have many friends.*
> *You are a good friend.*
> *It is easy for you to make and keep friends.*
> *I like the way you treat your friends.*
> *I like the way you treat me.*
> *Thank you for being my friend.*
> *I love you.*
> *Sweet dreams.* 》

There are times when we all doubt ourselves, and this script offers not only reassurance that the child has the ability to make friends but also an invitation to practice with the parent: I'm not just your mom; I can be your friend, too. In my case, I found that these issues would come up suddenly and that working them out was always a short-term situation with Sleep Talk.

Fingernail Biting

Just as thumb sucking was a problem with preschool kids, fingernail biting can be a problem with kids from five to twelve. Both behaviors are habits, and in order to break an ingrained habit, you need to offer children some alternative, something else they can do with their hands.

Eight-year-old Debbie was biting her fingernails until they bled, and her mother, Nona, who was a student in one of my classes, asked me for a script that would help her daughter get control of this self-destructive behavior. Here's the one I gave her:

> 《 *Debbie, this is your mom.*
> *I want to let you know how much I love you.*
> *I just want you to know how proud of you I am when you*
> *take care of your nails.*
> *I am proud of you because I know that you are proud of*
> *yourself.*

You have beautiful nails and hands.
Your hands and fingernails are pretty and healthy looking.
When you feel uptight, you can take a deep breath, relax, and
*   feel good inside.*
You leave your hands at your side or in your lap.
You are calm and confident.
I like your hands to look pretty.
I appreciate you being my daughter.
I love you.
Sweet dreams. »

Nona read this script to Debbie for about two weeks without a break. She also took Debbie to a local beauty college right at the beginning and got her a professional manicure. The nails began to look better after about a week, and Nona took Debbie back for another manicure. The manicurist encouraged the girl. In the first two visits, she used clear polish on Debbie's nails, but then during the third manicure, at the end of the second week, she painted the girl's nails with colored polish. It was a sort of graduation for Debbie, and she never bit her nails again.

Attitude Adjustment

In the Introduction, I described the situation of Kevin, the boy whose younger brother, Mike, was so terrified of swimming.

Kevin, at age ten, was determined to do everything well, and he was extremely capable and energetic. But he was so driven to do everything perfectly that it was impossible for him to take any joy in his own accomplishments. His mother told me that in school, if he misspelled a word in a paper he was writing, he wouldn't erase it but would instead crumple up the paper, throw it away, and start all over again. This was a kid who could talk about any topic intelligently and articulately, but he seemed to wake up mad every morning, ready to fight the world. Any little mistake he made would make him furious, and he'd strike out, totally frustrated.

I gave Lisa the following script to help Kevin adjust these attitudes, which were causing pain to himself and everyone around him:

« *Kevin, this is your mother.*
I want to let you know how much I love you.
I want to let you know how proud I am that you are my son.
I am proud of you when you wake up in the morning with
*   your smiling, shiny face.*
Seeing you happy makes my heart sing.
People comment on what a cheerful person you are.
You are fun to be around.
I enjoy being with you.
Thank you for being in my life.
I feel happy seeing you.
I love you.
Sweet dreams. »

The letter from Lisa that I quoted in that section describes the transformation of this angry, unhappy child to a much more contented individual. After a few weeks of his listening to this script, his disposition improved quite a bit, and he's been getting all As in school since then.

One interesting sidelight on Kevin's growth in this situation: a few years after Lisa read him the script, his teacher gave him and other children a group project. Though he did his part, the other kids didn't do theirs, and he got a lower grade as a result. The teacher came down pretty hard on all of them. Kevin went home and communicated to his mom about this, and she and his grandmother went to the school and talked it over with the teacher, explaining that he had done his part and was being penalized for other kids' failures. The important point here is that Kevin felt safe enough by that time to tell his mother what had happened.

Shyness

I began Chapter 1 with the story of Kelly, the seven-year-old daughter of my client Melanie. Kelly's painful shyness made it impossible for her to participate in class, and her teacher was concerned about the girl's withdrawn attitude. Here is the first script I wrote for Melanie to read to Kelly:

《 *Kelly, this is your mother.*
I want to let you know how much I love you.
I want to let you know how proud I am that you are my
　　daughter.
I want to let you know how proud I am of you when you do
　　well in school.
In class, you are eager to share and participate.
You are very smart.
You know lots of things and volunteer information in class.
You speak clearly and make eye contact with the people
　　around you.
I am very proud of you.
I love you very much.
Thank you for being in my life.
Sweet dreams. 》

As Chapter 1 explained, the results in this case were dramatic, so much so that Melanie called me three months later to ask for a script that would correct Kelly's new tendency to talk too much and show up as a know-it-all! That second script helped the girl achieve a good balance, and she has been doing fine in school ever since.

Helping One Another as a Family

Children at this age can be profoundly affected by stresses within the family, especially marital problems between the parents. When Corin, an only child, was eight, his parents separated, and he seemed to completely shut down. From the child's point of view, his family was falling apart and there wasn't anything he could do about it. So, he simply withdrew, refusing to extend himself in any way to help his mother or himself.

His mother wanted a script that would remind him that they were still a family, even though she and her husband were separated. Here's the one I gave her:

《 *Corin, this is your mother.*
I want to let you know how much I love you.

I want to let you know how very proud I am that you are my son.

I want to let you know how proud I am that you are part of my family.

You are so helpful.

I appreciate it when we pull together, keeping our family close.

I appreciate the active mutual support we exchange with each other.

Even when everyone is busy doing many things, we pull together as a family.

Thank you for being my son.

Thank you for being in my life.

I love you.

Sweet dreams. »

This script accomplished a rebonding between Corin and his mother, and he began connecting with her again. The parents were wise enough to include the boy in some of their sessions with a family therapist, which also helped. In the end, the parents reconciled, and Corin managed to rebond with both of them.

Relationship with Grandparents

Many families struggle with the problem of helping their children form positive relationships with grandparents. We've had some difficulties with this in our own family, and the stresses were compounded by George's mother and father's habit of coming to our house for extended visits.

Trey, Briana, and T.J. were able to accept their grandmother's criticisms without getting upset, but Tara became quite distressed about this situation. Tara is something of an activist, and she is very outspoken. I've always had some concern that we might have to go and get her out of jail at some point for marching or for putting her body in front of vehicles, defending animal rights. George's mother felt it was her mission to straighten Tara out, so grandmother and granddaughter were on a collision course.

I asked myself how I could help Tara through this difficult time. This is the script I devised to help her (and myself) make the best of this situation:

《 *Tara, this is your mom.*
I want to let you know how much I love you.
I want to let you know how proud I am that you are my
  daughter.
I want to let you know how proud I am of you when you
  treat your grandparents with respect.
You treat older family members with respect because of who
  you are and not because of who they are.
You are a wonderful person.
You know how to be kind.
You know how and when to say "yes" or "no."
Thank you for being my daughter.
I love you.
Sweet dreams. 》

This script addresses that third Rule of Life: Whoever is in your life is exactly who is supposed to be there. We don't always have a choice about having certain people in our lives, and I believe we learn more from difficult relationships than from easy ones. This script offered Tara some guidelines for coming to terms with that rule.

This is one of the biggies: while we would all like to be treated with respect, people treat you the way they do because of who they are, not because of who you are. You may not have a choice about the way they treat you, but you do have a choice about the way you respond to their treatment. Their behavior does not justify disrespectful behavior from you.

I'm so pleased about the way Tara has dealt with this problem. Even as an adult, she can sustain a good relationship with her grandmother (though she can get madder at the woman than at anyone else in the family). Grandma is now ninety-five, and Tara often takes her shopping or for a ride, or just stops by to see her. I think learning to deal with her grandmother has given Tara tools to cope with difficult people in her business life; she learned how to stand up for her own goals and beliefs without descending to anger or blaming others.

Safety

News reports today are full of horror stories about vicious things done to children, and I know of no way to eliminate these outrages from our lives. It's a hard fact of life that we as parents cannot always protect our children, but the more tools we can give them to protect themselves, the less likely they are to become an awful statistic. Instilling fear about the world outside the home is no solution. I've seen heartbreaking cases in which parents tried to do this, only to have their child face the outside world without inner resources.

The best way to keep them safe is to give them confidence in their own inner radar and permission to say no to adults when they sense potential danger.

Here is the script on safety:

« *Briana, this is your mother.*
I want to let you know how much I love you.
I want to let you know how proud I am that you are my daughter.
I want to let you know how much I appreciate your being safe.
Thank you for checking with me before you go anywhere.
Thank you for letting me know where you are going, how you will get there, who you will be with, and when you will be home.
Follow your hunches about who to trust.
Thank you for keeping yourself safe.
You deserve to feel safe and can say no to anyone who frightens or confuses you.
You are my special daughter.
Thank you for being my daughter.
I love you.
Sweet dreams. »

The way I see it, this kind of education in responsibility falls into the category of preventive medicine, and I see no need to apologize for it. Sure, you'll run into some adults who think it's more important to observe certain niceties than to keep a child safe. For instance, one time T.J. and I were flying back from Florida. He was about seven, and I made him come into the women's bathroom at the airport with me. It wasn't crowded, but an older woman walked in and said, "Son, aren't you a little old to be in here?" Then she said to me, "Just how old is he going to have to be before you let him go to the bathroom by himself?" I said, "Oh, about twenty-eight."

Sleeping

With children at this age having so much going on in their lives, it's no wonder they want to cut down on their sleep time to cram in more activities. This is an area in which guidance from parents can help the children establish sleeping habits that will serve them well over a lifetime.

Younger kids in this age group, from five to nine, still need about eleven hours of sleep. So, if they get up at 7:00 A.M., they should generally be in bed by 8:00 P.M. Most older kids, from ages ten to twelve, can get along on about ten hours, which means they will probably need to go to bed by 9:00 if they rise at 7:00.

Some kids (just like some adults) need more sleep than others, but a regular bedtime and a positive attitude toward it are worth encouraging. An important aspect of sleeping is healing, and the amount of sleep we need may depend on how much healing we need after the stresses and activities of a particular day. Sleep deprivation and sleep disorders are serious problems in our society, and many adults today get less sleep than they need to do their jobs effectively and maintain good health. (I can attest to the fact that mothers of babies and young children are chronically sleep-deprived.)

It's important for parents to recognize that sensible bedtimes for their kids may necessitate some adjustment in family mealtimes. If both parents are working outside the home, an early dinner may be difficult. But if a child needs to be in bed by 8:00, serving dinner at 7:30 isn't going to work very well.

Sam, a crack litigator, mentioned to me that his seven-year-old son, Zeke, resisted going to bed and was continually getting up in the middle of the night to join his parents in their bed. He just couldn't sleep, he'd tell them. Or he'd had a bad dream.

I asked Sam if Zeke generally watched television just before he went to bed. Sam said he did, but he wasn't sure what the programs were. I suggested that it might be a good idea to limit Zeke's television viewing in the hour before bedtime, since TV often overstimulates children and makes it harder for them to get to sleep.

I also suggested Sam try reading the following script to his son:

« *Zeke, this is your dad.*
I want to let you know how much I love you.
I want to let you know how proud I am that you are my son.
I appreciate it when you go to bed willingly and get a good night's sleep.
You sleep all night in your bed.
When you wake up, you feel happy and full of energy.
I love seeing your happy, smiling, shining face.
Thank you for being my son.
I love you so very much.
Sweet dreams. »

After a week, Sam reported that Zeke was sleeping through the night, with no forays in the wee hours into the parental bedroom. Sam also mentioned that he himself had been sleeping a few more hours in recent nights. "How long do you sleep now?" I asked. "About six hours," he said. I asked how long he had generally slept before. "About four hours." (I suspect that trial lawyers are another chronically sleep-deprived group.)

I'm always impressed with how much effect these Sleep Talk scripts have on both parent and child. Certainly a great many of the ones I've read to my own kids have made a big difference in my life. I've heard many teachers say that the best way to learn a subject thoroughly is to teach it, and it seems to me these scripts may work in a similar way. Expressing love and support and offering positive feedback to our children may have an impact on our own ways of thinking and our habits. I suspect Sam may be more effective in the courtroom on six hours' sleep, and I *know* I've been able to handle the stresses of my own life with more grace, thanks to the scripts on parent rebonding and improved relationships with grandparents, among others in this chapter.

Self-Confidence at School

There's always a lot for parents to juggle with kids at school age, and there are some specific ways you can help them deal with challenges related to their schoolwork.

Fran, the daughter of a nurse I knew at UCLA Medical Center, called to ask my advice about her seven-year-old daughter, Holly, who was doing poorly in second grade. Holly had no significant problems at home; she was confident with her parents and her four-year-old brother. But she never raised her hand in class and seemed terrified of her teacher. From Fran's description, the teacher sounded like one of those my-way-or-the-highway people who are in their element drilling Marine recruits. But it seemed Holly was stuck with this woman, and in order to change the situation, we had to start with Holly.

I suggested Fran read Holly the following script on self-confidence at school:

> « *Holly, this is your mother.*
> *I want to let you know how much I love you.*
> *I want you to know how proud I am that you are my*
>   *daughter.*
> *I want to let you know how proud I am of you when you do*
>   *well in school.*
> *In class, you are eager to share and participate.*
> *You are very smart.*
> *You know lots of things and volunteer information in class.*
> *You speak clearly and make eye contact with the people*
>   *around you.*
> *I am very proud of you and love you very much.*
> *Thank you for being my daughter.*
> *I love you.*
> *Sweet dreams.* »

An important aspect of this script is the information it offers the child. Rather than simply urging Holly to be more self-confident, it expresses confidence in her abilities and describes particular behaviors that reflect self-confidence: sharing and participating, volunteering information, and making eye contact with people around her. So, Holly had some guidelines as to specific things she could do to become more effective in class. Once she tried out these new behaviors, the response she got from her teacher and her classmates confirmed that she was on the right track—and this helped build her confidence even further.

The script worked wonders for Holly. She seemed much happier about going to school, and her grades improved. In this case, it's hard to assign all the credit for this transformation to Sleep Talk, because the teacher left at midterm and was replaced. I imagine that a woman with the attitudes Fran described would not be any happier teaching a roomful of seven-year-olds than they would be learning from her, so perhaps her exit was inevitable.

The important thing is that Holly learned to *show up* (Haddad's First Rule of Life). She also got a memorable introduction to two of the other Rules of Life: Whoever appears in your life is supposed to be there, and When it's over it's over.

If Holly hadn't been challenged by this difficult relationship, who knows how long she might have put off learning the primary lesson about showing up in her own life. The teacher's martinet stance, unpleasant as it was, got Fran's attention and led to Holly's getting the help she needed. When it was over, it really *was* over, but Holly came out of the situation with important new skills that have served her well in school and in life ever since.

Increasing Reading Fluency

My coauthor Judith Searle had trouble learning to read in the early grades despite a passionate desire to master this skill. She suspects she may have had a mild dyslexia, which is a problem more commonly recognized and dealt with these days than when she was in school. Some children who have difficulties with reading do need professional help, but all can benefit from parents' support for their efforts.

Joe, a loving father who is also something of a workaholic, called to ask me for a script that would help six-year-old Tony, a bright

boy who was unhappy about going to school because he couldn't
read as well as the other kids in his class. (You may remember previous scripts I wrote for Tony, about sleeping, in Chapter 7, and
behavior on the playground, in Chapter 8.)

Here is the script I wrote for Joe to read to Tony on increasing
reading fluency:

> « *Tony, this is your dad.*
> *I want to let you know how much I love you.*
> *I want you to know how proud I am that you are my son.*
> *I want to let you know how much I appreciate your learning*
>   *to read.*
> *As you learn to read, words are easy and fun for you.*
> *You have fun reading words everywhere.*
> *You can read so many words.*
> *It is exciting to hear you read words out loud and to know*
>   *you can read words in your head as well.*
> *You are a good reader.*
> *I love you.*
> *Sweet dreams.* »

Tony continued to struggle with reading for a few more weeks,
and Joe continued reading the script to him. Then all of a sudden,
the clouds seemed to part, and Tony "got it." His grades shot up,
and he's been enjoying school ever since. Like all other Sleep Talk
scripts, this one has a built-in "bonding" element that strengthens
the relationship between father and son at the same time it offers
encouragment in the specific skill of reading. At this time in the
child's life, his father's love and approval mean a great deal.

Assigned and Leisure Reading

My own kids have been avid readers from early ages, but many parents rarely see their children immersed in any book that isn't part
of a homework assignment. For better or for worse, television plays
a significant role in the lives of most of us these days, and some kids
may need to be reminded that reading can also be fun.

The only general rule about television in our household is that the set is turned off during mealtimes. Each of my kids had specific programs they liked to watch, and they were free to do that, so long as their homework and chores were out of the way. Nowadays, if T.J. has a lot of homework on a particular night, he might miss his program, but he can tape it and watch it at a later date. I see no point in using deprivation of television as a punishment—that would only make it more attractive.

I believe in encouraging recreational reading for several reasons. Computer literacy is a major tool of our society, and kids today need to be able to read in order to use their computers effectively. Children also need to be able to read in order to gather information they need in other areas. Last but by no means least, literature offers examples of human behavior and relationships that are more interesting and complex than most of what is offered on television.

Pam, a client of mine who is an avid reader of literary fiction, belongs to a book group that meets once a month. She was concerned because her nine-year-old daughter, Jenny, whose grades were above average, rarely cracked a book except to do her homework assignments. Here is a script I wrote for Pam to read to Jenny:

《 *Jenny, this is your mom.*
I want to let you know how much I love you.
I want to let you know how very proud I am that you are my daughter.
I want to let you know how much I value it when you do your reading assignments and fun reading.
Your love of words in reading is appreciated.
You feel good about your ability to read.
Reading is easy for you.
Thank you for being a good reader.
I love you.
Sweet dreams. 》

While I can't report that this script turned Jenny into a bookworm, she did express an interest in going along the next time her mother made a trip to the public library. Jenny got a library card of her own, and Pam would occasionally see her reading on weekends. Even though there was no dramatic transformation here, Jenny's willingness to try out reading for pleasure is creating the possibility of further interest and development later on. In this case, it's obvious that her mother's example is an important factor.

Reading for Memory and Test-Taking

Much of the reading children do is related to test-taking, and phobias about tests are common at this age. Though my own kids never had any serious problems in this area, many of my friends have reported that their kids' minds become blank when confronted with an exam paper.

It seems to me the basic difficulty here is that most children are never given one basic piece of information: that their reading for school is linked to taking tests on that particular subject matter. Just making them aware that when they read textbooks, they need to hold in mind the intention to *remember* the material can make an enormous difference.

Scott, the eleven-year-old son of my student Ramona, had a history of freezing up on tests. A lively and intelligent boy who was conscientious about doing his homework, Scott was extremely frustrated by his poor track record on exams. His C and occasional D grades seemed to contradict the potential his parents saw in him.

Here is the script I gave Ramona to read to Scott:

《 *Scott, this is your mother.*
I want to let you know how much I love you.
I want you to know how proud I am that you are my son.
I am proud of you when you remember things you read.
You have a good memory.
It is easy for you to read and remember what you read.
It is easy for you to take tests on what you read.
You let the information flow from your brain to the paper
    during tests.
Thank you for being my child.
Thank you for being such a good reader.

I love you.
Sweet dreams. »

Scott is one of my best Sleep Talk success stories. The week after his mother started reading him this script, he got an A on his history exam (his previous grade had been a D). His grades in all his subjects improved dramatically: on his next report card, he got a B in math and As in everything else. He is now in his senior year of high school, with an excellent record behind him, and has made applications to several Ivy League colleges. Test-taking no longer holds any terrors for him, and I expect this pattern to continue through his college years.

Increasing Math Fluency: Add, Subtract, Multiply, and Divide

My son Trey started Montessori school at two, and by age three he had taught himself to read. One day, I was taking him to the barbershop and was busy getting Tara out of the car, when he said, "Mom, we can go in now." I said, "How do you know?" He pointed to the sign: "It says they're open." Then I began to notice that when we were driving, he'd be in the backseat doing a singsong: "Motel, hotel, hotel, gas, Texaco, Texaco. . . ." And I realized he was reading the signs.

Even though Trey read everything he could get his hands on, he was completely uninterested in math. Fortunately, he had an excellent teacher who saw a way to help him. Instead of using numbers, she started writing out math situations in words; with that approach, she had no trouble getting him to do what he needed to do. (One of the great benefits of the Montessori schools is that the teachers there are especially skilled at using what a child can already do to move him into a new area.) And that's how Trey got hooked on math.

I'm aware that girls in our society generally have more problems with math than boys do. In some quarters, there's still an absurd assumption that being good at numbers is unfeminine, and I think some parents unconsciously transmit this belief to their daughters.

Jessica, a student of mine, told me that her ten-year-old daughter, Nicole, was close to flunking math, even though her grades in all other subjects were As and Bs. "I just can't do numbers, Mom," she said, when questioned about her D-minus grade. "How does your husband feel about this?" I asked Jessica. "He just laughs," Jessica said, "says she'll probably never need to use it anyway." Jessica had already used a number of Sleep Talk scripts with her daughter, to good effect. I knew from comments Jessica had made in my class that Nicole worshiped her father, and I asked if Jessica thought her husband might be willing to read a math script to Nicole.

In the end, he was the one who read the following script to his daughter:

« *Nicole, this is your dad.*
I want to let you know how much I love you.
I want you to know how proud I am that you are my
daughter.
As you learn your math facts and multiplication tables,
numbers are easy and fun for you.
You enjoy doing your math and studying each fact or times
table.
You are fascinated with numbers.
Math becomes easy and automatic for you.
Numbers tell stories, and you can write them.
I want to let you know how much I value it when you do
your math assignments.
Thank you for being my daughter.
I love you so much.
Sweet dreams. »

With her father expressing confidence that she could do well in math, Nicole went from a shaky D to a B on her next report card. Jessica told me that Nicole even remarked one night at dinner, "I think this math stuff is really fun." The girl beamed when her father said, "I always knew you could do it!" Jessica winked at me. "And you know what? I think he actually believes that now."

Math Test-Taking

Even kids who feel comfortable with numbers sometimes panic when confronted with tests in math. Although the children understand the process, the stress of being asked to perform mathematical computations on the spot under pressure of time may cause them to freeze up. As with tests involving reading, the math test situation can be eased by a parent's reassurance that the child knows how to solve the problems and can count on having a clear channel from brain to paper during the exam.

My client Pam (whose daughter Jenny started reading for pleasure after hearing a script on the subject) also has a son, Joel, who at age eleven suddenly developed a phobia about math tests. Joel had no problem taking tests about facts he'd read, and he had been getting Bs in math. Then one day, he came home and said, "Mom, I don't know what happened. I just got scared out of my mind—couldn't figure out how to do any of those problems. If I had that test in front of me right now, I could do them all."

Pam called and asked if I had a script to help Joel with math test-taking. Here's the one I gave her:

《*Joel, this is your mother.*
I want to let you know how much I love you.
I want you to know how proud I am that you are my son.
I just want you to know how proud I am of you when you remember your math.
You have a good memory.
It becomes easy for you to add, subtract, multiply, and divide and to know which function to use.
It is easy for you to take tests in math.
You let the information flow from your brain to your paper during your test.
You are a good math test-taker.
Thank you for being my child.
I love you.
Sweet dreams.》

The results with Joel were quick and gratifying. The week after his mother started reading this script to him, he had another test in math, and this time he sailed through it with an A. He's been doing fine in math ever since. It seems that his mom's confidence and pride in him renewed his own sense of being able to handle the stressful test situation, and he has never again frozen up on a test.

Academic School Behavior

School is a brand-new world for children, and they need to learn appropriate behavior in a classroom situation. If they've been in nursery school, they may already be familiar with some of the rules, but the greater structure of first and second grades may confuse some kids.

A big question for all of us in life is: *When should I assert myself, and when should I sit back and simply listen to what is going on?* The classroom provides the first laboratory for our personal experiments around this question, and some kids have trouble finding a workable balance.

Norma, one of my students, asked me for a script she could use with her son, Allen, who was having trouble figuring out the rules in first grade. Even though he was no longer solving conflicts with other children by hitting them (as I described in Chapter 8 in my script about action control), he was extremely vocal and assertive, and his teacher told Norma that he didn't seem to understand that he also needed to listen. "I don't want to squelch him," Norma told me, "but I need to tone him down."

Here's the script I gave Norma to read to Allen:

《 *Allen, this is your mom.*
I want to let you know how much I love you.
I want you to know how proud I am that you are my son.
I appreciate you being so well behaved.
I am proud that you know the answers.
I know that you can be assertive, or say what you need to
    say, but there are times when you listen.
Thank you for being my wonderful son.

I love you.
Sweet dreams. »

As with the earlier script, Allen responded promptly to Norma's suggestions. He was still quick with answers to the teacher's questions, but he was also able to sit quietly and listen to what others had to say.

Another problem some children have at this age is shyness. As kids struggle to learn the rules of appropriate classroom behavior, they may alternate fairly rapidly between one extreme and the other. This was the case with seven-year-old Kelly, who I discussed first at the beginning of the book and again earlier in this chapter. After listening to the Sleep Talk script on shyness, Kelly overcame her problem to such an extent that she needed another script to temper her bossiness. This second script (see Chapter 1)—similar to the one I wrote for Allen—was effective in helping her achieve a good balance.

Homework

Getting used to the idea of homework and taking responsibility for it is an important part of a school-age child's learning experience. With the enormous number of things children need to attend to at this age, it's no wonder that homework sometimes doesn't get done as well as it should, or doesn't get done on time, or doesn't get done at all.

Melody, the bright but distracted eight-year-old I wrote about earlier in the chapter, had a lot of trouble getting her homework done. She would forget her assignments, or lose them, or become interested in something else and fail to complete them.

Here's the script I wrote for Melody's mother to read to her:

« *Melody, this is your mom.*
I want to let you know how much I love you.
I want you to know how proud I am that you are my
    daughter.
I just want you to know how proud I am of you when you
    get all your homework done.

You go to school with your homework all finished.
I know you are proud of yourself.
You do a good job of completing your homework and
submitting it on time.
Thank you for being my daughter.
I love you.
Sweet dreams. »

Melody was not a shirker; she just kept getting distracted by more appealing activities. Once she realized the importance of doing her homework assignments, she became much more reliable about turning them in on time. This was an exceptionally spirited and creative child, and after she learned to follow through on tasks (including homework), her academic record was excellent.

Teamwork: Working with Others

Learning to work with others as a team is another new and important area for children in the elementary grades. Whether on the sports field, in a group art project, or in a class play, this is a skill children need to develop. Like all other skills, it comes more easily to some than to others. For children who are particularly aggressive or individualistic, learning to share tasks with others may be difficult.

Norma, who read my script on academic school behavior to Allen when he was in first grade, asked me the following year for a script that would help him work more harmoniously with others. Even though he was able to control his assertiveness in class, his teacher informed Norma that he became bossy and even bullying when assigned to create an art project with three other children.

Here is the script I gave Norma to read to Allen:

« *Allen, this is your mother.*
I want to let you know how much I love you.
I want you to know how proud I am of you.
I am inspired when I watch you work with others.
You are calm, confident, and cooperative.

You build wonderful, supportive structures in whatever
   project or activity you are participating in.
You are a good team player.
You and I make a special team.
Thank you for being on my team.
Thank you for being my son.
I love you.
Sweet dreams. »

A child like Allen may actually need information about what cooperation entails, and being encouraged to practice teamwork with his mother offered him a chance to see how this new skill might work in a familiar situation. Several weeks after Norma began reading this script to Allen, he worked with another small group of classmates on a skit to be presented to the class. His teacher called Norma to say that he had been extremely cooperative with the other kids and that his group's skit was outstanding, thanks in large part to his supportive leadership.

Learning to work with others requires combining all the Rules of Life introduced in this chapter. The child needs to (1) show up, (2) pay attention, (3) recognize that whoever appears in his life (and on his team) is supposed to be there, (4) understand that whatever happens is what is supposed to happen, and (5) be aware that when it's over, it's over. A complex lesson indeed for a seven-year-old!

During the school years, our children establish patterns for the way they will deal with others throughout their lives. This is a particularly sensitive period for them, and we as parents can contribute crucial information and encouragement through using appropriate Sleep Talk scripts. All that is required is that *we* follow the Rules of Life to our own best ability. Our love and support make these scripts effective, and our modeling of the behavior we encourage in our children adds even more power to our nightly readings.

10

SLEEP TALK
AND YOUR
ADOLESCENT

Many parents view adolescence as a kind of childhood disease; they hope it will run its course and be over as quickly as possible. Even in the closest of families, it is frequently a trying time. The teenage years are a time of rebellion, similar to that of the "terrible twos," except that the individuals are a lot bigger and the process lasts a lot longer.

You may find it helpful to see these years as a bridge between childhood and adulthood: a period during which the teenager grows in many ways and takes important steps toward independence. For boys and girls at this stage, the world often looks confusing, and you as a parent can offer support and encouragement as they try their wings, sometimes manage to fly—and sometimes crash to earth.

One of the major tasks of this stage of life is learning to establish intimate ties with people beyond the family. This includes coping with sweeping hormonal changes in the body and powerful sexual drives. The ways this manifests in teenagers' lives may range from hours spent on the phone to joining gangs, and from acquiring a girlfriend or boyfriend to becoming sexually promiscuous.

For many parents, this is a painful time because the teenager's movements toward independence may look to the parent like rejection, especially in families that have maintained close ties. Being currently in the process of seeing T.J., my youngest, through his adolescence, I know how frustrating this period can be for a parent. I also know that it is a natural and inevitable stage of growth that must be successfully negotiated if he is to become an independent, self-sustaining adult.

It's especially important at this time to offer teenagers support for shaping their own agendas, not pressuring them to live up to a specific program you have in mind. Having survived the adolescence of my three older children, I can testify that the reward you get at the end is wonderful: you get to have in your life adult children with qualities you would treasure in your best friend.

The big message for young people at this stage is that they have choices. With choices inevitably come mistakes, and mistakes are a way of learning to make better choices. One of the hardest parts of parenting at this stage is being patient as you watch your kids make mistakes, letting them learn their own lessons. The values you have taught them earlier are a part of them at this point, and it's important to trust that they will apply those principles to life situations. If you express love, trust, encouragement, and friendship, they will gain confidence in their own ability to cope. At this point, your acceptance of their independence—and your willingness to offer advice *if asked*—can be a major strength to them on their journey.

All of which is not to say that parents are bound to accept inconsiderate, self-destructive, or irresponsible behavior. But this stage of life is about learning self-control, and teenagers are especially sensitive to controls imposed on them by parents.

Are some controls necessary? Of course. With my kids, the problem of the telephone was a major one. Especially in families with one phone line, it may be necessary to limit time on the phone. I've been known to take an egg timer and say, "This is how long this call may last. When the bell goes off, it's over." Another constraint we have in our family is that if the grades aren't at a certain level, phone privileges stop.

Nowadays a lot of kids have phones in their rooms; most of the teenagers I know have cell phones they take everywhere, and many have beepers and e-mail addresses as well. It's important for them to communicate with their peers, because that's one of the ways they develop skills in interacting. But it's also reasonable for a family to have rules, and the obvious way to establish them is to sit down with your kids and work out appropriate boundaries. For example, my kids don't talk on the phone during family dinners, or when homework and chores haven't been done. Rules are important for the information they give a teenager about where she stands and how much latitude she has; knowing those limits can actually be reassuring for her.

Of course, teenagers learn more from their parents' example at this age than from any rules or advice. This is especially true when it comes to intimate relationships, a subject of absorbing interest to kids at this age. Most of the time they are going to handle relationships the same way they observed their parents doing it. But one of the benefits of opening up to the wider world during the teenage years is that kids get to see that other families do things differently. A teenager who comes from a loving, supportive family will probably observe among his circle some families in which the kids are put down or ignored or even beaten. It can be a shock. And for a child from a troubled family, it can be equally surprising to experience the warm, happy family relationships in a friend's home.

Awareness of these differences is the beginning of growth. Part of that growth is the establishment of moral values, and many of these we get from our families. But in the teenage years, there are inevitably challenges to the standards we got from our parents. I remember vividly, for example, the moment I decided that a life of crime was not for me.

My friends were on their way to steal some watermelons. Did I want to come along? Of course I did; I wanted to be included in the group. It was the dead of night, and we were giggling as we rode out into the country in an old jalopy, talking about where we'd go to eat the watermelons after we got them. But while we were in the process of stealing them, the farmer started shooting buckshot at us. I hit the dirt and dug my way back to the car. Of course I knew what I was doing was wrong; I knew it was stealing. But for a moment my desire to be part of the gang was greater than my scruples. The experience taught me an important lesson, and I remember making a specific decision that I would never do anything like that again. I got a powerful lesson with minimal risk.

Nowadays the stakes are often higher, and I sympathize with parents who fear, often with good reason, that their teenagers may not survive adolescence. It takes real intestinal fortitude to parent a teenager these days. It's no fun to sit back and watch your child take unnecessary risks and suffer the consequences. Of course you help where you can, but it's important to recognize that there are certain areas where you have to step back and trust the process.

Despite their need to disengage from the family, teenagers still need a home where they can be assured of love and support, lick their wounds when they fail, and celebrate their successes. Having a parent who makes a distinction between the teenager's essential value and his sometimes less-than-sterling behavior gives a child continuing strength for the battle.

What's crucial is keeping the lines of communication open. I wanted to make sure my kids knew I believed in their ability to make good choices, I accepted that there would be some mistakes, and I was available if they wanted to ask my advice about anything.

Self-Confidence

My kids have been quite different from each other as teenagers. Briana, for example, was very clear about her goals and comfortable about using me as a resource when she needed me. T.J., who is now a teenager, has needed a little more help in the area of self-confidence. Some of this may be due to some difficult life experiences he had before we adopted him when he was eighteen months old. I can't change the things that happened before he came into our family, but

I can continue to give him information that dilutes the negative aspects of what he has gone through and neutralizes feelings that could lead to his hurting himself or others.

In T.J.'s case, the bonding scripts have been especially important at every stage of his life, and the following script on self-confidence is the logical next step:

« *T.J., this is your mother.*
I want to let you know how much I love you.
I want to let you know how proud I am that you are my son.
I am so proud of you when you get clear on what you want.
Your willingness to work and accomplish tasks is such fun to
watch.
You are calm, confident, and energetic.
You know how to finish a job and get tasks done.
It is fun to watch you with your successes.
You look for "good things" in all kinds of situations.
You let those "good" things serve you.
I am happy to be in your life.
I love you.
Sweet dreams. »

The main message of this script is that the teenager has options. Expressing pride in the child's ability to decide what he wants and to finish tasks that he undertakes supports his independence. Having confidence that he will look for "good" things in his life supports his ability to make appropriate choices. While there is a reminder of the ongoing connection to the parent, it simply establishes that the parent is there for him as a resource, making no demands for particular behaviors or achievements.

Negotiating the teenage years is a problem for all children, and those who have had difficulties establishing basic trust in the world as infants and toddlers are likely to have a particularly hard time between the ages of thirteen and nineteen. In T.J.'s case, I feel the Sleep Talk work we have done together over the years has made for a far less troubled adolescence than I've observed in other adopted children.

Reading this self-confidence script to him has also given me a new perspective on the parent-child relationship. Because he has no genetic link to our family, I observe his unfolding in a different way than I did with my three birth children. I have fewer expectations, perhaps, and a deeper acceptance that he is becoming the person *he* needs and wants to be.

Caring

My husband usually drives T.J. to school, but one day not long ago, I took on the chauffeuring when George wasn't able to do it. Usually just before they leave the house, T.J. kisses me, but on this morning we left together. We drove up to the school just as a school bus was unloading, and the scene was chaotic, with a man directing traffic, lots of people walking, and kids moving into the fenced area of the school grounds. I stopped to let T.J. out, and he leaned over and kissed me on the cheek. I was surprised that, at age fifteen, he would let all these people see him kissing his mother.

Two boys who were walking by laughed, and as he got out of the car, they said something to him that I couldn't hear. The traffic director was waving me on, so I had to leave. That afternoon when I picked up T.J., I asked about his day and finally got around to asking if those boys had given him a hard time about kissing me good-bye. "Kind of," he said. "How did you handle that?" I asked. "Oh, I didn't," he said, "Michael did." Michael, his best friend, happened to be standing against the fence and saw the whole thing. "Those guys came over and were kind of giving me a bad time," T.J. went on, "and Michael just said, 'If you knew his mother, you'd kiss her too.'"

The teenager's stance of toughness often covers a terror that others may realize how vulnerable he feels inside. A common attitude is: "I can take care of myself—I don't ask anybody for anything." In cases like this, it's helpful for a parent to remind the child that establishing caring relationships with others is also important.

This isn't an area that T.J.—or any of my other kids—has needed help with, but I can imagine that a parent of one of the boys that was giving him a hard time might make good use of a script like the following to restore some balance to their son's life:

《 *Tom, this is your father.*
I want to let you know how much I love you.
I want to let you know how proud I am to be your dad.
I just want to let you know how much I appreciate your kind and gentle manner.
You are warm and gracious.
You look for harmony in situations.
You feel good about taking action when you see opportunities to assist others.
Thank you for being in my life.
Thank you for caring for me.
I like and appreciate the way you take care of me.
I love you.
Sweet dreams. 》

In a case like this, a father's reading a Sleep Talk script on caring would probably have an especially strong impact on a boy, since our society generally seems less positive about the quality of caring in males.

Perseverance

At this stage of life, the ability to follow through on tasks becomes a significant predictor of a person's success, both in school and in the outside world. For a child whose attention span is short, a parent's encouragement to see a project through to completion may help establish a habit of persisting in spite of difficulties or flagging interest.

Marjorie, one of my clients, asked me to write a script for her fifteen-year-old daughter, Vicki. Vicki's grades had suddenly plummeted—the classic "sophomore slump"—even though her test scores showed her to be of above-average intelligence and her previous grades had been good. Vicki seemed far more interested in boys than in studying (not unusual for girls at this age), and she found it difficult to complete papers she was assigned to write. "I try," she said, "I really do. Even with my best effort, I just can't finish this stuff."

Here is the script on perseverance I wrote for Marjorie to read to Vicki:

« *Vicki, this is your mom.*
I want to let you know how much I love you.
I want to let you know how proud I am that you are my daughter.
I just want to let you know how much I appreciate it when you create and accomplish the things you want to get done.
When your "best effort" is not enough, it only means you need to "stick with it."
Your concentration increases as you lengthen your attention to the task.
You enjoy seeing success in completion.
Like all achievers, you persist.
I am so proud of you.
Thank you for being my daughter.
I love you.
Sweet dreams. »

After Marjorie had read Vicki this script for several weeks, Vicki began finishing more of her projects, even though the final results were not always of the highest quality. My sense of the situation is that Vicki's heart and mind were otherwise engaged (and probably would continue to be during this volatile period), but that the habit of persisting in her tasks, once established, would stand her in good stead when the storms of adolescence were past.

With other teenagers, the failure to follow through may have different causes. Some kids feel put down by their peers for wanting a particular goal, and their inability to push through to completion may be rooted in a loss of confidence. Being clear about their needs is an important factor—not only understanding that their goal is important, but also believing that they themselves are important and deserve to have what they desire.

Of course, this script on perseverance is not applicable only to academic situations. Take a look at the state of the child's room. Is your son finishing his household chores? Is your daughter delivering on whatever she has committed herself to do? Parents don't always know exactly what psychological factors may be operating in their teenager, and the child often doesn't know how to ask for help, but when follow-through is a chronic problem in any area, this script can be helpful.

Homework

The common adolescent problem with follow-through has an obvious relationship to homework. With kids nowadays, there seems to be a more casual attitude about turning in assignments.

While T.J.'s behavior in this area has generally been responsible, I've been conscious of some situations in which reminders from me were important. Not long ago, he got an extension on some homework because of his involvement with a special after-school program, and he took the assigned work to school with him the day after most kids in his class were required to turn it in. As I was driving him home from school that day, I said, "Did you turn in that assignment you had an extension on?" "No," he said. "Why not?" "Well," he said, "the teacher didn't ask for it." I turned the car around and headed back toward the school. "It's your responsibility to see that she gets it," I said, "not to wait till she asks for it." I parked near the school and waited while he went in, found the teacher, and gave her his homework.

If this incident were to become part of a chronic pattern—and especially if his grades were affected—I might use a Sleep Talk script like the following one to help him become more aware of the issues involved:

《 *T.J., this is your mom.*
I want to let you know how much I love you.
I want to let you know how proud I am that you are
    my son.

When you get your homework done and do well in school, I
*   am proud of you because I know that you are proud of*
*   yourself.*
When there are interruptions, you stay on task.
You study your schoolwork and complete your homework.
I am so pleased when you turn in your homework on time
*   and make good grades.*
I can trust you to do what you say you are going to do.
Thank you for being my trustworthy son.
You are so important to me.
Thank you for being in my life.
I love you.
Sweet dreams. »

This script would be effective for any teenager who is having problems with homework. There could be many reasons for this kind of
lapse, and it's not necessary for a parent to perform complicated feats
of diagnosis in order to help a child change this negative pattern.

I'm aware that there seems to be a greater incidence of attention deficit disorder these days at all school levels. Some parents, at
their wit's end over how to deal with this problem, have resorted to
a written "contract" that the child is required to have the teacher
sign periodically to confirm that homework has been turned in. My
sense of the situation is that these ADD children are not being deliberately irresponsible; they simply haven't yet learned to pay attention when assignments are given. This script, as well as the previous
one on perseverance, can help children with this problem focus on
what they need to accomplish.

Common Sense

Children at this age may become distracted for a variety of reasons.
The hormonal surges in their bloodstreams might be the easiest factor to blame, but there are other elements as well. My son Trey—a
brilliant boy who could read at age three, entered high school at
eleven, and graduated at fifteen—was so focused on the world of

ideas that he often had trouble coping with aspects of life that a child with half his IQ might handle easily.

One continuing problem area for Trey during his teenage years was his trip home from school on the bus. I had to be sure to be home by 4:00 because he would call me from all over Orange County, having gotten absorbed with something he was reading and ridden past his stop. One day I said to him, "What do the bus drivers say to you when you miss your stop, when you don't get off?" He said, "Today the driver said, 'Son, son! Are you getting off?' I looked up and said, 'Well, where are we?' He said, 'We're at the end of the line.' I just told him, 'You went by my stop.'" So, Trey needed to understand that it was *his* responsibility to pay attention.

At that time, I wasn't consistent about using Sleep Talk scripts with my older kids, and I never developed one to help Trey with this problem. If I had, it might have helped him with the tunnel vision that is a problem for him to this day. Here's the script I wish I'd used with him:

« *Trey, this is your mom.*
I just want to let you know how much I love you.
I just want to let you know how much I appreciate it when
*   you think situations through.*
You can think problems through to a good solution.
You are a good worker.
It is fun to watch you at your best when you consider options
*   and make choices.*
It does not matter if I am there. You are capable.
I delight in and appreciate the fact that you use good
*   judgment.*
Thank you for being my son.
I love you so very much.
Sweet dreams. »

The applications of this script to safety are obvious. This is the age when kids begin driving, and not paying attention at the wheel is a common cause of accidents. Trey has always been a terrible driver, and he'd still rather take the bus wherever he's going (when he can remember to get off at the right stop) and be free to read on the way. One day when he was sixteen, I got a call from one of my neighbors: "Trey is down at the stoplight in the left-hand turn lane," she said, "and the cars behind him are honking." He was just sitting there reading a book, oblivious.

Leadership

When Trey was in high school, he achieved the highest scores in the county in four different areas, including math and physics. But instead of giving him all four awards, the powers that be decided he should receive only one, so that "other children would have a chance." To me, this seemed unfair, especially since they didn't let him choose which award he wanted, but simply assigned him one. The most important thing for me was that he had earned top status in four categories, and I was extremely proud of him, but I had to help him cope with his understandable disappointment.

At this age, children often experience negative pressure about leadership, and it's important for parents to recognize that situation when it exists and take steps to counter it. It's difficult to say just what makes many children with natural leadership abilities hold back—perhaps a misguided sense that if they're leaders in one area (such as being captain of the football team), they can't (or shouldn't) be equally prominent in another (such as running for class president). This attitude may come from their peers as well as from teachers and school administrators.

It is a fact of life that people gifted in one area are often gifted in others, and it seems unreasonable to put them down for aspiring to excel. I'm especially aware of this kind of pressure on teenage girls, and the work of such writers as Carol Gilligan (*In a Different Voice*) supports this impression.

By the time I became aware of this problem, my younger daughter, Briana, was a teenager, and she was already so confident about her leadership abilities that there would have been no point in writing a script on the subject for her. I developed the following script as a possible source of help for talented teenagers who seem to be putting the brakes on their own leadership abilities:

《Heather, this is your mom.
I want to let you know how much I love you.
I want to let you know how proud I am to be your mom.
Excellence is your middle name.
I am so proud that you are willing to be seen.
You are a trailblazer, innovative, and inspiring to be around.
You set an example with your peers and make good choices.
You carefully plan your course and stick to your convictions.
You are a strong leader, moving toward excellence.
Thank you for being my daughter.
You are so wonderful.
I love you.
Sweet dreams. 》

Initiative

Related to leadership is initiative. Even children who show no special gifts as leaders may benefit from support for striking out on their own to create their own agendas. What my script on initiative does is to make the teenage boy or girl aware that taking the initiative is important. Especially for the shy or timid adolescent, it can provide support for trying out new and positive behaviors.

Chapter 9 discussed the way a Sleep Talk script on self-confidence helped eight-year-old Jason, who had a history of childhood illnesses, to interact more positively with his teachers and peers. By the time Jason was fourteen, he still seemed reluctant to take the initiative, and his father, Nick, asked me for help with this problem. Here's the script I wrote for Nick to read to Jason:

《Jason, this is your dad.
I just want to let you know how much I love you.
I just want to let you know how proud I am to be your dad.
I am proud of you when you ask questions and look for
    answers.
You use initiative to seek new ideas.
You look for ways to improve.

You are positive and productive.
It is fun to watch you organize, begin something, and keep on
*   going.*
People comment on how you stay "on mission."
Thank you for being my son.
I am proud of you.
I love you.
Sweet dreams. 》

Notice that this script does not impose any particular parental agenda on Jason, but simply encourages his impulses toward setting his own agendas and following through on them. Like all the other scripts in this chapter, it reflects the parent's pride and confidence in the child's abilities.

Approaching Adults as a Resource

Chapter 9 also described how Nicole, the ten-year-old daughter of Jessica, one of my students, benefited from having her father read her a Sleep Talk script on increasing math fluency. Some years later, Jessica became concerned that Nicole seemed shy about seeking help from her teachers or adults other than her parents. When Nicole had been in charge of lighting for a school play, she resisted consulting the teacher who was directing the production about certain technical problems she was having. "I'm not sure why she couldn't just ask him for help," Jessica said, "but I got the feeling she didn't feel safe about it, and she wouldn't discuss it with me in any detail."

Here's the script I wrote for Jessica to read to Nicole:

《 *Nicole, this is your mother.*
I want to let you know how much I love you.
I want to let you know how proud I am that you are my
*   daughter.*
I want to let you know how proud I am of you in your
*   ability to seek and ask for help in your schoolwork.*
You find ways to make things happen for yourself.
It is easy for you to approach your teachers or an adult to
*   ask for help.*

> *You know when and how to effectively ask for help that*
>   *benefits all concerned.*
> *You continue to follow your hunches and keep yourself safe.*
> *You trust yourself.*
> *I trust you to negotiate school situations to a workable*
>   *solution.*
> *Thank you for being my daughter.*
> *I love you.*
> *Sweet dreams.* »

Jessica called about a month later to tell me that Nicole had requested a conference with her English teacher when she had trouble writing an assigned paper. The students had been given a list of poems they might choose to write about, and each person in the class signed up to write about a different poem, with the expectation of later reading the paper aloud to the class. Nicole had signed up for a particular poem but felt dissatisfied with her choice when she began working on the paper. In her meeting with the teacher, she described her problem, and the teacher suggested she switch to a poem that had not been on the original list, a selection Nicole felt enthusiastic about working on. In the end, Nicole got an A on her paper, and Jessica was delighted that her daughter had taken the initiative to approach her teacher as a resource.

Choices: Using Time

One of the major choices that teenagers have to make is about how to use their free time. Many kids this age spend hours on the phone with their friends, and their preoccupation with this activity often creates problems in meeting other commitments. Learning to manage limited resources such as time and money is a major task at this stage, and the child's struggles with this problem may be a major source of frustration to parents.

All of us need to learn the importance of keeping our time agreements, and this responsibility goes beyond simply showing up on time for dates we have made. It also involves consideration for the time management problems of others.

For example, one day recently I needed to pick up T.J. immediately after school to drive him to a special class he was taking
that met at 4:00. I had gone to a lot of trouble to rearrange my
own schedule so that I could arrive promptly. When he got into
the car, he smiled lovingly and said, "Oh, I don't have that class
today." "When was this decided?" I asked. "Oh, last time I was
in class, they announced it." His failure to tell me about the situation had put me to unnecessary trouble, and he seemed blissfully
unaware that it might be important to let me know about the
change earlier.

Here is a script parents can use to offer their teenager guidelines for using time responsibly:

《 *T.J., this is your mother.*
I want to let you know how much I love you.
I want you to know how proud I am that you are my son.
I want to let you know how much I appreciate it when you
    make conscious choices about your time.
When you use your time wisely, you get so many things done
    and completed.
When you do the things you say you are going to do, you
    keep your time agreements.
When you keep your time agreements, you tell the truth.
Thank you for telling the truth.
Thank you for keeping your time agreements with me.
Thank you for being my son.
I love you.
Sweet dreams. 》

One of the things this script does is to remind the teenager that
time has value not only to him but also to others on whom his time
choices impinge. Making this point effectively can be especially difficult when the child observes a casual attitude toward time commitments in one or both of his parents. In our family, my husband
is often careless about his time agreements, and that makes effective communication with T.J. on the subject more difficult.

Choices: Using Money

Teenagers today seem to have a lot of money, and many of them are already aware of the need to make good choices concerning it. My kids didn't get allowances; instead, they had an opportunity to sign up for various jobs I needed to have done, such as washing the front windows or the car. I would post a list on the refrigerator, and various jobs got paid various amounts. They could select the jobs they wanted and set up a time with me. In order to get paid, they had to finish the work and do it to my satisfaction.

My aim was to help my kids gain a sense of responsibility as well as an understanding that a job didn't just need to be done: it needed to be done *satisfactorily* in order to earn their pay. Which is exactly the situation they would be facing as adults in the business world.

When Tara was sixteen and Briana was twelve, we had poor janitor service at George's medical office. So, I told the girls I would pay them to clean the office. They did it until Tara graduated from high school, and it was the best cleaning job we ever had. There were certain side benefits for them: they got to see where their dad worked, they were part of a team, and they got a salary. If something they did wasn't exactly right, I or someone on the staff would call them on it, and the whole thing worked out extremely well for everybody.

There are a lot of jobs teenagers do these days. T.J. baby-sits. A lot of kids do yard work. My cleaning lady has a sixteen-year-old daughter who helps out at parties with her mom and is much in demand because she does such a good job. I know a woman who hired a thirteen-year-old boy to water the plants in office buildings.

When teenagers earn their own money, they get to decide how to spend it. In working to earn it, they give the best they have to offer in exchange for money, and it's important for them to exchange it for the best others have to offer and for things that really matter to their lives.

My kids have handled responsibilities involving money so well that I've never needed a Sleep Talk script on the subject for them.

But a lot of kids can benefit from support and encouragement for good choices, and the following script would work very well for them:

« *Lisa, this is your mother.*
I want to let you know how much I love you.
I want you to know how proud I am that you are my daughter.
I want to let you know how much I appreciate you using your money wisely.
You make good choices about how to use your money.
You make good choices about your money.
I appreciate it when you use your money wisely.
Money is the exchange you have to trade your best with the best of others.
I am proud of your choices with your money.
Thank you for being my daughter.
Thank you for being in my life.
I love you.
Sweet dreams. »

Will this script prevent mistakes? Of course not. But children learn from their ineffective choices, and those lessons are part of the process of becoming an adult.

Choices: Making Friends

One of the most important tasks of adolescence is learning to make close connections with other people. At this age, the child moves beyond simply looking for another kid or a group to play with to choosing good, trustworthy friends. The teenager is learning to look beyond surface attractiveness to assess people's inner qualities and form lasting friendships.

One of my clients, Trudy, told me that her family had recently moved to our area and that her son, Stan, who was a junior in high school, was having trouble making friends. He was a football player, but when he arrived at the school, football season was over. It seemed that all the good friends were taken and the cliques were established, so it was hard for him to make a space for himself. There were a few kids who had failed to make friends for good and sufficient reasons who were available to pal around with Stan, but he didn't really like them and was reluctant to settle for these makeshift connections.

Fortunately, he was close enough to his parents to let them in on what was happening, and they were wise enough not to push things but to trust him to find his own way. Here is the Sleep Talk script I wrote for Trudy to read to Stan:

> « *Stan, this is your mother.*
> *I want to let you know how much I love you.*
> *I want you to know how proud I am that you are my son.*
> *I want to let you know how much I appreciate it when you surround yourself with trustworthy friends.*
> *I enjoy seeing you happy and having fun.*
> *Good friends add to having a good time.*
> *Your choice of friends makes me proud of you.*
> *You pick and keep good people as your friends.*
> *You are a good friend.*
> *Thank you for being my friend.*
> *Thank you for being my son.*
> *I love you.*
> *Sweet dreams.* »

Things worked out well for Stan, in the end. He bided his time and resisted the temptation to make friends with just anybody. By the time football season arrived during his senior year, his excellence in that area allowed him to become part of the group he liked. His mother told me that coping with this situation made an enormous difference for him; for the first time in his life, he had to start on the outside and work his way into the inner circle. This challenge allowed him to develop a mature outlook about friendships that might have taken him years to achieve under normal circumstances.

Remember Haddad's Five Rules of Life? Stan got a crash course in all of them at once. He showed up, paid attention, accepted that whoever appeared in his life (or didn't) was right for him, accepted that what happened (the move and its consequences) was also right, and recognized that when his temporary isolation was over, it really was over. In the course of living through this difficult period, he developed skills that he'll be able to use to great advantage for the rest of his life.

Choices: Organizational Skills

The social calendars of teenagers are often incredibly crowded. Between the birthday parties, the dance recitals, the music lessons, the sports, and the continual rushing from one thing to another, being organized becomes essential to sanity. If, for example, your daughter's room is a chaos (as Tara's often was) and she isn't able to find her belongings when she needs them, arguments and accusations can disrupt the lives of everyone in the family.

At this point, you may want a Sleep Talk script that will encourage your teenager to get better organized. This script is a more sophisticated version of the "Keeping Room Clean" script in Chapter 9 for school-age children:

《 *Tara, this is your mom.*
I want to let you know how much I love you.
I want you to know how proud I am that you are my daughter.
I want to let you know how proud I am of you when you are organized.
Your room is neat and clean.
I am proud of you because I know you are proud of yourself.
You can find your things.
Your time is organized.
You find time to plan and keep your schedule on track.
Thank you for keeping your room neat and clean.
Thank you for being on time.
It helps me when you are on time, and I appreciate it.
Thank you for being my daughter.
I love you.
Sweet dreams. 》

Not every script in this chapter will be right for every teenager. Some children in this age group are beautifully organized; some are naturally self-confident; some instinctively consider the feelings of others. During adolescence, children's personalities become more and more individual. This is a time when it's important for you as a parent to pay close attention to what is going on in your teenager's life; even though they don't confide in you about everything, you can learn a lot from just keeping your eyes and ears open. The keynotes here, as throughout this book, are love, pride, and support.

Puberty

One of the major roadblocks along the way for adolescents is puberty. Not only do their bodies undergo enormous changes during this period, but they also have to cope with powerful sexual urges and volatile emotions. Although you as a parent can do nothing to prevent the inevitable upheaval, your expression of love, pride, and confidence in your child's ability to successfully negotiate this transition can provide important reassurance.

I've developed two Sleep Talk scripts about puberty: one for boys and one for girls. The reason for using different scripts is that the physical changes boys undergo during this period involve the maturing of existing structures, whereas girls develop new structures and processes. Both scripts express respect for the individual and for the process.

Puberty: A Boy's Maturing Body

Changes in the male body at adolescence are more subtle than for girls, but locker-room competition and comparisons can make life difficult for a boy who matures relatively late. The range of normal growth patterns is wide, and the teenage boy is likely to be insecure no matter what his particular rate of maturation.

The following script would be appropriate for any boy in the process of puberty:

《 *Doug, this is your dad.*
I want to let you know how much I love you.

I want to let you know how proud I am that you are my son.
I want to let you know how proud I am of you.
I appreciate it when you take good care of your growing
    body.
Your body is your vehicle to get you where you want to go in
    life.
As your body matures and changes, feel proud of it.
Thank you for keeping your body strong and healthy with
    exercise and good food.
I love you so much.
Sweet dreams. »

One of the important aspects of this script is the practical approach it takes toward the boy's maturing body. The body is treated as a means to get the child where he wants to go in life (like a car). The script also offers the boy specific information about ways to keep his body healthy: through exercise and good food. It treads a fine line between offering useful information and expressing confidence that the boy will take responsibility for his own health.

Puberty: A Girl's Developing Body

The girl's experience with puberty is dramatic. Not only does her shape undergo significant changes, but also her menses signal that her body is now capable of conceiving and bearing a child. As we see with boys, the girl who matures especially early or late may feel self-conscious, and her mother's confidence that she is developing normally may help defuse her insecurities.

This script would be appropriate for any girl in the process of puberty:

« *Amy, this is your mother.*
I want to let you know how much I love you.
I want to let you know how proud I am that you are my
    daughter.
I want to let you know how much I appreciate it when you
    take good care of your body.
Your body is strong and healthy.
Be proud of your body.

Be proud of who you are.
I feel so happy watching you grow.
As your body changes and develops, take good care of it.
I love you so much.
Thank you for being my beautiful daughter.
Sweet dreams. »

Since teenage girls are generally extremely conscious of their diet and exercise needs, it is important for parents to be alert to signs of eating disorders. With most girls, the parents' expression of love, pride, and admiration for a body that is strong and healthy offers a helpful perspective to girls who may be overly concerned with physical attractiveness.

These two scripts on puberty, like all the other Sleep Talk scripts in this chapter, are designed to offer validation to teenagers as they struggle to achieve the self-confidence and skills they will need for a satisfying adult life. Even though at this stage your role as a parent is less active, these scripts can help you maintain a loving connection with your teenager during this difficult time.

Have you ever stood along the last mile of a marathon race and seen how the applause of the bystanders seems to spur on the exhausted runners? Your teenager is into the last lap on the way to adulthood, and the applause and encouragement you supply through reading these scripts can make all the difference in your child's successfully moving on to the next stage.

11

SLEEP TALK

AND

RESPONSIBILITY

Throughout this book, I've presented Sleep Talk scripts that help children exercise a level of responsibility appropriate to their age. This chapter discusses ways parents can use these techniques to help teenagers deal with increasingly complex responsibilities as they move toward adulthood.

Adolescents often find it difficult to articulate their problems and ask for the help they need—especially in the area of moral and ethical standards. So, a parent sometimes has to be almost psychic to understand what is really going on with a teenager at any given moment. The Sleep Talk scripts I offer in this chapter can help you tune in to your child's unspoken difficulties—and offer timely help.

As in previous sections, the scripts in this chapter offer help in a context of love, pride in the child's accomplishments, and respect for the child's ability to grow and learn. With adolescents, respect for the individual's independence and trust in his or her judgment and goodwill are especially important. Learning to take responsibility depends to a large extent on being given responsibility, which includes implicit permission to make mistakes.

Children of every age learn responsibility primarily through watching their parents' behavior, and thoughtful parents are aware that their example in this area counts for far more than verbal advice.

A Big "Thank-You"

For each age group, I've offered a Sleep Talk script on bonding, and for adolescents this area is especially important. Kids this age are usually so caught up with their own activities that they have less contact with their parents. Despite teenagers' fierce assertions of independence, the challenge of coping with powerful physiological and emotional changes brings with it an equally strong need for reassurance and validation.

Above all, adolescents need to know that, despite the stresses their struggles create in the household, parents are grateful for their presence and appreciate their efforts. The following script offers the child a big "thank-you." I've seen its power with my own kids, and I've had reports from innumerable clients and students about its effectiveness in strengthening the bond between teenagers and parents:

《 *Barry, this is your father.*
I want to let you know how much I love you.
I want to let you know how proud I am that you are my son.
I want to let you know how safe I feel knowing you are a
*   responsible person.*
I feel confident that you know what is right and you do it.
You do things that are right for yourself and others.
Thank you for the help you give and the things you do for
*   the family.*
You feel good about who you are, the things you are doing,
*   and the places you are going.*
You feel good about who you are.
Thank you for being my responsible son.
I appreciate your being in my life.

> *I love you.*
> *Sweet dreams.* »

One of the things I especially treasure about this script is the way it has helped me stay in touch with the real gratitude I feel for and to my own kids. With the inevitable family conflicts at this stage, getting (and staying) in touch with the underlying love is just as important for the parent as for the teenager.

Using Effort/Inner Direction

As adolescents take on more and more complex tasks, they often reach a point of feeling overwhelmed and inadequate. Rather than throwing up their hands and abandoning a project, they need support for pushing on to fulfill their commitments despite exhaustion and a feeling of having spread themselves too thin.

The previous chapter presented a script on perseverance, a related subject. But where perseverance involves increasing attention span and concentration, the script I'm offering here is more concerned with resourcefulness. It supports the teenager's reliance on inner direction to find the means of fulfilling tasks she has agreed to do. It acknowledges the role of effort and determination in the face of obstacles and recognizes the adolescent's ability to come up with solutions to difficult problems.

Deborah, the sixteen-year-old daughter of one of my clients, had won a competition to design a mural for the lobby of a small theater at her high school. Part of her prize was a commission to paint the mural, and she had made a commitment to finish the project before the end of the school year. A girl of many talents, she had also been cast in a leading role in *Twelfth Night*, the drama club's last production of the year. Deborah's mother, Mary Louise, expressed her concern to me about her daughter's feeling overwhelmed with the demands of these projects in addition to her final exams. "I don't know what to tell her," Mary Louise said. "Between rehearsing for the play and trying to keep up with her schedule on the mural and studying for her exams, she's just exhausted. Something's got to give."

I suggested Mary Louise read Deborah the following script on using effort/inner direction:

《 *Deborah, this is your mother.*
  I want to let you know how much I love you.
  I want to let you know how proud I am that you are my
    daughter.
  I want to let you know how proud I am of you when you
    complete a job or task.
  I get so excited when you reach somewhere deep inside
    yourself to keep going on an activity you want done.
  Sometimes it is not easy in the beginning.
  As you continue using your energy and express yourself in
    action, you create marvelous things.
  Your effort moves you beyond barriers to a place of
    achievement.
  You are so wonderful.
  You make things easy and fun.
  I love you.
  Thank you for being my daughter.
  Sweet dreams. 》

Less than a week after Mary Louise and I talked about the problem, I received another phone call from her: "Lois, the most amazing thing has happened. Deborah has solved the problem! *I* couldn't have solved it, but *she* solved it—all by herself!"

What Deborah had done was to enlist the help of the students in her advanced art class to help her finish the mural. She had sketched the outlines of the forms on the wall, blocked her design into segments, and persuaded most of her fellow students to take part in what she called her "Tom Sawyer" project. She would mix all the colors for the mural herself so the segments would match, but her cohorts could complete their portions of the project whenever they had free time. All the students who helped Deborah were to be rewarded by having their names included on the plaque placed next to the mural. She got full credit for the design, but her helpers were also listed.

A few months later, after the school year had ended, Mary Louise called me again to say that not only had Deborah and her crew finished the mural on time, but also her performance in the play had received an enthusiastic review in the school paper, and her grades had been so good that she was considering applying to colleges under an early admission program.

Best of all, Deborah had gained confidence in her own ability to find solutions to difficult problems.

Improving Performance

When Tara and Briana took on the job of cleaning George's office (as I described in the previous chapter), they had never done professional cleaning, but they were willing to learn. When kids take on a big responsibility like this, sometimes the situation works out well with no special coaching from parents. In this case, both girls were bright and highly motivated, and they did a better job than any of the professional janitorial services we had employed. They were quick to see where improvements could be made and not shy about suggesting a better way when they saw one.

However, some teenagers are less confident about taking responsibility for doing a job more effectively, and for kids like this, encouragement from parents to take the initiative in improving their performance can be important.

The following Sleep Talk script would be helpful in providing this kind of support:

《 *Eve, this is your father.*
I want to let you know how much I love you.
I want to let you know how proud I am that you are my daughter.
I want to let you know how proud I am of your choices to get a job done.
You see something that needs to be done and you do it.
Often you improve it.
I appreciate it when you choose to improve a job or task that you have started.
Your help in completing the job or task is appreciated.
Thank you for all your help.

Thank you for being my daughter.
I am so proud of you and your ability to make good choices.
I love you.
Sweet dreams. »

Sometimes adolescents are simply not aware that doing a job differently (and better) is an option. Kids this age are often uncertain about the unwritten rules of the business world, and parents can use Sleep Talk to introduce possibilities that the teenagers may not have considered. They may feel that they have been instructed to perform a task in a certain way and that their input about improvements is not wanted. So, this script offers the information that their taking the initiative in suggesting a better way may be rewarding.

Manners

Children who have not been appropriately introduced to the practice of good manners are at a disadvantage in our society. The principle of consideration for others is basic to good manners, and many of the scripts presented earlier relate to this subject. My scripts for preschoolers on listening, getting along with others, and taking turns, for example, offer guidance about manners. And for school-age children, the scripts on listening, making friends, attitude adjustment, teamwork, and relationships with grandparents also address the issue.

When adults show respect for each other and for their children, manners are easy to learn. Even toddlers can learn to say "please" and "thank you." Our kids were invited to sit at the dinner table occasionally even as toddlers. Once their motor abilities are up to the task, children instinctively imitate their parents' table manners, and it's helpful for them to have opportunities to practice with their parents.

It can also be helpful—and fun—to practice with peers. For our son T.J.'s tenth birthday, he requested a skating party. The eight boys he invited came for lunch first. I set the table exactly as I would for adults: with soup spoons and forks that the kids could use for their spaghetti (T.J.'s favorite meal) and forks and spoons for the dessert. T.J. is a whiz at twirling his spaghetti with a fork and spoon, and even when he was five, when we went to a restaurant people would stop at our table to watch him twirl it and eat it. When I suggested that T.J.'s friends might want to practice twirling their spaghetti in case they received an invitation to a girl's house and needed to know how to eat it properly, they were eager to try, and everyone had a lot of fun.

During the teenage years, kids are extremely conscious of the way others see them, and they want to make a good impression if they are invited to dine at a friend's house or when they go with friends to a restaurant. At this age, nobody wants to look "gross." If they are in doubt about which fork to use, they watch to see what others do.

If your child needs some support and encouragement about table manners, the following Sleep Talk script may be helpful:

« *Tom, this is your father.*
I want to let you know how much I love you.
I enjoy being with you, especially at mealtimes.
You have such good manners at the table.
You know what to do.
It is fun to be with you and talk with you.
I am so proud of you when we visit or have company for
*   dinner.*
You are such a gentleman.
Thank you for being my son.
I love you.
Sweet dreams. »

Of course, good manners are not limited to correct usage of cutlery at the table. The basic principle of manners is kindness and consideration for others.

The following Sleep Talk script encourages this aspect of manners; like the preceding one, it could be used with children as young as three:

« *Betty, this is your mother.*
I want to let you know how much I love you.
I just want you to know how proud I am that you are my
*   daughter.*

I want to let you know how much I appreciate it when we
*   have company or go out, and you have such good*
*   manners.*
You are kind and polite.
I am proud of you.
You make being with others easy and fun.
I enjoy seeing you have a good time.
Thank you for being my daughter.
I love you so much.
Sweet dreams. »

When children feel confident about their manners, they feel good about themselves, and their thoughtfulness of others helps their friends feel comfortable and at ease around them.

Being on Time

One important aspect of good manners is being on time. This problem may arise at any age, and my Sleep Talk scripts on getting ready to go (for preschoolers) and morning preparation for school (for school-age children) have addressed the same issue.

Teenagers sometimes get so wrapped up in their own activities that they fail to show this basic consideration for others, and if being late becomes a chronic problem, you as a parent can help in several ways.

Often adolescents are dependent on parents to drive them to appointments, and their arriving on time may depend on your commitment to support them in their attempts.

When kids are chronically late through their own negligence, using a Sleep Talk script may be appropriate. Many of my clients and students have used the following script successfully:

« *David, this is your mom.*
*   I want to let you know how much I love you.*
*   I want to let you know how proud I am to be your mom.*
*   I want to let you know how much I appreciate it when you*
*   are going to school or have appointments and you are*
*   on time.*

*You start early enough to do what you need to do to be on
time.*
*Your time is valuable, and you are considerate of other
people's time.*
*Most of all, when you are on time, you are keeping your
word.*
Thank you for keeping your word.
I love you.
Sweet dreams. »

Just on the level of information, the teenager may need to be
reminded that starting early enough is essential to arriving on time.
As the script reflects, it's also important to help him make the connection between being considerate of other people's time and having others be considerate of *his*. Finally, a reminder that being on
time involves keeping his word emphasizes the seriousness of time
commitments.

Exchanging and Sharing Property

As I've discussed in previous chapters, I believe it is unreasonable
to expect anyone to share belongings without getting something in
return. In our household, everything is owned by someone, and the
owner of a thing has the ultimate right to decide what happens to
it. A child of preschool age may learn that getting along with others involves allowing them to play with his toys so that they will
allow him to play with *their* toys: exchanging value for value. The
scripts on teamwork and helping the family both make a similar
point for school-age children.

It's important for adolescents to learn a more advanced lesson
in this area: how to assess whether a particular person is likely to
respect their property if they choose to lend it or share it. When
they believe someone is likely to be careless with their belongings,
they have a right to say no.

Dorothy, one of my students, told me that her fifteen-year-old
son, Cal, was continually lending various items to friends. "All they
have to do is ask," she said, "and he lets them take it, no matter

what it is." After his bicycle was stolen while in the hands of a friend and several pieces of his sporting equipment were lost or damaged, she asked me for a Sleep Talk script that would offer Cal some guidance about being more discriminating in his lending. Here's the script I gave her:

《 *Cal, this is your mother.*
I want to let you know how much I love you.
I want to let you know how proud I am that you are my son.
I want to let you know how proud of you I am when you are responsible for your property.
You take good care of your things.
When it is appropriate to let others borrow or use your property, you know what to say and do.
You can say no as well as yes.
You are a very generous person.
You follow your "hunch" about who will be responsible and careful with your things.
Thank you for being my caring son.
I love you.
Sweet dreams. 》

Notice that this script makes a strong point about the child's being a generous person but also one who takes good care of his things. These two qualities are not contradictory but complementary, and both are important aspects of a mature person. The teenager needs to consider the habits and behavior of friends who ask to use his belongings, and he needs to be validated in his decision to say no when the would-be borrower has a track record of irresponsibility. This script offers the teenager guidelines for making the kinds of decisions he will continually need to make as an adult, whatever his job or profession. It also suggests that saying no can be as significant a source of self-respect as saying yes.

Cal's quickness in picking up on this lesson may have had something to do with the events that followed the theft of his bicycle. (The friend to whom he'd lent it had failed to use the lock Cal provided, and then disclaimed all responsibility for its being stolen. Cal ended up having to foot the bill for a new bike himself.) Dorothy told me her son developed such a humorous way of refusing to lend his belongings to certain people that he lost no friends as a result of his more stringent lending policy.

Protection of Property/Stealing

Respect for property is something I've addressed in previous chapters, beginning with the script for preschoolers on touching with one finger. Scripts for school-age children on keeping their rooms clean and helping the family also relate to the protection of property.

Everybody knows that stealing is wrong. But the underlying issue of protection of property is a more positive way of looking at the question. Teenagers and younger children need to be aware that protecting what belongs to them also involves leaving other people's property alone. The establishment of trust with others depends on having respect for their property.

A few years ago, I got a call from Claudia, a single mother who had recently moved to California from another state to take a nursing position. She and her fourteen-year-old son, Andy, had moved into a communal house that contained private bedrooms and bathrooms for each family but also common areas shared by all, an arrangement that provided affordable accommodations for everyone.

Andy would get home from school about 3:00, but Claudia didn't get home from her job until 6:00. It soon became evident that during this time, he would wander into other people's apartments and take things. She came to me for help with this problem, and I wrote the following script on protection of property for her to read to him:

≪ *Andy, this is your mom.*
I want to let you know how much I love you.
I want to let you know how proud I am that you are my son.
I want to let you know how proud I am of you when you
    respect other people's property.

You take care of your property and leave other people's
   property alone.
You know what it means to protect property.
You know how to respect other people's property.
I am so proud of you and love you so much.
Other people feel safe with you around and trust you.
I trust you to be proud of yourself.
Thank you for being my son.
I love you.
Sweet dreams. 》

After she had been reading this script to Andy for about a week, we had another phone conversation. There had been some improvement, she told me, but he was still wandering around the house and getting into other people's things. He made the stealing so obvious that it seemed clear he wanted to be caught. I arranged a session to discuss the situation with both of them, and what came out was that Andy felt lonely during the hours before his mom got home from work. Even though she would call to check up on him and ask if he was doing his homework, he resented her not being there with him. Since it was impossible for Claudia to adjust her work hours, and he needed some private time with her, we arranged that Saturday would be their day together, to go out to breakfast, visit the mall, and see a movie.

After a while, Andy's grades improved and he began to make friends at school. Claudia taught him to cook, and even when he had activities with friends, he would get home in time to make dinner on the days she worked. It seemed that his taking on that extra responsibility for helping his mother carried over into his taking more responsibility for the property of his fellow tenants as well. I wrote another script for Claudia to read to him:

《 *Andy, this is your mom.*
I want to let you know how much I love you.
I want to let you know how proud I am that you are my son.
I want to let you know how much I appreciate it when you
   are respectful of other people's property.
You know what is yours and what is not yours.

> *I am so proud of you when you take a stand and stay firm*
> *about respecting property regardless of what others are*
> *doing.*
> *You stand tall.*
> *People feel safe around you.*
> *I feel safe with you in my life.*
> *Our property is taken care of and is safe.*
> *Thank you for being my son.*
> *I love you.*
> *Sweet dreams.* »

This script acknowledges some progress on Andy's part, and Claudia continued to read it to him for almost two years.

Telling the Truth

Children who steal are likely also to lie in order to conceal their actions. I wrote another script for Claudia to read to Andy on the subject of telling the truth. Now, "truth" is a rather abstract concept for some kids, and it's important to indicate that telling the truth means giving accurate information. It's also important to point out the connection between expecting someone to tell you the truth and trusting that person.

Here is the script I gave Claudia:

« *Andy, this is your mom.*
> *I want to let you know how much I love you.*
> *I want you to know how proud I am that you are my son.*
> *I want to let you know how much I appreciate it when you*
> *tell me the truth.*
> *I depend on you to give me accurate information.*
> *I feel special and safe around you because I can trust you.*
> *That means so much to me.*
> *Thank you for being in my life.*
> *Thank you for being the truthful person you are.*
> *I love you so much.*
> *Sweet dreams.* »

In conjunction with the scripts on protecting property and stealing, this script on telling the truth had an impact on Andy's behavior. By the time he was sixteen, the problem that brought his mother to consult me had resolved itself.

Of course, it's important for parents to realize that telling the truth is a two-way street, and if we expect our kids to be truthful with us, we need to hold ourselves to the same standard. An incident that occurred during Briana's high school years vividly illustrates this point. A large group of her peers was going to Palm Springs during spring break, and she wanted to go with them.

At the time, it was common for the Palm Springs Police to arrest young people for creating disturbances and to jail them until the parents could arrange to pick them up. I didn't want Briana to go.

But she seemed determined to join her friends. "I won't do anything," she promised. "I'll be good."

Her father shook his head. "When you're with a bunch of kids and they're causing trouble, it doesn't matter whether *you're* doing something wrong or not. You're part of the pack!"

I decided to do some timely truth-telling. "Briana," I said, "I'll tell you what: you go ahead and go to Palm Springs. If you get thrown in jail, you can call me to come and get you. I'll come. No matter what the circumstances are, I'll come. However, as you're sitting there in that cell, you may hear some rumbling, you may feel the building shaking, you may hear people saying, 'Oh, my God! We've got this slightly overweight middle-aged blonde crazy lady here. This madwoman says we're holding her daughter.' Then, Briana, you'll know I've arrived to pick you up."

Briana gave me a look. "Oh, Mother!"

"Even though I can't say what kind of condition I'll arrive in," I concluded, "I promise I'll come and pick you up."

Briana went to her room and thought about this for a while. When she came out, she announced she'd decided to stay home and make other plans.

I had told her the truth: *that I didn't know how I would behave* if I had to go and collect her from a Palm Springs jail. She became part of the decision-making process, with a share in the ultimate responsibility for whatever happened. Her mother's feelings and limitations were an important part of the picture in this case, and her decision took those factors into account.

Honesty

To many people, truthfulness and honesty are synonymous, but even though the two often go together, there is a basic distinction between them. Telling the truth refers to the *words* that come out of one's mouth. Honesty involves gearing one's *actions* to a code of ethics.

There are many pressures on adolescents today to make high grades, and it's not uncommon for high school kids to pay someone to write a paper for them. (Among college students, the sale of term papers and theses has become a thriving industry.) Cheating on exams is far more common than it was when I was in high school (when we had something called the "honor system"). No matter how many of your child's peers indulge in this kind of behavior, it's important for you to make clear that you expect a different standard.

One way to do this is through a Sleep Talk script that expresses your love and pride in your child's honesty:

《 *Annie, this is your mom.*
I want to let you know how much I love you.
I want you to know how proud I am that you are my
  daughter.
I want to let you know how much I appreciate it when you
  are honest with me.
When you are honest in words and actions, you take good
  care of me.
I appreciate living in this caring way.
When you are honest with yourself and others, I am proud of
  you.
Thank you for being the honest person you are.

*Thank you for speaking the truth and behaving with honest
    actions.
You are a wonderful daughter.
I love you.
Sweet dreams.* »

The habit of speaking and behaving honestly engenders self-
respect. When teenagers see their parents telling the truth and
behaving with integrity, their own commitment to high standards is
strengthened. The script's pointing out the connection between honesty and caring helps the child see how essential trust in the other
person's integrity is to all intimate relationships.

Being Assertive While Calm and Relaxed

Adolescents sometimes run into problems with adults in authority
who treat them insensitively or disrespectfully. Responding to such
situations maturely and effectively is a skill everyone needs to learn,
and you can help your teenager make the crucial distinction between
assertiveness and aggressiveness. If a teacher or a coach gets on your
child's case about something, the child has a choice about getting
upset or remaining calm and in control, and habits he forms at this
age are likely to stand him in good stead in any career he chooses.

Here is a script that many of my clients have found effective in
this common situation:

« *Owen, this is your mom.
I want to let you know how much I love you.
I want to let you know how much I appreciate it when you
    go into a situation calm and collected.
Regardless of what is going on, you remain calm.
In a situation where others are upset, you can remain in
    control.
You feel good about who you are and what you are doing.
You can be cooperative if appropriate.
You are a gentleman.
Thank you for being my son.*

I love you.
Sweet dreams. »

Note that this script does not suggest that cooperation is *always* appropriate. The child is not being encouraged to passively accept abuse, but he is being offered the alternative of resisting without getting aggressive about it. Sometimes people in authority are unfair. The teenager is bound to encounter this situation in the business world as well as in school, and being able to assess the situation calmly and act without anger will always be an important asset.

Dealing with Anger

In our increasingly violent society, there is a serious lack of understanding about the psychological processes involved with anger. It's important for you as a parent to offer your children information about how anger works so that when they find themselves in the throes of it, they will have tools to avoid doing damage to others or to themselves.

Having children is a great way for adults to understand the mechanism behind anger, since we get so many opportunities to observe ourselves being furious with them. For example: While you're talking with a neighbor in the yard, your son darts into the street, and you hear the screech of brakes. You run, grab your child, and begin scolding him furiously. "I told you not to go into the street." And you spank him all the way back into your yard. Were you angry? You bet! But more important, you were afraid your child might be seriously injured or killed. Were you thinking clearly and making appropriate choices? Of course not.

When you are in the grip of anger, you allow yourself to become a victim, and there seem to be only two possible things you can do with your fury: (1) strike outward and hurt others, or (2) strike inward and hurt yourself.

But let's take a closer look at what happens when you get angry. Your first feeling is not anger. In the example I just described, your first feeling is fear. You're terrified for your child's life (and understandably so). *Anger is always a second feeling.* Once you understand this, you are in possession of the major tool you can use to teach your child how this overwhelming and often destructive emotion works.

When you are able to confront your own initial feeling (in this case, fear) before the anger swept over you, you can acknowledge that feeling to your child. While you are hugging him after scooping him up off the street, you can let him know how frightened you were that he might have been hit by the car. Letting him see your anxiety acknowledges your own vulnerability and shows him the connection between that and your caring. It also offers him a model of the way he might deal with his own feelings in a crisis situation.

This is not a lesson to be learned from a single incident, but when you make a habit of discussing your child's anger as situations come up, he comes to understand that this kind of self-examination is a tool that he can use in his life.

Let's say your teenage daughter is angry because her younger sister borrowed a sweater without asking. Talk to her about what happened. Try to identify what the first feeling was: hurt, disappointment, embarrassment, fear, exasperation, frustration, sadness? "I felt betrayed and hurt when you took my sweater without asking." Once she knows her initial feelings, she can follow through with appropriate behavior.

Or say your son is angry because he lent his bike to a friend and it was stolen (as happened with Cal in an incident previously described in the chapter). What was his first feeling, before the anger? "I am sad and disappointed that I don't have my bike anymore." Once he has solid information about his initial feeling, he can make better choices and accept responsibility for his feelings.

Children love success, and all the Sleep Talk scripts in this book are based on this principle. With the tools I've just described, your child can be successful even in difficult situations. And this lesson is not applicable only to adolescents; even preschoolers can begin to understand the way anger works.

For example, one time when T.J. was two, he was whining and crying, and I said to him, "T.J., it's time for you to go to bed." "I'm not sleepy, I'm not sleepy," he said, still whining. "Oh, yes you are," I said. Tara, who overheard our conversation, commented, "Boy, I never would have thought of *that* answer." But T.J. didn't know what was wrong. He was just upset because he was tired. It was time for him to go to bed, and I took him to bed and he went to sleep.

It's important for parents to get into the trenches with kids of every age when anger comes up (either for the parent or for the child). Reading scripts on anger while the child is sleeping can reinforce these techniques at a moment when the child is calm.

Slightly different scripts may be appropriate for different children (or for the same children at different times). For example, Beth, a sixteen-year-old daughter of one of my clients, had a tendency to turn her anger inward and fail to confront people. The following script was extremely helpful for her:

《 *Beth, this is your mother.*
I want to let you know how much I love you.
I want to let you know how proud I am that you are my daughter.
I want to let you know how proud of you I am when you handle your anger.
When you get angry, you always feel something else first.
Maybe you are tired, disappointed, embarrassed, or scared before you feel angry.
Go back to that first feeling and let people know what is going on for you.
I love you, and we can talk about feelings anytime you want.
I am proud of you handling your anger because I know that you are proud of yourself.
Thank you for being my daughter.
I love you.
Sweet dreams. 》

For seventeen-year-old Bernie, whose short fuse led him to lash out at others and physically assault them, a different variation was appropriate:

《 *Bernie, this is your mother.*
I want to let you know how much I love you.
I want to let you know how proud I am that you are my son.

I want to let you know how proud I am when you handle
   your feelings of anger.
If you are upset, you do not hurt others.
You calm down so you can make a good choice about what
   to do and say.
I am proud of you when you are effective in your behavior
   and feelings.
I am proud of you when you make "good" choices because I
   know that you are proud of yourself.
Thank you for being my son.
I love you.
Sweet dreams. »

The more aware your child becomes about techniques for controlling his rage, and the more support he gets from you in practicing these techniques, the more likely he is to develop habits that will stand him in good stead for a lifetime. As in every other area I've discussed in this chapter, your handling of your own feelings serves as a significant model for your kids. Letting them see, through your example, that there truly is a better way is essential to their learning these lessons.

Showing Up Differently

The first of Haddad's Five Rules of Life is to *show up*, and one of the things children learn during their teens is that it's possible to show up differently. Once they accept responsibility for what's going on within themselves, they can decide to act in new ways. They don't necessarily need to be victims of other people's feelings and actions; they can make up their own minds about how they are going to behave. This may involve breaking patterns they've observed in their own family or in their peer groups. To an adolescent, such a new way of being in the world may feel tentative at first, but it becomes more confident when validated by parental support.

Here is a Sleep Talk script you can use to encourage your child to trust her own instincts about becoming who she really wants to be:

« *Daphne, this is your mom.*
I want to let you know how much I love you.
I want to let you know how proud I am that you are my daughter.
I want to let you know how proud I am of you.
When you get upset, tired, or fussy, you take a deep breath, relax, and become calm.
You are calm, confident, and in control of yourself.
When you are calm, you think of better choices to make.
You learn to show up differently.
I love you so much.
I appreciate it when you are in control of your emotions and actions.
I trust you.
You earn trust.
I like who you are.
Thank you for being my daughter.
I love you.
Sweet dreams. »

Even though teenagers may be unable to articulate these issues with their parents, their need for encouragement in their struggle to find and claim their best self is very real. This is a time when the child's emotions are often volatile, and the parent's encouragement through Sleep Talk can have a powerful effect. Using a script like this one also shows real trust on the part of the parent that the child's emerging best self is worthy of love and respect, despite the inevitable mistakes that have been made along the way.

Emotional Upset

Anger, of course, is not the only emotion the teenager must learn to cope with. Sadness, hurt, disappointment, failure, rejection, and insecurity are all so much a part of the adolescent landscape that most of us are glad to put these years behind us. But moving through this stage and engaging fully with these problems is the only way an individual can achieve adulthood. We all know people who have failed to complete this journey, and therapists' calendars are filled with their names.

Your concern and love for your teenager cannot eliminate the necessity for him to go through this stage. But like steel that has been tempered by fierce heat, most adolescents become stronger through experiencing the stresses of the teenage years. Your serenity in the face of their mood changes and your honest acknowledgment of your own emotional responses give them confidence that they will survive the perils of this new territory that they are exploring.

Here is another Sleep Talk script that offers your child support, love, and tools with which to hack his way through the emotional jungle:

« *David, this is your dad.*
I want to let you know how much I love you.
I want to let you know how proud I am that you are my son.
When you get upset, tired, fussy, take a deep breath.
You take a deep breath, relax, and become calm.
You are calm, confident, and in control.
You think of better choices to make.
You learn to show up differently.
I love you so much.
I appreciate it when you are in control of your emotions and
*   actions.*
Thank you for behaving differently when it is appropriate.
I like who you are.
Thank you for being my son.
I love you.
Sweet dreams. »

The simple technique of taking a deep breath and relaxing can be a physiological trigger for calming overwrought emotions, so this script offers teenagers important information. Because they are taking in this information while asleep, they can assimilate it in a way that would be difficult or impossible in the midst of emotional upheaval.

At no time is your sensitivity as a parent more crucial than when helping your adolescent move toward a consciousness of responsibility. Your personal example is of course vital. I believe that most parents try to set a good example for their kids, and teenagers are quick to point out any discrepancies between your advice to them and your own behavior. We all have our lapses. (When I lose my temper, my kids delight in saying, "Now, Mom, take a deep breath, relax, and become calm.") But your habitual responses to these ethical questions are likely to set the tone for your children's overall attitudes toward responsibility as adults.

12

SLEEP TALK

AND

RECREATION

Children learn some of their most important life lessons during their leisure time, and Sleep Talk offers a valuable technique for helping your child grow through activities in the arts, sports, public speaking, and involvement with pets. When the path of least resistance may be to sit passively in front of a television set, parental guidance through Sleep Talk can offer kids tools that encourage them to explore various activities, learn to cope with success and failure, and take pride in their ability to improve.

Many of the scripts I discussed in the last chapter, "Sleep Talk and Responsibility"—using effort/inner direction, improving performance, being assertive while calm and relaxed, showing up differently, and emotional upset—are related to the subject of this chapter. But the scripts here are more specific. In addition to expressing your love and pride in your child, they offer the child information about techniques for improving performance and attitude in a variety of applications.

One of the essential things we all need to discover is what gives us joy and satisfaction. Children are bursting with creative energy, and expressing it in music, dancing, artwork, writing, or sports is no burden to them. Watching my own kids explore various activities has been one of the most satisfying aspects of motherhood for me. Parents who ignore this area of a child's life are missing one of the most important ways they can both strengthen their present relationships with their children and ensure continuing close connections with them as adults.

Music

Chapter 1 described a Sleep Talk script I wrote for Dr. Jack Gutman to read to twelve-year-old Molly, a gifted pianist who became discouraged when she failed to win first place in a piano competition. Once Molly understood that her father loved her, delighted in her musical abilities, and was proud of her regardless of whether she won or lost any contest, she was able to resume playing and go on to excel in other creative areas as well. Molly's story illustrates a major theme of this chapter that applies as much to sports as to the arts: *You never lose unless you quit.*

Most children who study an instrument, play in a school music group, or participate in choirs do not go on to professional careers in music. But playing the piano for one's own pleasure, accompanying group singing at parties with a guitar, or singing in a church choir are all ways adults make music a fulfilling part of their lives. For children who are interested in music, a parent's encouragement can strengthen their motivation to stick with lessons in the face of other time demands or fear of on-stage performance.

Stage Fright/Performance Anxiety

A parent who is comfortable in the public eye may find it difficult to understand a child's terror at the prospect of performing in public. Sam, the successful trial lawyer I described in Chapter 9 (who used Sleep Talk to help seven-year-old Zeke get a good night's sleep), asked for my help again a few years later. Zeke was so upset at the prospect of playing in an upcoming piano recital that he was considering stopping his lessons. "I don't want to force him to do this," Sam said, "but it just kills me to see him quit when he gets such a kick out of playing."

Here's the script I wrote for Sam to read to Zeke:

« *Zeke, this is your father.*
I want to let you know how much I love you.
I want to let you know how proud I am of you when you play the piano in front of other people.
You create beautiful music.
You are calm, confident, and prepared when playing in front of an audience.
People enjoy hearing you play.
I enjoy seeing you perform.
I am proud of you because I know you are proud of yourself.
Thank you for being my son.
I love you.
Sweet dreams. »

The week after Sam started reading this script, he called to tell me Zeke was feeling better about the recital and had invited his parents to listen to a "preview" of the selection he was scheduled to play. After that home performance, they expressed their enthusiasm, and Sam continued reading the script to his son. The following week, I got another call from Sam, bursting with pride as he described Zeke's fine performance at the recital and his poise in taking his bow afterward.

Practicing

Over the years, I've written many scripts for Melody, the bright but distractible girl I described in Chapter 9. Melody predictably had trouble maintaining a regular practice schedule for the saxophone lessons she had begged to be allowed to take. Her mother, Iris, called when Melody was in ninth grade to tell me that the girl's music teacher had threatened to stop giving her lessons if she didn't come to the sessions prepared.

Here's the script I gave Iris to read to Melody:

《 *Melody, this is your mother.*
I want to let you know how much I love you.
I want to let you know how much I appreciate it when you
    practice your music on your saxophone.
You fit practicing into your schedule so you are prepared
    before your lesson.
Thank you for practicing your music.
I am proud of you when you are ready for your lesson
    because I know you are proud of yourself.
Thank you for being my daughter.
I love you.
Sweet dreams. 》

A few months later, Iris told me that Melody was practicing more—at least enough to satisfy her teacher, who had said nothing further about stopping the lessons. During her high school years, Melody became part of a jazz group that played occasionally at parties and school events. For a girl who today would probably have been diagnosed with ADD, this is an impressive achievement.

Singing: In Performance and for Fun

Jenny, the daughter of my client Pam (for whom I wrote a script on assigned and leisure reading, discussed in Chapter 9), used to enjoy singing on family trips in the car. Abruptly, she stopped, and Pam asked her why. Ten-year-old Jenny, who sang in the church choir connected with her school, was reluctant to discuss the subject at first but finally admitted that the director of the choir had told her she should just mouth the words, since her off-key singing was disrupting the whole alto section. "I guess I don't have as good a voice as I thought," she told her mother with tears in her eyes.

"I wanted to call up that choir guy and fry him with a few choice words," Pam told me, "but Jenny said she'd die of embarrassment if I did. So, I'm holding my tongue, even though I'm pretty burned up. Is there anything I can do to help my daughter deal with this?"

I suggested Pam try reading Jenny the following Sleep Talk script:

《 *Jenny, this is your mom.*
I want to let you know how much I love you.

> *I want to let you know how proud I am that you are my
> daughter.*
> *I want to let you know how happy I am when you sing.*
> *You have a beautiful voice.*
> *I love hearing you sing.*
> *You do such a good job when you use your singing voice.*
> *Thank you for being my daughter.*
> *I am happy to have you in my life.*
> *I love you.*
> *Sweet dreams.* »

The next time the family went on a car trip, Jenny joined in the singing—softly at first, but her confidence seemed to grow as she got into it. A few weeks later, Pam asked Jenny if she'd enjoy taking some private singing lessons. Jenny said yes, and they found a teacher she liked. Jenny continued her lessons for several years and participated in a vocal ensemble when she was in high school. Her mother's timely use of Sleep Talk made it possible for her to keep this important pleasure in her life.

Dancing

When T.J. was four, I enrolled him in a dance class with my friend and client Barbara (whose use of Sleep Talk with her daughters' health problems I described in Chapter 1). He was the only boy in the class, but that didn't seem to bother him. He had a lot of energy, and the dancing seemed a wonderful outlet for it. At the class's first recital, Barbara placed him right in the center (since he was the only boy). When the curtain went up, the girls on either side of T.J. began dancing away like mad, but he just stood there smiling at the audience. He didn't look scared, but he never moved. We made a videotape of the recital, and after T.J. watched it, he said, "Next time I think I'm going to move my feet."

To this day, I'm not sure whether he was paralyzed with fright or simply distracted by the presence of the audience, but after he finished this course of dance lessons, he decided not to continue.

When I talked the situation over with Barbara, she suggested I write some Sleep Talk scripts that she could give the parents of her dance students, since reactions like T.J.'s were not uncommon. I wrote three different scripts for Barbara. Here's the one on performance:

> « *Kelly, this is your mother.*
> *I want to let you know how much I love you.*
> *I want to let you know how proud I am that you are my*
>   *daughter.*
> *I want to let you know how proud of you I am when you*
>   *dance.*
> *Your movements are smooth and fluid.*
> *You know what to do and when to do it.*
> *Your feet and hands are flexible and in tune with your music.*
> *Your body is strong, and you have a lot of energy.*
> *I am proud of you because I know you are proud of yourself.*
> *I love you.*
> *Sweet dreams.* »

I wrote two other scripts for Barbara's students: one on the need for practice and one on remaining calm and confident when dancing in front of an audience. These scripts, which are similar to the ones on music I wrote for Zeke and Melody, are included in Appendix A at the end of this book. Also included in Appendix A are additional scripts related to instrumental music and singing.

Public Speaking

Respondents to a national survey ranked public speaking above death on a list of their greatest fears. This is probably because the fear of being laughed at, of being publicly humiliated in front of the tribe, is the worst fate most adults can imagine.

Stage fright or performance anxiety is a problem that afflicts not only musicians, dancers, and actors but also many nonperformers who need to speak in front of a group. This would include not only the child who becomes involved with the debating society but also the one who is required to give an oral book report in class.

The ability to feel at ease in front of a group is a major asset in any profession, and parents can do their children an immense service by encouraging them in their public speaking efforts. Here's a Sleep Talk script that would be helpful in defusing the anxiety many kids feel when speaking in front of a group:

« *Frank, this is your mother.*
I want to let you know how much I love you.
I want to let you know how proud I am that you are my son.
When you speak, your voice is strong and clear.
Your posture shows poise.
You speak with conviction and authority.
You are calm and confident.
I am very proud of you because I know you are proud of
   yourself.
Other people comment on what a fine public speaker you are.
I love you very much.
Thank you for being my son.
Sweet dreams. »

The first of Haddad's Five Rules of Life is to *show up*, and this script can offer your child important help in showing up with confidence, whether running for class office, presenting a science project, or making an announcement at a school assembly. Of all the activities I discuss in this chapter, public speaking probably has the most significant relation to a child's success in later life.

Acting

For some children, speaking in front of an audience holds no terrors. In fact, they delight in being allowed to perform roles in class plays and community theater productions. The ability to imaginatively inhabit another person's skin, to speak, move, and behave in ways that are completely different from oneself, is a distinct talent. For kids who have natural gifts for acting, playing a part on stage can be a great satisfaction as well as a way of learning about human psychology.

If your child enjoys this form of self-expression, the following
Sleep Talk script may offer encouragement and information that help
her improve her performing skills:

> « *Eleanor, this is your mother.*
> *I want to let you know how much I love you.*
> *I want to let you know how proud I am that you are my*
>   *daughter.*
> *When you perform a role on stage, you project your voice so*
>   *you can be heard in the last row of the theater.*
> *The presence of an audience stimulates you and gives you*
>   *energy.*
> *You use your imagination to behave as if you are the*
>   *character you are portraying.*
> *Your voice and movements on stage are always "in character."*
> *I am very proud of you because I know you are proud of*
>   *yourself.*
> *Other people comment on what a fine actress you are.*
> *I love you very much.*
> *Thank you for being my daughter.*
> *Sweet dreams.* »

Most children who are active in school productions and community theater do not go on to become professional actors. But the
sensitivity to others and awareness of human differences they develop
through this form of recreation will be major assets in life, no matter what career they choose.

Artistic Ability: Drawing, Painting, Sculpture, and More

One evening when T.J. was twelve, he, George, and I went out to
dinner at a restaurant, and T.J. took along his sketch pad with a
drawing of a wolf he was working on. As a couple walked by our
booth, the man looked down at T.J.'s work, then came back and
said, "That's really good, Son. That's a fine drawing." T.J. thanked
him, tore out the drawing, and said, "Would you like to have it?"

The man said, "Oh, no, I couldn't do that." He and his wife sat down in the booth behind us, and after a while he reached around and held out a $10 bill. "I'll buy that picture from you," he said. "You date it and sign it. And when you become famous, I'll sell it back to you for $10."

One of the special joys of raising an adopted child is the talents he has that bear no relation to the family genetic endowment. T.J. has needed no special encouragement from me to develop his artistic gifts. However, for a child who shows interest in art but lacks T.J.'s confidence, the following script might be helpful:

《 *T.J., this is your mom.*
I just want you to know how much I love you.
I want to let you know how proud of you I am.
I love seeing your artwork and drawing [or sculpture, etc.].
Your creative energy flows from your brain through your
*   hands and fingers, creating beautiful works of art.*
I am so proud of you.
You direct your energy into such creative pieces.
I love you.
Sweet dreams. 》

Children gifted in one area of the arts often show ability in other arts as well, and T.J. is a good example of this. Even though he has not studied piano for three years, he occasionally sits down at the keyboard and plays as well as I've ever heard him play. The stories he writes are imaginative and interesting (despite a few errors in spelling and punctuation). Although my older kids were stronger in academic work, T.J. is by far the most artistically talented of the four, and having him as part of our family has given me a greater understanding and appreciation of the creative process.

Creative Writing

Particularly during adolescence, many children write stories and poems as a way of expressing their feelings, and sometimes the works they produce, like T.J.'s artwork, show real talent. Simply putting their thoughts and emotions into words gives children a sense of control in the face of fears, angers, and hurts that they inevitably experience as part of the normal growing process. Writing is another skill (like public speaking) that is important in many professions, and a parent may want to encourage the child's efforts through a Sleep Talk script:

> « *Wendy, this is your mom.*
> *I just want to let you know how very much I love you.*
> *I just want to let you know how proud I am that you are my*
> *   daughter.*
> *I love seeing you write. I love reading your writing.*
> *Your creative energy flows from your brain through your*
> *   hands and fingers, creating beautiful stories [and/or*
> *   poems, compositions, etc.].*
> *I am so proud of you and your work.*
> *Thank you for being my daughter.*
> *Thank you for directing your energy into such creative pieces.*
> *I love you.*
> *Sweet dreams.* »

It's important to recognize that not every child who writes stories or poems is going to see this work published in *The New Yorker*, but writing can be a powerful avenue to self-understanding and valuable communications skills. A parent's love and appreciation of the child's efforts offers encouragement for further growth.

Sports

Like the arts, sports offer children excellent opportunities for self-development. Parents can use Sleep Talk to help kids gain self-confidence, physical and mental skills, and a determination to be all they can be. Through participating in sports, kids learn how to handle competition and how to cooperate when teamwork is required. Both winning and losing offer important lessons that will have reverberations throughout the child's life.

Participation in sports is fun, and when children are enjoying themselves, working for improvement becomes part of the package. When parents watch their child taking part in sports, their presence testifies to their love and pride, no matter what the outcome.

This section offers scripts for several individual and team sports appropriate to different ages, and you'll find additional scripts in Appendix A.

Beginning Baseball

Little League baseball is a milestone in many children's lives, with avid parents cheering their kids on from the bleachers. These games can be a lot of fun for everybody and a wonderful learning opportunity for the boys and girls who play.

My heart goes out to the kids on the field as they struggle with what is for many the first serious competition of their lives. When I see a little boy standing at the plate with the bases loaded and all the responsibility for his team's success on his narrow shoulders, I can't help hoping he'll get a hit even when he's on the opposing team. When I see him swing and miss and I hear an adult voice yell, "Strike out the bum!" (bringing a glint of tears to the kid's eyes), I want to rush over and shake that thoughtless adult!

Some people might say I'm being overly sensitive, but I like to think parents can express support for their own child without savaging somebody else's. Certainly there is enough opportunity for any kid to get bruised, both mentally and physically, without this kind of added insult. Some kids are better natural athletes than others, but all of them can get better at the game.

The following Sleep Talk script can offer timely support, help, and encouragement:

《 *Bobby, this is your mother.*
I want to tell you how much I love you.
I want to let you know how proud I am that you are my son.
I want to tell you how proud I feel when you play baseball.
I enjoy watching you play baseball.
I enjoy watching you bat the ball.
You watch the ball and keep your eye on it while you bat.

I love to see you run.
Even when there is not much to do in the field, you are
    important.
You are important to the team.
You are important to me.
Thank you for being my son.
I love you.
Sweet dreams. 》

Note that this script includes some gentle coaching—reminding the child to keep his eye on the ball while he's batting—as well as confirming his importance to the team even when there is no immediate activity on the field. All my Sleep Talk scripts on team sports involve some element of coaching and also a reminder that the child is part of a team.

Learning to work toward a goal in cooperation with others is one of the most important lessons a child takes away from any team sports competition, for this is a skill adults need in almost every line of work. Little League baseball is an important first step on the road to success in life, and Sleep Talk can help get your child off on the right foot.

Beginning Soccer

One of my students, Kristine, asked me to write a Sleep Talk script for her seven-year-old daughter, Dana, who was a member of her class soccer team. The team had scored no goals at all halfway through the season, and even though Dana was a good athlete who loved the game, she was discouraged. She was neglecting her homework, and her grades had gone from above average to mediocre.

Here's the script I gave Kristine to read to Dana:

《 *Dana, this is your mother.*
I want to let you know how much I love you.
I want to let you know how proud I am that you are my
    daughter.
I enjoy watching you play soccer, especially when you enjoy it
    so much.
I am so proud of you because you are proud of yourself.

When you play soccer, you are strong and fast.
When you play soccer, you are confident and accurate with
    your kicks.
You are a good player.
I enjoy seeing you have a fun time.
Thank you for being my daughter.
I love you.
Sweet dreams. »

After only a few days of Sleep Talk, Kristine told me she could see a change in Dana's attitude. The girl seemed more confident, more focused. Kristine continued reading the script, and after two weeks, the team scored two goals in one game—both made by Dana. As her performance continued to improve, the coach moved Dana to center forward position, where she continued to excel. By the time the team made it to the second play-off game, Dana had become a star player, whom her teammates nicknamed "the Boot." Not only was she delighted with her achievements in soccer, but her grades also showed marked improvement as her self-confidence increased.

Swimming

In Southern California, where many children have access to private pools as well as the ocean, learning to swim is essential for safety. My kids started their lessons early: Trey at three, Tara at two, and Briana at six months! (We belonged to a club that had a program designed to teach infants to swim before they could walk.)

The two girls had strong natural abilities in the sport, but Trey had a chunky build that was not ideal for swimming. He did well enough in the breaststroke, but when he swam backstroke his body was a foot underwater. He'd come up for breath, then sink back down, and all you could see most of the time was his forearms coming up out of the water.

All the kids participated in swimming meets, and when I was in the bleachers watching Trey, I'd often hear people say, "Whose kid is *that*?" But he kept working at it, kept competing, didn't quit. In the breaststroke competition, he often came in first, second, or third, but he never had much success with his unorthodox backstroke style.

The girls were consistently first in their events, and they had to deal with the same ego problems I was dealing with when we were on the sidelines watching Trey swim. I think the experience was good for all of us—for Trey because he hung in there and did his best, for the girls and me because listening to other people's comments about him helped us keep clear in our minds what was important to us: that even though his performance wasn't stellar, we were immensely proud of *him*.

The following Sleep Talk script would be appropriate for any child who needs support and encouragement as a beginning swimmer:

« *Karen, this is your mom.*
I want to tell you how much I love you.
I want to tell you how proud I am that you are my daughter.
I am so proud of you when you swim.
You are such a good swimmer.
I enjoy watching you at the swim meet, at practice, or having
     a fun time in the pool.
Your energy builds.
I appreciate your effort to improve.
Thank you for being my daughter.
I love you.
Sweet dreams. »

Teamwork

In any team sport, learning to be a team player is an important key to success, and these skills and attitudes are just as important to success in life. Various books on business have pointed out that women have often been handicapped in corporate life because they lacked the experience most men had in playing team sports, an experience that serves as a model for much of corporate culture.

Nowadays there are many more opportunities for girls in team sports. When Tara was in college, she played touch football on a collegiate team. Briana's sport was crew, and she got excellent experience on her college team. I know a private elementary school that has two basketball teams, one for boys and one for girls; the boys' team has girl cheerleaders, and the girls' team has boy cheerleaders.

Whatever team sport your child is involved in, the following Sleep Talk script can offer the child support for learning to be a team player.

《 *Linda, this is your dad.*
I want to let you know how much I love you.
I want to let you know how proud I am that you are my daughter.
I am proud of you because you seem to know what it takes to be a team player.
By playing your game, you learn how to direct your energy in a constructive way.
You learn teamwork by participating.
You accept good coaching.
Your leadership qualities assist your teammates.
You display the spirit of victory and still have independent thinking.
Thank you for being my daughter.
Thank you for keeping yourself in good physical condition and safe.
I love you.
Sweet dreams. 》

Beginning Golf

Participating in individual sports can also teach a child important lessons about commitment, involvement, and focus, in addition to preparing them for a lifetime of enjoyable recreation.

Chapters 9 and 10 described Sleep Talk scripts on self-confidence and initiative that I wrote for Nick to read to his son Jason, a frail boy who had a history of childhood illness. By the time Jason was fifteen, he was in good health, and he asked his father, an excellent golfer, to teach him the game. Nick showed Jason the basics and also arranged for him to have some private lessons with the pro who worked at the local country club.

When Jason showed signs of becoming discouraged because he wasn't progressing faster with his game, Nick asked me for a script to encourage him.

Here is the script I gave Nick to read to his son:

« *Jason, this is your dad.*
I want to let you know how much I love you.
I want to let you know how proud I am to be your dad.
There is no commitment without involvement.
When you practice hitting golf balls, you do a good job.
Your drives show strength and accuracy.
Your putting is on target.
You focus on what you want to happen during your play.
I am proud of you because I know you are proud of yourself.
When you are involved, your level of commitment is
    wonderful to watch.
I love you.
Sweet dreams. »

After a week of nightly Sleep Talk readings, Nick told me Jason's attitude toward the game had improved enormously. His skills continued to improve over the next few years, and now father and son frequently play eighteen holes together on weekends. Nick still has the edge, but he says with a twinkle in his eye, "That kid is giving me a run for my money!"

Animals

Almost from the time she could walk, Tara was continually bringing home an assortment of animals. Clearly in love, she would stroke the fluffy ball of fur in her arms, look up at me, and say, "Isn't he cute? Can I keep him? I'll take care of him."

The Haddad household has always included dogs, cats, and horses, and our kids learned early to love and be responsible for animals. Having a pet encourages children to go beyond themselves, to protect the animal and keep it safe, and to develop a sympathetic understanding of its needs. Having a dog or cat in the household also guarantees that children will have a loving and uncritical friend at those moments when the whole world seems to be against them.

Of course, having an animal as a friend is a two-way street, and no one knows this better than Tara, who is now a veterinarian. When she was in veterinary school, a calf only a few days old was brought into the hospital. He was very small and weak and had been run over by a truck. Tara named him Solomon and cared for him until he became strong enough to undergo surgery for his broken leg. He continued to heal and was almost ready to leave the hospital when Tara came home for a brief visit. During her absence, Solomon became very ill, and the clinician at the hospital delayed the warranted euthanasia until Tara's return so she could say good-bye.

After the calf's death, Tara wrote a poem about her experience with Solomon called "Will I Take Care of You?" The last two stanzas express the attitude that makes her such a fine doctor and friend to animals:

> Will I take care of you?
> Well, I might cry when you have gone,
>   but don't feel sad for me.
> The care I give is a piece of myself
>   I give up willingly.
>
> Will I take care of you?
> And risk the loss if it means
>   I might be one friend less.
> The answer to your question
>   is simply, "YES."

For a child who is getting a first pet, a Sleep Talk script may be helpful in offering support and information about what is involved in caring for it. The following script would be appropriate for a child from school age through adolescence:

《 *Chris, this is your dad.*
I just want you to know how much I love you.
I just want you to know how proud I am to be your dad and how proud I am that you are my son.
I want you to know how much I appreciate it when you take good care of your pet.

You are so good with animals.
You are caring and tender with your pet and other animals.
You care for your pet.
You feed it and keep your pet clean.
I thank you for keeping your animal fed and clean.
I am so proud of you.
I love you so very much.
Sweet dreams. »

For preschool children, you can refer to two scripts in Chapter 7: one on bugs and insects and one on animals. Both are concerned more with safety than with responsibility, and this is appropriate for the younger child.

In Appendix A I've included a script on competition with an animal, which would be suitable for a child who is involved with dog or cat shows, 4-H shows, or riding a horse in competition.

Through all the Sleep Talk scripts in this chapter, you have an opportunity to express your love and pride in your child's recreational activities. A thoughtful and appropriate use of these scripts can strengthen the bond between you and your child and foster your child's enjoyment of life as an adult. As you work with these scripts, it's important to keep in mind that they are designed to support your child's choices of leisure involvements. Your love and pride in your child's efforts to improve (irrespective of who wins) are the crucial elements in enhancing the child's experience and growth. When you keep that in mind, everybody wins (no matter what the score is).

13

SLEEP TALK

AND

SPECIAL NEEDS

Few families get through their children's growing up without a share of difficult or frightening experiences. Sleep Talk's power becomes especially impressive in challenging situations, and this chapter discusses the ways you can use it to help a child reduce tensions related to adoption, cope with crisis situations such as a death or divorce, deal with various health problems, and learn to live with physical or mental disabilities.

Adoption

Raising our adopted son, T.J., has been an experience the Haddad family wouldn't have missed for the world. I'm puzzled when I hear parents express concern about whether, if they add an adopted child to their family, there will be enough love to go around. I don't see love as a finite quantity like a pie that gets cut into smaller portions

237

as new members are added to the family. Our experience with adopting T.J. was that the whole pie got bigger, so that everyone both gave and received more love.

Adopting a child is a major decision for any family, and I think it's important to take a hard look at your motives before taking this step. Prospective adoptive parents who are simply seeking a love object guaranteed to always love them back might be better advised to get a dog. Raising any child can be a frustrating, exhausting, surprising, and magnificent experience for parents who are willing to take the emotional risks involved with letting that child into their lives and fully bonding with him. When the child is adopted, the emotional risks may be even greater, but the rewards can also be extraordinary.

One of the surprises for me in raising T.J. has been not having the same ego investment in him that I experienced with my three older kids. When we decided to adopt him, I had almost no expectations. My own responsibilities were primarily to love him and to educate him. Loving him was easy, but educating him has been more of a challenge. In order to cope with his attention deficit disorder, I've had to learn to pay attention in a new way myself—to look at what *this* child needs at *this* moment and to be more flexible.

Because my three older children are so close to each other in age, I basically raised them all at once, but T.J., whom we adopted when the others were grown, has been more like an only child. I've been able to focus my attention on his particular needs because I'm not as stressed or as busy as I was when Trey, Tara, and Briana were growing up. My priorities have shifted in the process, and some things I insisted on with them now seem less vital. For example, it's not as important to me that T.J. make his bed every day (though it is important that he know how to make his bed). If I'm going to get on his case about something, it's more likely to be brushing his teeth every day, which *is* important.

My experiences with the other three kids have allowed me to be more effective with T.J. and to appreciate his unique qualities, such as his creativity.

Bonding with an Adopted Child

Adopted children need to be reassured that they are lovable and worthy of being cared for and that they are a valid addition to the family. The script on bonding with an adopted child that I described in Chapter 6 has been especially important for making T.J. a part of our family. When he was twelve years old, someone asked him what it was like to be raised in our family. He thought for a minute, then said: "I can go to the store, I can go to school, I can even run away, but *I'll still be a Haddad*."

One of my students asked whether I would recommend using this same script for bonding with a foster child for whom formal adoption papers have not yet been signed. In this tricky situation, I recommended that she use instead the standard script on bonding with a parent that I also discussed in Chapter 6. This script simply expresses love and pride in the child and says nothing about the child's being "a valid addition to the family." My caution about using the script on bonding with an adopted child before an adoption is finalized is based on my concern that the child might be devastated if he had to leave the family with whom he had fully bonded. Especially with an adopted child, it's essential not to make promises you may not be able to keep.

Releasing Worry from the Past

When T.J. first came to live with our family, he came as a foster child, and as his foster mother I was required to take him to visit his birth mother. So, he knew from the beginning who she was. I think it's important to let a child know he's adopted, even if he has been with you since birth. It's also important, when he raises questions about why he was adopted or why his parents gave him up, to offer reassurance that what happened before the adoption has no bearing on his secure place in the family.

Questions of this kind can come up in various ways. Sometimes a classmate's casual remark—"Oh, I understand you're adopted"—can set a child's concern in motion. When T.J. was eight or nine, he asked me, "Do you think Mama Mary is still alive?"

I said I'd try to find out, and I did. I called the social worker on the case, but she was not able to give me any information, and I explained this to T.J. When he was eleven, he mentioned the subject again. I told him that when he was eighteen, they would give him the information that they weren't legally able to give me now. I assured him that if he wanted to go looking for his birth mother then, I'd do my best to help him.

The first time he asked about his origins, I started using the following script:

> « *T.J., this is your mother.*
> *I want to let you know how much I love you.*
> *I want to let you know how proud I am that you are my son.*
> *You are so special and important in my life.*
> *There is a powerful reason you are with us.*
> *It doesn't matter what has happened before we came together.*
> *I love being your "real parent for keeps."*
> *I am so glad you were born.*
> *I feel special having you in my life.*
> *Thank you for being my son.*
> *I love you.*
> *Sweet dreams.* »

Adopted children need to be assured that their acceptance as a family member is in no way provisional. It's important for them to feel confident that there is nothing that could be revealed about their past that would challenge their status as a member of the family. This releases their worries about the past and helps them focus on the present.

Releasing Worry from Conflict

All families have incidents of conflict and upset, and it's important for an adopted child to understand that she bears no special responsibility for them, that they are an inevitable part of life. If Mom and Dad have a fight, the child needs to be reassured that she is loved and valued despite their conflict.

The following Sleep Talk script would be appropriate for any adopted child at any stage, but especially at times when there are unusual tensions in the family:

> « *Cindy, this is your mother.*
> *I just want to let you know how much I love you.*
> *I just want to let you know how proud I am that you are my*
>   *daughter.*
> *I want to let you know that even when there are family upsets,*
>   *I love you, and it is good to have you as my daughter.*

> *Today I thought again how glad I am that you were born and became my daughter.*
> *I am happy to have you in my life.*
> *I love to watch you grow.*
> *Thank you for being my daughter.*
> *I love you.*
> *Sweet dreams.* »

Wise parents know that it's important with all children not to use love as a means of control: "I will love you if you clean up your room" or "I will love you if you get a B average." Adopted children are especially sensitive to manipulations of this kind, and their self-respect can easily be undermined. This script helps defuse the adopted child's all-too-ready assumption that if only she were different, all would be well in the family.

Note that the script says, "Today I thought again how glad I am that you were born and became my daughter." Many adoptive parents are tempted to say instead, "how glad I am that you were born *to become* my daughter." But this variation implies a cause-and-effect situation that is basically false. The child was born and then became the adopted child of this family, but *the purpose of the child's birth was for her to be herself.* It's important for the parent to accord the child the respect for her individuality implied in the statement as written in the script.

Also, my version of this line makes allowances for imperfections and dissatisfactions on both sides of the parent-child relationship. The child can make mistakes and still be seen as worthy of love, just like the parents. People sometimes say to us, "Boy, is T.J. ever lucky, getting adopted into your family." I think George's response to that comment is exactly right: "*We're* the lucky ones."

Crisis Situations

We all do our best for our children, but there are times when we cannot shield them from the losses and anxieties that are part of the human condition. During these difficult times, it is more important than ever for the child to feel loved and valued. One of the greatest challenges for a parent under these circumstances is to understand how much the child needs to be included in the situation, dealt with honestly, and reassured that life will go on in spite of grief. At such times, the child needs to know that there is an adult in control and taking responsibility for the child's health and safety.

Death of a Family Member

For a child, the most devastating event of all is the death of a parent or family member. No one can eliminate the fact of death from our lives or explain away the emotional damage it leaves in its wake. Even though what is lost can never be restored, if children are encouraged to share their feelings at such times, the hurt can begin to heal.

Sleep Talk offers a way of helping you and your child stay connected as you move together through the experience of grief:

« *Artie, this is your father.*
I want to let you know how much I love you.
I want to let you know how proud I am that you are my son.
You are my brave, wonderful son.
It hurts when you are not going to see someone again.
It is OK to feel upset.
It is OK to be sad.
When people die, their eyes are closed, and their lips are
    silent.
But your heart beats with love.
You remember the good, loving times.
They are stored in your memory.
Stay in touch with your feelings.
Talk about your feelings whenever you want to.
I will talk with you about your feelings.
Remember the good times with love.
I love you.
Thank you for being my son.
Sweet dreams. »

When you read this script to your child, you offer him a model of love, courage, and responsibility that he will never forget. The bond between you becomes stronger than ever through this gift you give him in the midst of your own pain. Staying in touch with your child's needs at such a time also has the unexpected benefit of promoting your own healing.

Death of a Friend

A child whose contemporary dies not only suffers the loss of a friend but also feels anxieties about her own mortality and that of others close to her. In this moment of special vulnerability, a Sleep Talk script can offer reassurance that she is not alone and that her parents are also her friends:

> « *Carolyn, this is your mother.*
> *I want to let you know how much I love you.*
> *I want to let you know how proud I am that you are my daughter.*
> *I feel sad because of your loss.*
> *The death of _____ is difficult.*
> *Being "alone" is not fun. Feeling "alone" hurts.*
> *_____ did not leave you alone.*
> *You have many friends.*
> *I am your friend.*
> *_____ is on his/her path.*
> *You remember the good times with pride.*
> *You remember the happy times.*
> *They are stored in your memory.*
> *Thank you for being my brave and wonderful daughter.*
> *I love you.*
> *Sweet dreams.* »

The sentence "_____ is on his/her path" is consistent with Haddad's fourth and fifth Rules of Life: *Whatever happens is supposed to happen; When it's over, it's over.* (The Rules of Life are discussed in Chapter 9.) The most important aspect of this script is that it offers the child assurance that the parent loves and values her and sympathizes with her distress. It may also encourage the child to talk to the parent about her feelings.

When "Bad Things" Happen

There are times when parents sense that their child is seriously troubled about something, yet even the most tactful questioning brings forth a quick "Nothing's wrong, Mom. I'm fine." One of my clients told me that she learned, long after the event, that her seventeen-year-old son had been deeply distressed when his girlfriend, pregnant with his child, had gotten an abortion. Since his parents didn't even know he was having sex with the girl, he felt he couldn't share anything about this situation with them. He didn't tell his mother about it until years later, after he had graduated from college.

In a situation like this, if you sense that your child is going through difficulties but is unable to share them with you, you can still offer support through the following Sleep Talk script:

« *Cary, this is your mother.*
I want to let you know how much I love you.
I want to let you know how proud I am that you are my son.
When "bad things" happen to you or around you, I feel sad.
When people you depend on let you down, it hurts.
I hurt when I see you hurt.
I am proud of you when you move from a place of "hurt" to
  a place of "new beginnings."
I am proud of your new level of self-confidence.
Thank you for being my son.
Thank you for being in my life.
I love you.
Sweet dreams. »

This script could be effective in a wide variety of situations and for children as young as four or five. Even when your child is confronting problems he doesn't know how to solve and is unwilling to share with you, this script reassures him that you love him, trust him, and feel confident that he will find his way through the difficulty. (It's possible that, with the pressure to "tell all" off his back, he may decide to confide in you.)

Disappointments

Sometimes the reasons for a child's hurt and sadness are all too apparent. When a teenage girl goes out for a cheerleader position, feels her performance is the best, yet is turned down, she can be crushed. When a boy with a straight-A average fails to get into the college of his choice, he may be outraged. Especially in adolescence, when kids are continually putting themselves on the line and sometimes failing to achieve their goals, this Sleep Talk script can help them put things in perspective:

> « *Dickie, this is your father.*
> *I want to let you know how much I love you.*
> *I want to let you know how proud I am that you are my son.*
> *I know how it feels when you look forward to something*
>   *special and it doesn't work out the way you want.*
> *There is disappointment.*
> *It feels as if it isn't fair.*
> *I am proud of you when you become quiet, calm, and*
>   *relaxed.*
> *You draw on your inner strength.*
> *You become strong and positive.*
> *You look for new ways to succeed.*
> *You are a wonderful person.*
> *You move beyond barriers.*
> *You turn disappointments into learning experiences.*
> *I love you so much.*
> *Sweet dreams.* »

When a child feels he has "gone for the big one" and missed it, he needs reassurance that you love him and are proud of him just as he is, apart from his achievements. Your empathy is especially important in this situation because it acknowledges that disappointment is a fact of life—something that you, too, have experienced and survived. This script offers him important information about how to move forward after a disappointment so that his future efforts will be more likely to succeed.

Divorce

For a child, divorce is a trauma second only to the death of a family member. Not only does it plunge the child into emotional upheaval, but it also calls into question all the things she has taken for granted, beginning with her parents' love for her. *If they can stop loving each other*, she reasons, *they might also stop loving me*. The split-up certainly will change her lifestyle, perhaps necessitating a move to less costly accommodations and/or a change in schools.

In the midst of grieving for her lost security, the child may well feel that she is in some way responsible for the breakup of the family: "If only I had been less demanding, gotten better grades. . . ."

You as a parent in this situation may also be struggling with volatile feelings: about your soon-to-be ex-spouse, your child, the changes the divorce imposes on your own life. Yet, at this time, it's especially important to be sensitive to your child, to reassure her that the divorce is not her fault: No matter how her parents may feel about each other, they both love *her*, and it is possible to adjust to the necessary lifestyle changes. At this moment, she needs more than ever to feel secure, valued, cared for.

The following Sleep Talk script would be appropriate for a child of any age:

« *Denise, this is your mother.*
I want to let you know how much I love you.
I want to let you know how proud I am that you are my
    daughter.
I want to let you know that it is all right to feel and think
    many different things now.
Things are going to be OK.
Days get better, and life will feel good again.
Let me know when you need extra hugs and kisses.
I need hugs and kisses from you, too.
No matter what your dad and I decide about our marriage,
    you are a wonderful child.
"I love you" does not change.
We are still a family.
Thank you for being my daughter.
I love you.
Sweet dreams. »

The last thing a child in this situation needs is a series of long diatribes blaming the other parent for the breakup: "If he hadn't . . .";

"If she had only . . ." The main thing your child needs to know is that her parents will continue to be responsible for feeding and clothing her, keeping a roof over her head, and protecting her. If possible, she needs to be included in the planning for the new lifestyle. She also needs to feel confident that things will get better, that her pain and grief will diminish with time.

Health

As soon as children are old enough to spend large chunks of time with others in preschool or day care, they begin bringing home respiratory ailments that spread through the family like wildfire. Most households with preschool and school-age children are hotbeds of colds and flu throughout the winter months. Ours was no different, and the parade of fevers, coughs, and runny noses prompted me to write scripts for my own kids to help them become conscious of the way the body's immune system can protect them from illness.

Chapter 8 discussed one of the Sleep Talk scripts I wrote for Briana when she was at preschool. Once I started using these scripts with my kids, the incidence of illness in our family decreased dramatically.

Immune System: Younger Child

In the first chapter of the book, I mentioned a script that I suggested on the immune system for Dr. Jack Gutman to read to his six-year-old daughter, Gracie. That script is slightly different from the one I did for Briana, and it acknowledges that nobody really understands exactly how the body's immune system works. No one knows how aspirin works either, but we know it is effective in certain situations. I have seen evidence in my own family, as well as in reports from my clients and students, that the following script is a powerful aid to healing:

《 *Gracie, this is your dad.*
I want to let you know how much I love you.
I want to let you know how proud I am that you are my daughter.

    Let your body activate your immune system so you have a
        strong, healthy body.
    I do not know how to do this, but your body knows how.
    I love seeing your happy, healthy, smiling face.
    I love you so much.
    Thank you for being in my life.
    Sweet dreams. »

Trust is the key to the effectiveness of many of the scripts in this book. Here, because the child trusts her father, she will automatically assume that it is possible for her to activate her immune system when he assures her that her body knows how to do this. I never cease to be impressed by the power of love to promote growth and healing.

The script would be appropriate for any preschool child. In addition to the usual run of respiratory ailments and childhood illnesses, it can be effective for allergies, which represent another kind of imbalance in the body. The body has the power to neutralize the irritants that cause allergic reactions, and Sleep Talk can help your child mobilize these natural defenses.

Immune System: Older Child

For an older child, a more sophisticated script may be appropriate, but the same principle is at work:

  « *Paul, this is your mother.*
    I want to let you know how much I love you.
    I want to let you know how proud I am when you keep your
        body strong and healthy.
    Even when people around you are sick or have colds, you
        stay healthy most of the time.
    Your body knows what to do to keep your immune system
        active and working.
    You stay healthy because your body knows what to do.
    Your body knows how to activate your immune system and
        keep you healthy.
    I appreciate your ability to do this.
    Thank you for being my healthy son.

> *I love you.*
> *Sweet dreams.* »

Does this script guarantee a cold-free school year? Of course not. But a child who is conscious of the invisible shield his immune system provides for his body is likely to have a much smaller incidence of illness. Many children, even at the junior high school level, are familiar with the idea of the immune system from their science classes and discussions in the media. Using this script moves the idea from the abstract realm to the child's own body and encourages children to "turn on" this invisible switch that can protect them against the ailments afflicting their peers.

Hospital Stay

Hospitals can be frightening for children, especially when they find themselves separated from their parents and traumatized by intrusive and often painful medical tests and treatments. You as a parent can take certain steps to make your child's hospital stay easier. If the hospitalization is not due to a sudden emergency, you can gather information from your child's doctor or the hospital medical staff to let everyone know what to expect.

If you can find out what tests will be performed and how they will look and feel to your child, your explanations can go a long way toward defusing her anxieties. Even answers to such questions as whether she will be allowed to wear her own pajamas and who is allowed to visit her (and when) can help allay her fears. Many hospitals today have Child Life programs designed to help children and parents understand medical treatments and procedures before they are performed.

In this situation your child may not know what kind of behavior is appropriate and she is likely to take her cue from you. A Sleep Talk script can provide reassurance and information that promote healing.

When Jennifer, the ten-year-old daughter of Alice, one of my clients, had to spend time in the hospital recovering from serious burns, I gave her mother this script to read to her in the hospital as she slept:

《 *Jennifer, this is your mom.*
 I want to let you know how much I love you.
 I want to let you know how proud I am that you are my
    daughter.
 I want to let you know how proud I am of your willingness
    to do what it takes to get better.
 You are a good team player with the doctors and nurses to
    get yourself well.
 Regardless of what is happening or happens to your body, I
    love you so much.
 Thank you for cooperating with your treatment.
 You are my calm, matter-of-fact daughter.
 You open yourself up to heal.
 I care so much about you.
 Do what it takes to activate your immune system.
 Let your body do what it knows how to do.
 I love you.
 Sweet dreams. 》

Alice reported that Jennifer's grafts "took" well, and that the girl was able to go home a few days earlier than anticipated. Her healing was complete, with less scarring than usual for this kind of injury. Remembering the anguish of the boy I nursed at the beginning of my career (which I described in the Introduction), I felt especially good about being able to offer Jennifer and her mother a technique with this kind of power.

Surgery

The most common operations in childhood are appendectomies and tonsillectomies, and children nearly always have uneventful recoveries from these. The major problem is often not the surgery itself but the anesthesia, which makes the child feel "sick." I used the following Sleep Talk script with T.J. when he had his tonsils out, and it would be appropriate for any child undergoing general anesthesia:

《 *T.J., this is your mother.*
 I want to let you know how much I love you.
 I want to let you know how proud I am that you are my son.

> *I want to let you know how proud I am of your willingness*
>   *to do what it takes to get better.*
> *You will get medicine to sleep during your surgery.*
> *While you sleep, the operation will be done.*
> *You keep the medicine in your body as long as you need it to*
>   *keep you comfortable.*
> *When you no longer need the medicine, you release it from*
>   *your body.*
> *Thank you for being cooperative with your treatment.*
> *Thank you for healing so quickly.*
> *I love you so much.*
> *Sweet dreams.* »

Just as the body knows how to switch on its immune defenses, it also knows how to release medication once its function is completed. So, one of the most important aspects of this script is the information it gives the child: that his body knows how to eliminate the anesthetic once the operation is over. T.J.'s recovery after his tonsillectomy was rapid, and I've had similar reports about all children whose parents have used this script.

Wearing a Brace

When Trey and Tara were preschoolers, they both needed to use a brace at night to correct the tendency of their feet to turn inward. This device had a horizontal bar linked to shoes, and it was attached to the foot of the bed; putting the kids' feet in the shoes while they slept stretched their muscles to prevent them from walking pigeon-toed. There was quite a bit of tension in our household as bedtime approached, and I wish I had thought of using a Sleep Talk script with them to help them with this unpleasant situation. (A much better solution than the brace—one I didn't know about then—would have been to put the children in shoe skates and let them skate on the carpet. It's impossible to skate with your feet turned in, so that kind of exercise automatically stretches the muscles in the right way—in the process of having fun.)

Many children who suffer from scoliosis (curvature of the spine) need to wear a brace for long periods. The following Sleep Talk script would be helpful for a child of any age who has to wear a brace:

《 *Joan, this is your grandma.*
I want to let you know how much I love you.
I want to let you know how proud I am that you are my granddaughter.
I think you are wonderful.
You are wonderful the way your body knows what to do to be straight and strong.
You handle wearing your brace better than anyone I know.
I love your happy, smiling face and healthy body.
Thank you for being my granddaughter.
I love you.
Sweet dreams. 》

Especially when a child is dealing with a long-term health situation such as scoliosis, it's important for a parent to offer continual support for a positive attitude toward the corrective device she needs to wear. This script also offers the information that, even though the child may not understand exactly how the process works, her body knows how to use the brace to straighten and strengthen itself.

Healthy Eating

Kids seem to be born knowing about fast foods, and French fries (especially when consumed regularly) are not the best fuel for growing bodies. Children generally have choices of foods in the school cafeteria and from various food vendors after school hours. They also have choices of snacks at home, especially if they arrive home before their parents.

The following script would be helpful in encouraging a child of any age to be conscious of healthy eating:

《 *Nick, this is your dad.*
I want to let you know how much I love you.
I want to let you know how proud I am that you are my son.
I am so happy to see your healthy, smiling face.

You eat foods to keep your body strong and well.
I am so proud that you keep your body sound and robust.
Your body knows what to do to keep it healthy.
Choosing good foods helps your body stay well.
Thank you for being my wonderful child.
I love you.
Sweet dreams. »

Obviously, healthy eating habits are easier to establish when a child sees the parent regularly snacking on fruit or raw carrots rather than ice cream and cookies.

Dental Visits

Nowadays children are generally introduced to the dentist at age two or three. Many insurance plans support taking kids to the dentist's office for a preparatory visit. They get to climb up into the chair, look at the light and the equipment, and even get a little water splashed in their mouths. This generally defuses the anxiety around a trip to the dentist and makes the first "real" visit less traumatic.

Dentists now fill cavities even in baby teeth when a child is four or five, so that decay won't spread to other teeth. Some children may need significant dental work at fairly young ages. For example, Briana's teeth were very large, and at age nine she needed to have some of them pulled. She was accustomed to dealing with pain effectively from the time she was very young (the Introduction described the way she stopped the pain in her injured foot when she was three), so I knew she would need very little anesthesia. I explained this to the dentist, but unfortunately he didn't believe me, and he used the conventional dose on Briana, who had a bad reaction.

She still needed to have a couple more teeth pulled, and at that point, I wrote the following Sleep Talk script for her:

« *Briana, this is your mother.*
I want to let you know how much I love you.
I want to let you know how very proud I am that you are my daughter.

When you go to the dentist, you are calm and relaxed.
It is easy for the dentist to work on your teeth.
You lose very little fluid and heal quickly.
When you take deep breaths and relax, you are calm and
*   confident.*
Everyone remarks how quickly you heal.
I am so proud that you are my daughter.
Thank you for being my daughter.
I love you.
Sweet dreams. »

Before she had the teeth pulled, we changed dentists, and the new man heeded my instructions to give her no anesthetic at all. I think the situation was harder on him than on her. She breezed out of there, and the next thing I knew, she was sitting on the curb in front of our house waiting for our other kids to come home from school. Pain was obviously not a problem for her.

Orthodontics

By the time T.J. got his braces, at age ten, I was aware of the importance of encouraging him to keep his braces and his teeth clean. Here is the Sleep Talk script I used with him:

« *T.J., this is your mom.*
I want to let you know how much I love you.
I want to let you know how proud I am of you.
I am proud that you decided to correct the arrangement of
*   your teeth.*
Working with the orthodontist, you achieve your goal in a
*   short amount of time and with ease.*
I appreciate your attentiveness in achieving tooth correction.
I am proud of you wearing braces and bands [headgear] as
*   instructed.*
You brush your teeth and appliances, keeping them clean.
Only you can take care of them.
Thank you for paying attention to your eating habits.

You use common sense in your food selection.
Thank you for being my son.
With or without braces, I enjoy seeing your beautiful smile.
I love you.
Sweet dreams. »

It's extremely important for children who wear braces to be aware of their diet; certain foods tend to get stuck in the appliances. Without proper cleaning (which requires care and a fair amount of elbow grease), the teeth can decay. T.J. has been conscientious about keeping his braces clean, and I give a lot of credit to this script, which I see as a kind of preventive medicine.

Physically and Mentally Challenged Children

One of my students, Deena, a woman in her early thirties, is physically disabled. Afflicted with muscular dystrophy, Deena was run over by a fire truck when she was in her twenties and has undergone numerous surgeries on her legs over the past ten years. The combination of her illness and the injury has left her extremely short in stature and dependent on crutches and leg braces. She has a degree in physical education and, despite her personal limitations, works in a hospital with children who are physically disabled. A large part of her effectiveness in working with these kids is the implicit statement she makes by her own life: *If I can do it, so can you.*

Deena is one of the most courageous people I know, and becoming better acquainted with her has helped me understand the problems of people who struggle with challenges of this kind.

Parents of disabled children need a special kind of courage to support the child's efforts to live a life beyond the inherent physical and/or mental limitations. They continually walk a fine line: taking responsibility for the child's physical and emotional needs while supporting her in becoming as independent as she can be. In this heartbreaking situation, wise parents understand that to expect less from a disabled child than she is capable of is ultimately to *add* to her disability.

Encouragement to "Go for It"

A child living with a disability is first of all a human being, a person with the same needs for love and validation as one who is free of these limitations. For such a child (as for any child), having the courage to "go for it," to set goals and strive to attain them, is essential to developing self-respect.

The following Sleep Talk script would be appropriate for any child who is struggling with a physical or mental impairment:

《 *Samantha, this is your mother.*
I just want to let you know how much I love you.
I just want to let you know how proud I am that you are my daughter.
I want to let you know how proud I am of your courage.
You want something good in your life and decide to get it.
You look for ways to bring new, exciting experiences your way.
You do not let your disability keep you from achieving your goals.
You live your life beyond your disability.
I am so proud of you.
I am grateful you are in my life.
I love you.
Sweet dreams. 》

No matter how young or mentally limited your child may be, the basic message of love, pride, and support for her efforts toward independence will come through if you persist in reading this script. When the child feels valued, striving to do her best is no hardship.

Responsibility

The following script carries much the same message, but in language suitable for an older child:

《 *Norman, this is your dad.*
I just want to let you know how much I love you.
I just want to let you know how proud I am that you are my son.

> *I want to let you know how proud I am of your willingness*
> *to learn.*
> *You choose and learn what is good for you.*
> *That makes me happy.*
> *I feel happy because of who you are.*
> *I am proud that you do not live your life around your*
> *disability.*
> *You decide what you want and go for it.*
> *You focus on what is important in your life and find ways to*
> *make it work.*
> *You live your life with what you create.*
> *You are responsible.*
> *Thank you for being so responsible.*
> *Thank you for being my son.*
> *I appreciate you being in my life.*
> *I love you.*
> *Sweet dreams.* »

Adolescents, like younger children, need reassurance that they are valued for who they are rather than what they are able to achieve. Note that the message of this script is similar to that of scripts in Chapter 10, "Sleep Talk and Your Adolescent," on perseverance, initiative, and choices. Only the context is different. Behind all these scripts is the basic idea that a child (disabled or not) becomes a grown-up by taking responsibility for his life to the full extent of his capacities. Any human being who does this earns self-respect as well as the respect of others.

Encouragement for Surgery(ies)

Sandi, who was born with a harelip and a cleft palate, needed a series of surgeries to correct the problem and give her face a normal appearance. Her mother, Willa, asked me for a Sleep Talk script to read to her daughter in preparation for each of these operations, and this is the one I gave her:

> « *Sandi, this is your mom.*
> *I just want to let you know how much I love you.*
> *I just want to let you know how proud I am to be your mom.*

《 *I want to let you know how proud I am of your willingness*
    to do what it takes to get better.
Any surgery you have is for you.
A surgery is a plan to assist your ability to be better.
I appreciate it when you display your positive attitude.
I am proud of you for cooperating with your treatment.
I am proud of you for doing what it takes to be the best you
    can be.
I love you so much.
Thank you for being my daughter.
Thank you for being in my life.
Sweet dreams. 》

This script would be appropriate for a child of any age who has to undergo surgery to correct a physical disability. Most often, a series of surgeries is necessary, and it's important for the child to understand that the operations are designed for her benefit and that her cooperation with her treatment is important for its success.

Asking for Help

People who are "differently abled" in our society have to cope with the temptation to manipulate others into doing things for them rather than finding the way to do things for themselves. Given the intense feelings that parents and caretakers often have for a disabled child, the temptation to encourage him to become an expert manipulator is almost irresistible. But this attitude does the child a real disservice. Loving parents need special fortitude to steel themselves against *being* manipulated while at the same time encouraging their child to ask for the help he needs to become as independent as possible.

Here is a Sleep Talk script that can help both you and your child achieve these goals:

《 *Aaron, this is your mom.*
I want to let you know how much I love you.
I want to let you know how proud I am that you are my son.
I want to let you know how proud I am of your willingness
    to learn.

You open yourself to many lessons.
When you need help, you ask for it.
I am so proud when I see you not using your disability to get
*   what you want.*
Instead, you ask, figure it out, and do something to achieve
*   what you want.*
I am so lucky to have you in my life.
I love you so much.
Thank you for being who you are.
Sweet dreams. »

The vital message of this script is that, while it's OK for the child to ask for help when he needs it, it's not OK to use his disability to avoid learning to do whatever he can for himself.

Letting People into Your Life

Associations between people are built on exchanges through which all parties benefit. Because it's easy for people to overlook a disabled child, he may need to take the initiative in pointing out a contribution he is able to make. For example, a paraplegic child may not be able to play on the football team, but he can keep score.

Through Sleep Talk, parents can help children muster the courage to put themselves forward in this way:

« *Robert, this is your mom.*
I just want to let you know how much I love you.
I just want to let you know how proud I am to be your mom.
I want to let you know how proud I am that you are my son.
I want to let you know how proud I am of you when you
*   make choices about your life regardless of your disability.*
When you need help or a friend, you know how to let people
*   into your life.*
I watch you with friends and people.
You build support structures in your life.
You know when and how to effectively ask for exchanges that
*   benefit all concerned.*
I am so proud to have you in my life.
You are responsible and fun to be with.

I love you.
Sweet dreams. »

This script would be appropriate for a child of junior high school age or older.

Friends and Friendships

All children experience some awkwardness in learning how to relate to others, and the temptation to avoid making social connections for fear of rejection is especially strong for a child with a disability. Children who have a physical or mental disability often feel more comfortable with others who have equivalent problems. It's important for kids to move beyond this kind of self-imposed limitation and include in their circle of friends at least some people who are not disabled.

The following Sleep Talk script can offer support to your child for establishing relationships with a variety of people:

« *McKenzie, this is your mother.*
I want to let you know how much I love you.
I want to let you know how proud I am that you are my daughter.
I appreciate your friendship.
You are a good friend to me.
You have many friends.
Some of your friends may have disabilities similar to yours.
Some friends do not.
People are happy and comfortable around you.
I am happy and comfortable around you.
Thank you for being my friend.
Thank you for being in my life.
I am so proud of you.
I love you.
Sweet dreams. »

Note the way this script offers reassurance to the child through using her friendship with her parent as a model for other friendships. If her mother is comfortable around her, it stands to reason that other people would be also, even if they do not share her disability. This script would be appropriate for any child of school age.

Sports Participation

One of the things I find particularly inspiring about Deena is her willingness to put herself out there and become involved in sports. With leg braces and crutches, she participates in a 5K race a couple of times a year. Many races—even marathons—include wheelchair competitors, and other events such as the Special Olympics are designed for participants with a variety of disabilities.

Here is a script you can use to encourage your child to participate in sports to the limit of her abilities:

« *Jenna, this is your dad.*
I just want to let you know how much I love you.
I just want to let you know how proud I am that you are my daughter.
I want to let you know how proud I am of the way you respond to your physical [mental] challenges.
Your willingness and determination to participate in sports are apparent.
Your willingness to practice is appreciated.
You practice over and over with a good attitude.
Thank you for being the best you can be.
You are a joy and a delight to me.
Thank you for being in my life.
I love you.
Sweet dreams. »

Note that, in addition to offering the child her father's love and support, this script offers her pertinent information: that practicing is effective in achieving improvement and that maintaining a good attitude is important.

All the scripts in this chapter are based on the same principles I've emphasized throughout this book. Even in situations involving extraordinary challenges, a parent's love and validation is the key to helping children be the best they can be. Every one of these Sleep Talk scripts offers a rebonding experience for the parent, as well—a gentle reminder of the deep connection between you and your child that helps you sustain the courage you need in order to cope with even the most difficult times.

A FINAL NOTE

Parenting is an extraordinary adventure, and ultimately the best part of it is having in your life adult children you enjoy and admire—and knowing they also enjoy and admire you.

In our rapidly changing world, being a parent has never been more challenging or more potentially rewarding. Children have an amazing ability to grow and adapt to new situations, and your use of the Sleep Talk techniques described in this book can give them tools for achieving success throughout their lives (whatever their definition of success might be).

I believe that Sleep Talk, widely used, can produce a very special generation of children who are confident, loving, capable, and conscientious—young adults whose upbringing has supplied them with the skills to do an exceptional job of raising their own children.

As I come to the end of this book, I am witnessing this process in my own family. My younger daughter Briana has just given birth to her first child, a daughter, my first grandchild—and already I can see that my use of Sleep Talk with Briana since she was born has given her tools to be a better parent than I was capable of being at her stage of life.

For me, this is the ultimate satisfaction, as I believe it would be for any parent. I wish you the same joy in your own children and grandchildren.

Because Sleep Talk is a technique that is still in development, I would be most grateful for any feedback you are willing to send me about how it has worked in your family.

Please send your feedback to:

Lois Haddad
Sleep Talk Feedback
c/o NTC/Contemporary Publishing
4255 W. Touhy Ave.
Lincolnwood, IL 60646-1975

ADDITIONAL SAMPLE SCRIPTS ON RECREATION

Included in this Appendix are scripts related to the arts and creative energy, animals, and sports. These scripts, as well as those in the main text of the book, are indexed in Appendix B.

The Arts and Creative Energy

Piano: Practice

《*Jody, this is your mother.*
I want to let you know how much I love you.
I want to let you know how proud I am that you are my daughter.
I want to let you know how much I appreciate it when you practice your music on the piano.
Practicing creates the results you want and enjoy.
You practice frequently.

Thank you for practicing your music.
I am proud of you because I know that you are proud of
*   yourself.*
Thank you for being my talented daughter.
I love you.
Sweet dreams. »

Instrumental Music: Stage Fright/Performance Anxiety

« *Doug, this is your father.*
I want to let you know how much I love you.
I want to let you know how proud I am that you are my son.
When you play in front of other people, you are calm,
*   confident, and at ease.*
I feel proud when you play your music.
I enjoy hearing you and seeing you on stage.
You create and play beautiful sounds.
Thank you for your music.
Thank you for being my son.
I am proud of you because I know you are proud of
*   yourself.*
I love you.
Sweet dreams. »

Singing: Stage Fright/Performance Anxiety

« *Helen, this is your mother.*
I just want to let you know how much I love you.
I just want to let you know how proud I am that you are my
*   daughter.*
When you have a singing performance, I enjoy you so much.
You are wonderful.
You are calm, confident, and at ease because you are so well
*   prepared.*
You feel good about who you are, and it shows in the
*   performances you give in front of an audience.*
People enjoy hearing your talent.
I enjoy your singing, and I am very glad you are my daughter.

I am proud of you because I know you are proud of yourself.
I love you.
Sweet dreams. 》

Dancing: Practice

《 *Kelly, this is your mother.*
I want to let you know how much I love you.
I want to let you know how proud I am that you are my
daughter.
When you practice your dancing, it is fun to watch you.
You practice your dancing frequently.
Your mind and body create the movements that give you
pleasure.
You enjoy the results of your practicing.
Thank you for practicing your dancing.
Thank you for your strong, willing body.
Thank you for being my daughter.
I love you.
Sweet dreams. 》

Animals

Competition with an Animal: Dog, Horse, 4-H Shows, Etc.

《 *Karen, this is your mom.*
I just want you to know how much I love you.
I just want you to know how proud I am to be your mom.
I want to let you know how much I enjoy seeing you in
competition.
You are calm and confident.
You transfer this confidence to your animal, _____
[name].
You do a good job of becoming "as one" during competition.
You feel good about who you are and the job you do.
You feel pleased at expressing yourself in this manner with
your animal.

The trust between the two of you stands out.
I am so proud of you.
Thank you for being my daughter.
I love you.
Sweet dreams. »

Sports

Wrestling

« *Randy, this is your father.*
I want to let you know how much I love you.
I want to let you know how proud I am that you are my son.
I want to let you know how much I appreciate your
   individual effort when I watch you wrestle.
Your balance is unique.
You shift your weight to counter any move to "stay on top."
For every move, there is a countermove.
"Shoot"—standing face-to-face.
"Takedown"—to the mat.
"Cross face"—are all moves you execute with strength and
   accuracy.
You stay in shape.
You move quickly.
You are aggressive to stay off your back.
Thank you for being my son.
I enjoy your successes.
I enjoy you.
I love you.
Sweet dreams. »

Tennis

« *Loretta, this is your mother.*
I want to let you know how much I love you.
I want to let you know how proud I am to be your mother.

You have a good eye following the tennis ball.
Your swing is smooth and powerful.
Your endurance and timing are phenomenal.
Your practice pays off.
*No matter how fast the ball is coming, you have time to get
    there.*
It is a pleasure to watch you play tennis.
I enjoy seeing you have fun.
Thank you for being my daughter.
I love you so very much.
Sweet dreams. »

Track

« Ted, this is your mother.
I want to let you know how much I love you.
I want to let you know how proud I am of you.
I am proud that you are my son.
I enjoy seeing you participate in your track events.
When you run, you fly like the wind.
It looks as if you have wings on your heels.
I enjoy watching you.
You are a good runner and team member.
Your level of expertise is wonderful.
Thank you for being my son.
I love you.
Sweet dreams. »

Ice or Field Hockey

« Wayne, this is your mom.
I want to let you know how much I love you.
I want to let you know how proud I am to be your mom.
When you skate [run], you have such stamina and strength.
*I appreciate it when you take care of yourself and are healthy
    and fit.*
Your movements when you're playing are quick and flexible.

It is fun to watch your accuracy in shooting goals.
Your attitude includes working together with your teammates.
I am proud to be your mother.
Thank you for being my son.
I love you.
Sweet dreams. »

MASTER INDEX
TO SCRIPTS

References are to page numbers.

Academics

Adolescence

Approaching adults as a resource (184)
Choices: organizational skills (190)
Choices: using time (185)
Homework (179)
Initiative (183)
Perseverance (177)

School age

Academic school behavior (166)
Homework (167)

Listening (144)
Math fluency, increasing (163)
Math test-taking (165)
Reading, assigned and leisure (160)
Reading fluency, increasing (159)
Reading for memory and test-taking (162)
Self-confidence at school (158)
Staying on task (145)

Adolescence

Approaching adults as a resource (184)
Being assertive (210)
Being on time (202)
Caring (176)
Choices: making friends (148, 188)
Choices: organizational skills (190)
Choices: using money (187)
Choices: using time (185)
Common sense (180)
Dealing with anger (211)
Dental visits (253)
Drinking (55)
Eating, healthy (252)
Emotional upset (215)
Homework (179)
Honesty (209)
Immune system (247)
Improving performance (199)
Initiative (183)
Leadership (182)
Manners (200)
Orthodontics (254)
Perseverance (177)
Property, exchanging and sharing (203)
Property, protection of (205)

Puberty: female (192)
Puberty: male (191)
Self-confidence (174)
Showing up differently (214)
Smoking (55)
Stealing (205)
"Thank you" for being responsible (196)
Truth-telling (207)
Using effort/inner direction (197)

Adoption

Bonding with an adopted child (84, 238)
Releasing worry from the past (239)
Releasing worry from conflict (240)

Anger

Adolescence: being assertive while calm and relaxed (210)
Adolescence: dealing with anger (211)
School age: dealing with anger (150)

Animals

Caretaking (235)
Competition with an animal: dog, horse, 4-H shows, etc. (267)

Arts/Creative Energy

Acting (225)
Artistic ability: drawing, painting, sculpture, and more (226)
Creative writing (227)
Dancing: performance (224)

Dancing: practice (267)
Dancing: stage fright/performance anxiety (224)
Instrumental music: practice (222)
Instrumental music: stage fright/performance anxiety (266)
Piano: practice (26, 221, 265)
Piano: stage fright/performance anxiety (221)
Public speaking (224)
Singing: performance (222)
Singing: stage fright/performance anxiety (266)

Bonding

Adopted child (84, 238)
Infant: adoptive parent (84)
Infant: parent (80)
Infant: sibling (85)
Prenatal: father (75)
Prenatal: mother (72)
Prenatal: siblings (76)
Preschool: grandparent (18)
School-age: parent (27, 142)
Toddler: parent (87)
Toddler: working parent (88)

Crisis Situations

Brace, wearing a (251)
Death of a family member (242)
Death of a friend (243)
Disappointments (244)
Divorce (245)
Health (247)
Hospital stay (249)
Immune system (247)
Surgery (250)
When "bad things" happen (244)

Day Care

Action control: biting (135)
Action control: hitting (137)
Doing well in school (127)
Getting along with others (129)
Getting ready to go (120)
Health (134)
Listening (128)
Paying attention (132)
Playground behavior (131)
Taking turns (130)

Disabilities

Asking for help (258)
Encouragement for surgery (257)
Encouragement to "go for it" (256)
Friends and friendships (260)
Letting people into your life (259)
Responsibility (256)
Sports participation (261)

Health

Body control: preschool (106)
Brace, wearing a (251)
Crisis (24)
Dental visits (253)
Eating, healthy (90, 252)
Hospital stay (249)
Immune system: older child (248)
Immune system: younger child (58, 247)
Nurse to patient (58)
Orthodontics (254)
Preschool (134)

Self-healing (24)
Surgery (250)

Infant

Bonding: parent with adopted child (84)
Bonding: parent with infant (80)
Bonding: sibling with baby (85)
Caretaking: sibling with baby (86)

Manners

Adolescent (206)
School age (206)

Physical and Mental Challenges

Asking for help (258)
Brace, wearing a (251)
Death of a family member (242)
Death of a friend (243)
Disappointments (244)
Divorce (245)
Encouragement for surgery (257)
Encouragement to "go for it" (256)
Friends and friendships (260)
Health (247)
Hospital stay (249)
Immune system (247)
Letting people into your life (259)
Responsibility (256)
Sports participation (261)
Surgery (250)
When "bad things" happen (244)

Prenatal

Bonding: father (75)
Bonding: mother (72)
Siblings (76)

Preschool

Animals (113)
Arguing (100)
Bed-wetting (106)
Bonding: grandparent with child (17)
Bonding: parent with child (102)
Dental visits (253)
Eating, healthy (90)
Fears: bugs and insects (112)
Fears: new experiences (111)
Fears: scary events (110)
Focusing energy (18, 104)
Helping others (18, 103)
Injuries: being brave (109)
Phobias (2)
Safety: talking to strangers (114)
Sleeping (116)
Thumb sucking (105)
Touching with one finger (98)

Responsibility

Adolescence

Being on time (202)
Disabled child (256)
Honesty (209)
Improving performance (199)
Manners (200)

Property, exchanging and sharing (203)
Property, protection of (205)
Stealing (205)
"Thank you" for being responsible (196)
Truth-telling (207)
Using effort/inner direction (197)

Preschool

Touching with one finger (98)

School age

Being on time (202)
Dealing with anger (150)
Homework (167)
Keeping room clean (146)
Manners (200)
Morning preparation for school (143)
Protection of property (205)
Safety (155)
Staying on task (145)
Truth-telling (207)

School Age

Academic school behavior (166)
Attitude adjustment (150)
Bonding with a parent (2, 142)
Dealing with anger (150)
Dental visits (253)
Eating, healthy (252)
Fingernail biting (149)
Grandparents, relationship with (153)
Helping one another as a family (152)
Homework (167)

Immune system (247)
Keeping room clean (146)
Listening (144)
Making friends (148)
Manners (200)
Math fluency, increasing (163)
Math test-taking (165)
Morning preparation for school (143)
Orthodontics (254)
Protection of property (205)
Reading, assigned and leisure (160)
Reading fluency, increasing (159)
Reading for memory and test-taking (162)
Safety (155)
Self-confidence (141)
Self-confidence at school (158)
Shyness (151)
Sleeping (156)
Staying on task (145)
Teamwork (168)
Truth-telling (207)

Sports

Baseball: beginning (229)
Disabilities, sports participation for children with (261)
Golf: beginning (232)
Ice or field hockey (269)
Soccer: beginning (230)
Swimming: beginning (231)
Teamwork (232)
Tennis (268)
Track (269)
Wrestling (268)

Toddler

Bonding: parent with toddler (87)
Bonding: working parent with toddler (88)
Picky eater (90)
Sleeping (93)
Toilet training (92)

INDEX

Academics
  homework, 167–68, 179–80
  math fluency, 163–66
  reading, 159–63
  school behavior, 166–67
  scripts, 14–15, 144, 145–46,
    158, 160, 161, 162–63,
    164, 165, 166–67,
    167–68, 177, 179–80,
    183, 184–85, 185–86,
    190
Acting, 225–26
  script, 226
Adolescence, 55–56, 171–93
  adults and, 184–85
  attitudes toward, 171
  changes during, 171–72

choice and, 172, 185–91
control and, 172–73
initiative and, 183–84
perserverance and, 177–79
responsibility and, 195–217
self-confidence and, 174–76
work and, 199–200
Adoption, 23, 84–85, 237–41
  adopted children-parent
    bonding, 238–39
  family conflict and,
    240–41
  past family and, 239–40
  scripts, 84, 240–41
Adulthood, 56–57, 58–59,
  184–85
Anesthesia, 35–37

Anger, 211–14
  scripts, 213, 213–14
Animals, 105, 113–14, 234–36,
    267–68
  scripts, 114, 235–36, 267–68
Arguing, 100–101
  script, 101
Arrien, A., 140
Art, 226–27
  script, 227
Assertiveness, 210–11
  script, 210–11
Attention deficit disorder, 238
Attitude adjustment, 1–3,
    72–74, 150–51
  scripts, 1–2, 151
Auditory arousal thresholds
    (AATs), 32

Baseball, 229–30
  script, 229–30
Bed-wetting, 106–8
  script, 107–8
Bell, using, 147–48
Bennett, H., 36
Birth memories, 70–71
Birth process, 74–75
Biting, 135–36
  scripts, 135–36, 136
Bonding
  adolescent and parents, 175
  adopted children and
      parents, 238–39
  prenatal bonding, 22–23,
      51–52, 61–76
  preschool children and
      parents, 102–3

school-age children and
    parents, 142–43
  scripts, 18, 27–28, 72–73,
      75, 76, 81, 84, 85, 88,
      102, 142, 143
  toddler and parents, 80–82,
      87–90
Boundaries, 98, 104, 126
Braces, 251–52
  script, 252
Brain, 2
  EEG-pattern, 34
  information processing and,
      133
  waves, 34
Breast feeding, 67–68
Burn patients, 6–7

Cheating, 209–10
Cheek, David B., 35, 70, 71
Choice, 15, 172, 185–91
  friends and, 188–90
  organizational skills and,
      190–91
  scripts, 55–56, 185, 186, 187,
      188, 190
  using money and, 187–88
  using time and, 185–86
Cleaning rooms, 146–47
  script, 147
Cleft palate, 257–58
Common sense, 180–82
  script, 181
Communication. See
    Language issues;
    Nonverbal
    communication

Compassion and caring, 103–4,
130, 140, 176–77
script, 177
Confidence. *See* Self-confidence
Control issues
adolescence and, 172–73
assertiveness and, 210–11
bed-wetting, 106–8
biting, 135–36
hitting, 137
pain management, 137–38
Creative writing, 227–28
script, 228
Crisis, 57, 241–47
scripts, 242, 243, 244, 245,
247–48, 248–49, 249,
250, 250–51
Cycles
benevolent versus vicious,
11–12, 25

Dancing, 223–24, 267
scripts, 224, 267
Day care, 119–38
alternatives, 122–23
choosing a facility, 123–24
getting ready to go, 120–22
scripts, 121, 127, 128–29,
129–30, 130–31,
131–32, 133, 135–36,
137
Death, 5–8, 242–43
scripts, 242, 243
Dental visits, 253–55
scripts, 253–54, 254–55
Depression, 10, 66. *See also*
Emotional upset

Disabled children, 255–61
independence and, 258–59
scripts, 256, 257–58, 258,
259–60, 260, 261
Disappointment, 244–45
script, 245
Divorce, 245–47
script, 246

Eating
healthy, 252–53
picky eaters, 90–91
scripts, 91, 252–53
self-feeding, 91
Emotional upset, 215–17. *See
also* Anger
scripts, 215, 216
Empowerment, 99
Energy focusing, 17–19,
104–5, 127
script, 127
Erikson, Erik, 79

Family
dysfunctional, 20–21
helping one another, 152–53
moral values and, 173
script, 152–53
Fathers, 64, 75–76, 82–83
script, 75
Fear, 110–11
of insects, 112–13
of new experiences, 111–12
of water, 1–2, 11
scripts, 2, 110–11, 111–12,
113
Field hockey, 269–70

Fingernail biting, 149–50
  script, 149–50
Fist-clench responses, 33
Friendship, 148–49, 188–90
  disabled children and,
    259–61
  scripts, 149, 189, 259–60

Getting along with others,
    129–30
  on the playground, 131–32
  scripts, 129–30, 131–32
Gilligan, Carol, 182
Golf, 233–34
  script, 234
Grandfather-grandson
    relations, 17–19
  script, 18
Grandparents, 17–19, 153–54
  script, 154
Gratitude, 196–97
  script, 196–97
Gutman, Jack, 26–28, 88, 247

Haddad, Lois, viii, 140–41. *See
    also specific topics*
Harelip, 257–58
Health and healing, 9, 11,
    24–25, 28, 108–9,
    134–35, 247–55
  dental visits, 253–54
  diet, 252–53
  hospitals, 249–50
  immune system, 247–49
  orthodontics, 254–55
  pain control, 137–38

scripts, 24, 58, 91, 109, 134,
    247–48, 248–49, 250,
    250–51, 252–53,
    253–54, 254–55
  surgery, 250–51
  wearing a brace, 251–52
Helping others, 103–4
  script, 103–4
Hitting, 137
  script, 137
Hockey, 269–70
Hoffman, Lois, 120
Home care, 124
Homework, 167–68, 179–80
  scripts, 167–68, 179–80
Honesty, 207–10
  scripts, 207–8, 209–10
Hospital stays, 249–51
  script, 250
Hyperactivity, 17–19, 104–5,
    127
  script, 127

Ice hockey, 269–70
Illness. *See also* Health and
    healing
  children versus adult
    reponse to, 6
  secondary gains of, 6
Imagery, 6, 11
Immune system, 247–49. *See
    also* Health and healing
  scripts, 247–48, 248–49
Infancy, 52, 65
Initiative, 183–84
  script, 183–84

Language issues
  language ability and sleep
    talk, 100
  newborn reactions to
    language, 65
  nonverbal communication,
    50–51
  open communication, 174
  phrasing positively, 53
  prenatal, 61. *See also*
    Prenatal bonding
  words and vocabulary,
    50–51
Leach, Penelope, 120
Leadership, 182–83
  script, 183
Lieberman, Michael, 65
Listening, 128–29, 144–45
  scripts, 128–29, 145
Love of individual, 16
Lukesch, Monika, 66–67
Lying, 207–9
  scripts, 207, 209–10

Manners, 200–202
  scripts, 201, 201–2
Manrique, Beatriz, 64
Math fluency, 163–66
  scripts, 164, 165
Memory, 35–37, 162–63
  birth memories, 70–71
  script, 162–63
Mentally challenged children,
  255–61
  scripts, 256, 256–57, 258–59,
    259–60, 260, 261

Mind-body connection, 37
Mind-Body Therapy, 35
Mistakes, 50
Montessori methods, 124–25
Moral values, 173
Morning preparation for
  school, 143–44
  script, 144
Music, 220–23
  piano playing, 26–28, 265–66
  practicing, 221–22
  scripts, 26–27, 200, 221,
    222, 222–23, 265–67
  singing, 222–23, 266–67
  stage fright, 220–21, 266–67

Neonate intensive care units, 74
Non-REM sleep, 32
Nonverbal communication,
  50–51, 82
Nursery school, 121, 127–28.
  See also Day care
  scripts, 121, 127

Organizational skills, 190–91
  script, 190
Orthodontics, 254–55
  script, 254–55
Oxytocin, 70

Pain. *See* Health and healing
Pain management, 137–38
Parent-child relationship,
  vii–viii. *See also*
    Bonding; Parenting
  teamwork, viii

Parenting, 77–78, 263–64
  guilt, 21–22
  learning from children, 23
  mistakes, 19–20
  purpose of, 51
  script, 89
  teaching, 19–20
  working parents, 88–90,
    102–3
Parke, Ross, 83
Paying attention, 132–33, 140
  script, 133
Pearce, Joseph Chilton, 125
Perseverance, 145–46, 177–79
  scripts, 145–46, 178
Personal property
  protection of, 205–7
  scripts, 204, 205–6, 206–7
  sharing versus exchanging
    property, 125–27,
    203–5
Pert, Candace, 37
Phobia. See Fear
Physically challenged children,
    255–61
  scripts, 256, 256–57, 257–58,
    258–59, 259–60, 260,
    261
Placenta, 70
Policy Analysis for California
    Educators (PACE), 11
Positive reinforcement, 33–34,
    53, 130
Possessions. See Personal
    property
Pregnancy, 61–76. See also
    Prenatal bonding

depression and, 66
easing birth, 72–74
father's role, 64, 75–76
labor, 72–74
perceptions in utero, 63
smoking and, 65
stress and, 66, 73
as temporary, 77–78
Premature birth, 73
Prenatal bonding, 22–23,
    51–52, 61–76
  child's role, 69–70
  communication channels,
    68–69
  depression and, 66
  scripts, 72–73, 75
  stimulation, 64
  stress and, 66, 73
Prenatal sleep talk, 22–23
Preschool children, 53–54,
    97–117
  day care, 119–38
Psychological receptivity, 8
Puberty, 191–93
  female, 192–93
  male, 191–92
  scripts, 191–92, 192–93
Public speaking, 224–25
  script, 225
Punctuality
  script, 202–3

Quality time, 29

Reading, 159–63
  scripts, 160, 161, 162–63
Rebirthing, 71–72

Recreation. *See also specific types of recreation*
REM sleep, 32
Resourcefulness, 197–99
  script, 198
Responsibility, 15, 99
  adolescence and, 195–217
  disabled children and, 256–57
  effort and, 197–99
  gratitude and, 196–98
  inner direction and, 197–99
  possessions and, 126
  punctuality and, 202–3
  resourcefulness and, 197–99
  scripts, 99, 147, 196–97, 199–200, 202–3, 204, 205–6, 207, 209–10, 256–57
  by stages, 50
  work performance and, 199–200
Ritalin, 104
Rossi, Ernest Lawrence, 35
Rules of life, 140–41

Safety issues, 155–56
  scripts, 115, 155
  talking to strangers, 114–16
School-age children, 54, 139–69
  attitude adjustment, 150–51
  cleaning rooms, 146–47
  homework, 167–68
  math fluency, 163–66
  morning preparation for school, 143–44
reading, 159–63
school behavior, 166–67
self-confidence in school, 158–59
staying on task, 145–46
teamwork, 168–69
test-taking, 162–63, 165–66
School behavior, 166–67
Scripts
  appropriate, 46
  index by subject, 271–80
  preparation, 40–41
  readers of, 57–58
  reading, 42–43
  stages of, 49–50
Searle, Judith, 81, 159
Secret Life of the Unborn Child, The (Verny), 64
Self-confidence, 141–42
  adolescence and, 174–76
  resourcefulness and, 197–99
  in school, 158–59
  scripts, 142, 158, 175, 198
Self-identification, 41–42, 214–15
Self-respect, 16
Sharing versus exchanging property, 125–27, 203–5
  script, 204
Showing up, 140, 214–15
  script, 215
Shyness, 13–14, 151–52
  script, 152
Siblings
  new baby and, 76–77, 85–87
  scripts, 76, 85, 86

Singing, 222–23
   scripts, 222–23, 266
Skills
   stages of, 49–50
Sleep, 156–57
   auditory arousal thresholds
      (AATs), 32
   bedtime issues, 93–94,
      116–17
   fist-clench responses, 33
   K-complexes, 33
   learning during, 34–35
   negative reinforcement
      during, 33–34
   positive reinforcement
      during, 33–34
   scripts, 94, 116–17, 157
   stages of, 32
   subject's name and, 33
Sleep Talk
   adolescence and, 55–56,
      177–93, 195–217
   adulthood, 56–57, 58–59
   crisis periods, 57
   everyday uses, 25–28
   infancy, 52
   language ability and, 100
   manipulation and, 29
   medical applications, 58
   positive expectations, viii, 43
   prenatal, 22–23, 51–52,
      61–78, 97–117
   preschool age, 53–54,
      97–117, 119–38
   process, 37–38
      approach sleeping child,
         41–42

   discussion of process,
      44–45
   identify needs, 39–40
   length of process, 44
   results, 45–47
   script preparation, 40–41
   script reading, 42–43
   self-identification, 41–42
   quality time and, 29
   recreation and, 219–36
   responsibility and, 195–217
   school-age children and, 54,
      139–69
   special needs and, 57, 255–61
   toddlerhood and, 52–53,
      79–95
Smoking, 65
   script, 55–56
Soccer, 230–31
   script, 230–31
Speaking in class, 14–15
Special needs, 57, 255–61
Spontaneous abortion, 70
Sports, 228–34. *See also*
      specific sports
   disabled children and, 261
   scripts, 229–30, 230–231,
      232, 261, 268–70
Staying on task. *See*
      Perseverance
Stealing, 205–7
   scripts, 205–6, 206–7
Stott, Dennis, 66
Stress, 66, 73
Success, 124–25
Surgery, 250–51, 257–58
   scripts, 250–51, 257–58

Swimming, 231–32
   script, 232

Taking turns, 130–31
   script, 130–31
Talking to strangers, 114–16
   script, 115
Teamwork, viii, 168–69,
      232–33
   scripts, 168–69, 233
Telephone use, 172–73
Tennis
   script, 268–69
Test-taking, 162–63, 165–66
   scripts, 162–63, 165
Thomas, Lewis, 31
Thumb sucking, 105–6
   script, 106
Toddlerhood, 52–53, 79–95
Toilet training, 92–93
   script, 92–93

Touching with one finger, 53,
      98–100
   script, 99
Track
   script, 269
Truth telling, 207–9
   scripts, 207, 209–10
Two-year olds. *See*
      Toddlerhood

UCLA pediatrics ward, 5–8

Verny, Thomas, 64, 67, 82
Visualization, 6, 11

Wilson, Patricia, 17–19, 123
Working parents, 88–90,
      102–3
   day care, 119–38
Wrestling
   script, 268